The Information Retrieval Series

Volume 50

Information Retrieval (IR) deals with access to and search in mostly unstructured information, in text, audio, and/or video, either from one large file or spread over separate and diverse sources, in static storage devices as well as on streaming data. It is part of both computer and information science, and uses techniques from e.g. mathematics, statistics, machine learning, database management, or computational linguistics. Information Retrieval is often at the core of networked applications, web-based data management, or large-scale data analysis.

The Information Retrieval Series presents monographs, edited collections, and advanced text books on topics of interest for researchers in academia and industry alike. Its focus is on the timely publication of state-of-the-art results at the forefront of research and on theoretical foundations necessary to develop a deeper understanding of methods and approaches.

This series is abstracted/indexed in EI Compendex and Scopus.

Markus Schedl • Vito Walter Anelli • Elisabeth Lex

Technical and Regulatory Perspectives on Information Retrieval and Recommender Systems

Fairness, Transparency, and Privacy

Springer

Markus Schedl
Institute of Computational Perception
Johannes Kepler University Linz
Linz, Austria

Vito Walter Anelli
Polytechnic University of Bari
Bari, Italy

Elisabeth Lex
Institute of Interactive Systems and Data Science
Graz University of Technology
Graz, Austria

ISSN 1871-7500 ISSN 2730-6836 (electronic)
The Information Retrieval Series
ISBN 978-3-031-69977-1 ISBN 978-3-031-69978-8 (eBook)
https://doi.org/10.1007/978-3-031-69978-8

This Springer imprint is published by the registered company Springer Nature Switzerland AG
The registered company address is: Gewerbestrasse 11, 6330 Cham, Switzerland

To our families, friends, colleagues, and all researchers and developers who are looking beyond the mere technical aspects of retrieval and recommendation systems.

Foreword

It is Time.[1] I had the great opportunity to collaborate with Elisabeth Lex and Markus Schedl on two outstanding tutorials that delved deep into the ethical and regulatory dimensions of information retrieval (IR) and recommender systems (RecSys) in recent years: the SIGIR tutorial titled *Retrieval and Recommendation Systems at the Crossroad of Artificial Intelligence, Ethics, and Regulation*[2] in 2022 and the WSDM tutorial on *Trustworthy Algorithmic Ranking Systems*[3] in 2023. My contributions were linked to and motivated by my current research at the European Commission's Joint Research Centre on the impact of algorithmic systems on human behavior and my experience providing scientific evidence to European policies.

In these tutorials, I could witness the fact that, for technical communities, ethics and regulation topics are still seen by most as outsider discussions beyond technical research, in contrast with other research networks where algorithms are developed and studied as socio-technical systems and where the need to integrate these views from the very first stages of the technical development process is widely recognized. So I realized that incorporating such topics in technical fora is an urgent need for a true advancement of human-centric algorithm design.

As a consequence, when Markus, Elisabeth, and Walter invited me to write the foreword for this book, I was thrilled! This book is precisely what our community needs: a timely and comprehensive exploration of ethical and regulatory considerations tailored to technical audiences. It is an honor for me to provide a brief introduction to this crucial topic in the foreword.

On the Sunny Side of the Street.[4] I started to work in the field of IR and RecSys in the 2000s as a junior engineer and amateur musician, joining the *Acoustics, Signal Processing, and Computer Science Applied to Music* (ATIAM) Master's

---

[1] Lion Guard tune.

[2] https://github.com/socialcomplab/Retrieval-RecSys-AI-Ethics-Regulation-Tutorial-SIGIR22

[3] https://github.com/socialcomplab/Trustworthy-ARS-Tutorial-WSDM22

[4] Jazz standard.

program at the *Institute for Research and Coordination in Acoustics/Music* (IRCAM) in Paris. This was followed by a PhD focusing on melody and tonality at the Music Technology Group in Barcelona, Spain. In 2002, I joined for the very first time the *International Society for Music Information Retrieval* (ISMIR) conference as an early researcher. It has become one of my favorite research networks due to its interdisciplinary character (musicologists, engineers, and librarians gathering there, united by the love for music), its optimistic view of IR, and its strong focus toward applied research on applications to support music listening, discovery, and analysis. In this context, at the start of my scientific career, I perceived algorithmic systems as a means to provide users access to vast amounts of music data and information, in fact, to all music in the world—algorithms to democratize music discovery beyond mainstream hits! Looking back, I realize how naive my perspective was, but it fueled my passion for exploring the potential of algorithms in music.

In the last decades, I have been researching in this field, developing algorithms for music content description for retrieval and recommendation, based first on low-to mid-level music features such as pitch, melody, timbre, key, or tempo. In addition, thanks to novel data-driven techniques and the consideration of multiple music characteristics, we started using algorithms to model semantic concepts such as musical style or emotions. During these years, our field has witnessed, on the one hand, a paradigm shift from knowledge-driven to data-driven algorithm design, thanks to new developments in computing, access to data, and powerful machine learning algorithms. On the other hand, the field also experienced an increasing presence of industry researchers, given the economic value that algorithms bring in commercial products, namely, music platforms, education tools, or search engines.

The Dark Side.[5] The bloom of practical applications linked to IR and RecSys has also brought new challenges to be addressed by the research community. Personally, I felt the social impact and related ethical concerns while addressing technical research goals and challenges. For instance, the fact that I worked on projects dealing with non-mainstream music styles such as flamenco or classical music in the European project *Performances as Highly Enriched aNd Interactive Concert eXperiences* (PHENICX) made me experience the fact that music IR algorithms had been developed having mainstream popular music in mind—music for Western listeners and technology by Western developers. As a consequence, many corresponding human assumptions and design choices were propagated to systems that could not cope well with other styles or repertoires.

This was when the topics of *bias and fairness* became relevant in my research. In particular, when looking into adaptations of evaluation methods and personalization algorithms to different repertoires and user groups so that they can all have fair access and visibility. In addition, working as a woman in a male-dominated field, I became aware of diversity needs and became interested in contributing to fostering diversity during my service as a board member and president of the ISMIR and contributor to the *Women in MIR* (WiMIR) initiative. As diversity in teams is later

[5] Muse.

reflected in the developed algorithms, methodologies and tools that integrate varied perspectives are vital. Moreover, contributing to projects with strong social impact, e.g., a personalized music recommender system for Alzheimer patients or a music emotion recognition system, made me confront the potential risks of the algorithms we develop, in particular those linked to privacy issues or the impact on mental health. Finally, the recent evolution of generative models we are experiencing, especially their increased expressivity and naturalness, stimulates discussion on their impact on the jobs of artists and musicians, on creativity, and on the importance of transparency when interacting with state-of-the-art generative AI systems.

Across the Universe.[6] The study of the societal impact of IR and RecSys technology has become my core area of research in the last years, where I transitioned from a technical to a socio-technical research perspective for algorithm development and evaluation at the *European Commission's Joint Research Centre*. There are so many exciting opportunities: exploring the transformative potential of algorithmic systems, assessing their societal risks, devising mitigation strategies, and many more. This opens new avenues for research and technical development in the fields of IR and RecSys and beyond. In addition, regulatory approaches our research considers, notably the EU *Digital Services Act* and the *AI Act*, necessitate legal considerations when incorporating regulatory perspectives in technical development—a truly inspiring, interdisciplinary challenge!

This book addresses three key areas of ethical and regulatory discussions in the context of IR and RecSys: (1) bias, fairness, and non-discrimination; (2) transparency and explainability; and (3) privacy and security. It takes the needed interdisciplinary approach, covering perspectives from computer science, cognitive science, social sciences, and law, but is tailored to a technical audience. The book offers unprecedented insights into the ethical implications of algorithmic approaches and presents recent policy initiatives and their implications for IR and RecSys—a highly valuable and timely resource for anyone involved in research and development in these fields!

As we continue to shape the future of IR and RecSys, it is vital to address technical development, ethical challenges, and regulation in a holistic way, resulting in responsible innovation that serves society. Giving an overview on these crucial topics in the context of IR and RecSys is exactly what this book does. I am sure the reader will enjoy it!

Seville, Spain
April 2024

Emilia Gómez

[6] The Beatles.

Preface

In today's world, we are surrounded by data. Massive amounts of it are stored on private computers, reside on large-scale servers of big tech companies, or circulate the Web. This data comes in an unprecedented variety, ranging from low-quality user-generated multimedia content to expert-curated high-quality blogs, from publicly available status updates on social media to highly sensitive health data of hospital patients, and from automatically generated metadata about the users' exact location and activity to users' interaction logs with contents such as movies, songs, or news.

In fact, more information than ever before is available at everyone's fingertips. At the same time, it has become increasingly difficult to identify high-quality and trustworthy information. Fortunately, recent advancements in deep learning, large language models, and learning-to-rank algorithms have fueled research and development of recommender systems (RSs) and information retrieval (IR) systems, such as those used in search engines. These systems have tremendously facilitated the search for and discovery of new information in huge repositories of multimodal data. These systems influence our decision-making processes by preselecting and ranking the contents we are exposed to on the Web, such as products to buy, jobs to apply for, or movies to watch.

However, with these great advancements comes great responsibility—for tech companies, content creators, and consumers alike and, maybe most importantly, for researchers and developers of corresponding technologies. In recent years, the trustworthiness of information retrieval and recommender systems (IRRSs) has become a popular topic in the public debate—issues like unfair job recommenders that suggest lower-paying vacancies to female job seekers, generative language models that become racist after a short time, or search and recommendation systems that can easily be attacked to reveal sensitive user information. All these factors have contributed to many initiatives for regulating the use of artificial intelligence technologies, therefore, also for most IRRSs. In particular, the European Union has been at the forefront of regulating such technologies, evidenced by the approval of the *AI Act* by the European Parliament in early 2024. Likewise, countries like the USA and China have recently enacted AI regulations. Noteworthy, there exist big differences regarding the goals of these regulations between geographic regions. Based on our studies of the materials, we find that regulations in the USA are rather fragmented, and several states have enacted their own AI regulations. Europe, in contrast, has taken a more comprehensive approach through the AI Act. China's approach to AI regulation is centered on social security and national security.

Many of the existing regulations address one or more of the trustworthiness dimensions laid down by the European Commission's High-Level Expert Group on AI: human agency and oversight; technical robustness and safety; privacy and data governance; transparency; diversity, non-discrimination, and fairness; societal and environmental well-being; and accountability. While all of these are important, we concentrate our investigation in the book at hand on the three aspects of *fairness*, *transparency*, and *privacy* (and closely related topics), because these are among the most frequently discussed and impactful aspects in the context of IRRSs.

The book comprises five chapters. After a brief introduction to IRRSs, their stakeholders, and methods to evaluate them (Chap. 1), we provide an overview of recent initiatives to regulate AI technology and discuss them in the context of IRRSs, particularly focusing on Europe, the USA, and China (Chap. 2). Subsequently, we provide an overview of various biases, discuss their relation to fairness and non-discrimination, and present methods to quantify and mitigate undesired biases, all in the context of IRRSs (Chap. 3). After that, we introduce major facets of transparency, including explainability, justification, and interpretability, and present common strategies to achieve explainability in IRRSs together with concrete methods to generate explanations (Chap. 4). Thereafter, we elaborate on privacy and security aspects in IRRSs; present approaches to mitigate the risks of data breaches, e.g., through anonymization and encryption; and discuss security threats to ranking models, such as adversarial attacks, as well as defenses against them (Chap. 5). Finally, we provide a brief outlook on the grand challenges we identified for researchers and practitioners in IRRSs as related to the addressed trustworthiness dimensions (Chap. 6).

Throughout the book, we refer to three specific use cases to exemplify and illustrate the concepts and methods presented: *music information retrieval*, *recruitment-related recommender systems*, and *health-related search and retrieval*. We use these examples to discuss the real-world impact that the presented technical solutions have.

Basic knowledge of IRRSs is necessary to fully comprehend the more technical and algorithmic parts of the book. Nevertheless, even a lay audience in terms of technical background should benefit from the book.

While the book targets a mostly technical audience, we adopt an *interdisciplinary perspective* by incorporating views from computer science, psychology, social sciences, and law. Our aim is to equip its readers with the necessary understanding of the ethical implications of their research and development and of the potential impacts of recent policy initiatives and regulations.

In summary, by discussing the *technical challenges*, *societal impact*, *ethical considerations*, and *regulatory approaches* to IRRSs, we hope to give the reader a helpful overview of the challenges and possible solutions related to building trustworthy IRRSs.

Linz, Austria
Bari, Italy
Graz, Austria
July 2024

Markus Schedl
Vito Walter Anelli
Elisabeth Lex

Acknowledgments

We sincerely want to thank our colleagues and collaborators for the many hours of fruitful discussions on the topics covered in this book. In particular, we would like to emphasize the great contributions of Emilia Gómez (Joint Research Centre of the European Commission) with whom we delivered several tutorials on various subject matters covered in this book. Furthermore, we would like to express our gratitude to our colleagues, especially to Stefan Brandl, Gustavo Escobedo, Tommaso Di Noia, Antonio Ferrara, Christian Ganhör, Simone Kopeinik, Dominik Kowald, Oleg Lesota, Alessandro B. Melchiorre, Felice Merra, Marta Moscati, Markus Reiter-Haas, and Navid Rekabsaz. In addition, we would like to thank Elisabeth Greif, Tessa Grosz, and Emma Lantschner who provided invaluable insights into non-discrimination law.

Furthermore, we would like to acknowledge the funding bodies that enabled us to conduct the exciting research on recommender systems and information retrieval that substantially contributed to the foundations of this book. Concretely, we received support from the Austrian Science Fund (FWF), the State of Upper Austria, and the Austrian Federal Ministry of Education, Science, and Research. Some of the illustrations in this book have been designed using images from https://Flaticon.com.

Contents

Acronyms

AI	Artificial Intelligence
AIR	Adverse Impact Ratio
ALS	Alternating Least Squares
AML	Adversarial Machine Learning
APT	Average Percentage of Tail Items
ARP	Average Recommendation Popularity
BPR	Bayesian Personalized Ranking
CBF	Content-Based Filtering
CBR	Case-Based Reasoning
CCPA	California Consumer Privacy Act
CF	Collaborative Filtering
CLPRC	Cybersecurity Law of the People's Republic of China
COPPA	Children's Online Privacy Protection Act
CPRA	California Privacy Rights Act
CS	Computer Science
CV	Curriculum Vitae
DL	Deep Learning
DMA	Digital Markets Act
DNN	Deep Neural Network
DSA	Digital Services Act
DPO	Data Protection Officer
EC	European Commission
EEA	European Economic Area
EHR	Electronic Health Record
EMD	Earth Mover's Distance
ERM	Empirical Risk Minimization
EU	European Union
FL	Federated Learning
FTC	Federal Trade Commission
GAP	Group Average Popularity
GDPR	General Data Protection Regulation

GLBA	Gramm-Leach-Bliley Act
HCI	Human-Computer Interaction
HE	Homomorphic Encryption
HIPAA	Health Insurance Portability and Accountability Act
ID	Identifier
IR	Information Retrieval
IRRS	Information Retrieval and Recommendation System
JSD	Jensen-Shannon Divergence
LIME	Local Interpretable Model-agnostic Explanations
LLM	Large Language Model
LRP	Layer-wise Relevance Propagation
LTR	Learning To Rank
MF	Matrix Factorization
MIR	Music Information Retrieval
ML	Machine Learning
MLP	Multi-Layer Perceptron
MPC	Multi-Party Computation
NDCG	Normalized Discounted Cumulative Gain
NGO	Non-Governmental Organization
NHTSA	National Highway Traffic Safety Administration
NIST	National Institute of Standards and Technology
NLG	Natural Language Generation
NLP	Natural Language Processing
PIPL	Personal Information Protection Law
PL	Popularity Lift
PLD	Product Liability Directive
POI	Point Of Interest
QI	Quasi-Identifier
RAG	Retrieval-Augmented Generation
RS	Recommender System
SAC	Standardization Administration of China
SHAP	SHapley Additive exPlanations
SVD	Singular Value Decomposition
TAI	Trustworthy Artificial Intelligence
TPRP	True Positive Rate Parity
UGF	User Group Fairness
VAE	Variational Auto-Encoder
XAI	eXplainable Artificial Intelligence

Chapter 1
Introduction

Many decisions we make in our daily lives are affected by algorithmic ranking systems. In fact, the algorithms underlying modern information retrieval (IR) and recommender systems (RSs) influence our decision-making processes by preselecting and ranking the contents we are exposed to on the Web, such as products to buy, jobs to apply for, movies to watch, music to listen to, people to meet, or hotels to stay at. While underlying machine learning (ML) and deep learning (DL) methods have tremendously improved the accuracy of information retrieval and recommendation systems (IRRSs), they result in the creation or amplification of a narrowed view of our world by creating personalized filters for content the system does not deem important to the user.

As a result of these two observations, i.e., the prevalence of IRRS technologies in today's society and their strong influence on the digital content humans are exposed to, considering aspects beyond mere technical ones has become a necessity for developers and researchers in the areas of IR and RSs alike. In particular, many ethical and regulatory questions have arisen in the past few years in this context. For instance, is it necessary to impose regulations on IRRS technology—and, more broadly, artificial intelligence (AI) technology—to avoid negative effects on individuals and our society as a whole? If so, which parts of the systems should be regulated? Should these decisions about regulation depend on the domain, e.g., medicine versus entertainment? What is the trade-off between innovation and regulation? What are the consequences of unrestricted technical innovation of IRRS technology? What responsibility and accountability do developers, researchers, managers, and politicians have in this context? Giving answers to some of these questions is an overarching goal of this book.

In the following, we introduce the main objectives and target audience of the book (Sect. 1.1), provide a brief introduction to the fundamentals of IR and RSs (Sect. 1.2), raise awareness of the various stakeholders involved in IRRSs (Sect. 1.3), and delineate some use cases to illustrate concepts and solutions discussed throughout the book (Sect. 1.4). We end this introduction with an outlook to the subsequent chapters (Sect. 1.5).

M. Schedl et al., *Technical and Regulatory Perspectives on Information Retrieval and Recommender Systems*, The Information Retrieval Series 50,
https://doi.org/10.1007/978-3-031-69978-8_1

1.1 Objectives and Audience

This book provides an in-depth treatment of three important topical areas when it comes to ethical and regulatory discussions in the context of IRRSs: *(1) bias, fairness, and non-discrimination*, *(2) transparency and explainability*, and *(3) privacy and security*. We analyze these aspects, sometimes referred to as trustworthiness dimensions, taking an interdisciplinary perspective and incorporating views from computer science, cognitive science, social sciences, and law. We particularly consider the related technical challenges, societal impact, ethical considerations, and regulatory approaches.

The book targets a mostly technical readership and aims to equip its readers with the necessary understanding of the ethical implications of their research and development in IRRSs and of recent policy initiatives, including regulatory approaches. We assume basic knowledge of IRRSs to fully comprehend the more technical and algorithmic parts of the book. Nevertheless, even a lay audience in terms of technical background should benefit from the book. Furthermore, there exist several introductory books and surveys on IR and RSs. As for the former, popular examples include *Modern Information Retrieval* [41], which presents traditional approaches, and *An Introduction to Neural Information Retrieval* [267], which focuses on more recent DL-based methods. For RSs, we would like to refer to the *Recommender Systems Handbook* [321], which provides a solid, up-to-date treatment of all major topics relevant to RSs research. We do not assume previous knowledge of the non-technical disciplines the book discusses, such as policy, ethics, or law.

1.2 Retrieval and Recommender Systems

While the borders between retrieval and recommender systems are becoming increasingly blurred, in this book, we follow the traditional definitions of the underlying tasks, as explained below. From an ML point of view, both IR and RSs are applications of learning to rank (LTR) methods that can create a ranked list of contents based on some ranking model. This ranking model is commonly trained with associations between queries and documents (IR) or interactions between users and items (RSs).

Traditionally, the *information retrieval* task has been defined according to the Cranfield paradigm [397]. An illustration of the common pipeline of a retrieval system is provided in Fig. 1.1. It can be broadly summarized by considering a user who has a certain information need, which they express as a (most often textual) query q. Based on q, the retrieval system then generates a ranked list L_q of k documents $\{d_1, d_2, \ldots, d_k\}$, which form a subset of the entire document collection D, for instance, composed of Web pages in case of a Web search engine. An important assumption of this traditional perspective is that each of the d_i's is either relevant or irrelevant to the query q. This relevance information can be used to evaluate the accuracy of a retrieval system, for instance, in terms of traditional performance metrics from ML, such as precision and recall, or rank-aware metrics, such as normalized discounted cumulative gain (NDCG). An overview of the most common rank-agnostic and rank-aware accuracy metrics is provided in Tables 1.1 and 1.2, respectively. The former considers the result list of k documents as an unordered set, giving equal importance to each document regardless of its position. The latter, in contrast, assumes that users give higher priority to documents that occur in the top positions of the search results than to those filling the lower positions. We will refer to many of these rank-agnostic and rank-aware metrics throughout the book.

A *recommender system*, on the other hand, does not require a query to create ranked lists of items, such as products, movies, or songs. A simplified illustration of the recommendation pipeline is shown in Fig. 1.2. Its main ingredients to learn a ranking model are explicit preference expressions of users U for items I or P (e.g., ratings or "Likes")[1] or other data describing interactions between users and items that can be interpreted as implicit preference indicators (e.g., mouse clicks or purchasing actions). Such rating or interaction data is commonly represented as a user-item rating matrix or user-item interaction matrix R (rows denoting users, columns referring to items). A RS then learns a model from R that allows it to predict the rating of the target user for an unknown item or the likelihood of an interaction between the target user and the candidate items. Based on these predictions, the ranked list L_u of items for the target user u is created and presented to u. The recommendations for a given user u are, therefore, based on u's user profile that constitutes their ratings or interactions over all items, formally given by the corresponding row vector of R.[2] Traditionally, the evaluation of a RS is carried out by approximating the utility of the recommendations for its users. In the case of rating prediction, for instance, error measures that quantify the mismatch between the predicted and the true rating of the items in the test set can be applied, e.g., mean average error (MAE) or root mean squared error (RMSE). Also, ratings can be interpreted in a categorical manner as classes, enabling the computation of standard ML metrics such as precision and recall. Alternatively, rank-aware metrics such as NDCG can be applied, similar to the retrieval task. This is the common approach for RS algorithms that create a ranking based on their predictions of the interaction likelihood and, in turn, produce an ordered list of recommended items. Please refer again to Tables 1.1 and 1.2 for an overview of common accuracy metrics.

Despite the widespread use of the accuracy metrics described above, they only give a narrow view of the performance of IRRSs. In recent years, it has become standard to report also beyond-accuracy performance. Corresponding metrics include novelty, diversity, or coverage of retrieval and recommendation results. Since these metrics go beyond an introductory treatment of IRRSs, we will detail them in the corresponding book chapters where suited, for instance, in Table 3.1.

---

[1] Using the term P to denote items has historical reasons since P referred to products in e-commerce settings, one of the earliest areas in which RSs have been used.

[2] Many RSs leverage additional information about users (e.g., demographics) or items (e.g., content descriptors).

Metric	Formula	Description
Mean average error	$\frac{1}{\lvert T\rvert}\sum_{r_{u,i}\in T} \lvert r_{u,i} - \hat{r}_{u,i}\rvert$	MAE computes the average mismatch or error between predicted ratings $\hat{R}$ and true ratings R in the test set T of user-item ratings on which the RS is evaluated. $r_{u,i}$ and $\hat{r}_{u,i}$ refer to the actual and predicted ratings of item i for user u, respectively.
Root mean squared error	$\sqrt{\frac{1}{\lvert T\rvert}\sum_{r_{u,i}\in T} (r_{u,i} - \hat{r}_{u,i})^2}$	RMSE is similar to MAE, but, due to the squaring, gives more weight to larger discrepancies between predicted ratings $\hat{r}_{u,i}$ and true ratings $r_{u,i}$ than to smaller errors.
Recall	$\frac{\lvert L_u \cap T_u\rvert}{\lvert T_u\rvert}$ $\frac{\lvert L_q \cap T_q\rvert}{\lvert T_q\rvert}$	In the case of a RS (top), recall denotes the fraction of correct interaction predictions in the result list L_u created for user u among the true interactions of u in the test set T_u. Intuitively, how many of the items liked by u the RS can find. Usually, recall is computed for a list of recommendations capped at N items, i.e. $\lvert L_u\rvert = N$, commonly denoted as *Recall@N* (or $R@N$). Analogously, for IR tasks, recall denotes the fraction of documents L_q correctly retrieved for a query q among all documents T_q relevant to q.
Precision	$\frac{\lvert L_u \cap T_u\rvert}{\lvert L_u\rvert}$ $\frac{\lvert L_q \cap T_q\rvert}{\lvert L_q\rvert}$	Precision intuitively denotes how many of the recommended or retrieved items in the result list L_u or L_q are indeed relevant to the query q or liked by user u (concerning the items in the test set T_q or T_u). It is expressed in relative numbers with respect to a given result list of size N, i.e. $\lvert L_u\rvert = N$ or $\lvert L_q\rvert = N$, commonly denoted as *Precision@N* (or $P@N$).
Hit rate	$\frac{1}{\lvert U\rvert}\sum_{u\in U} \text{sgn}\lvert\{L_u \cap T_u\}\rvert$ $\frac{1}{\lvert Q\rvert}\sum_{q\in Q} \text{sgn}\lvert\{L_q \cap T_q\}\rvert$	Hit rate (or hit ratio) measures the fraction of users U for which the RS can suggest at least one relevant (liked) item; or the fraction of queries Q for which the IR system can identify at least one relevant document.

Table 1.1: Common *rank-agnostic accuracy metrics* to evaluate IRRSs. Notation: R and $\hat{R}$ denote actual ratings and predicted ratings, respectively; L_u and L_q represent, respectively, the result list for a user u or query q created by the IRRS; T_u and T_q, respectively, refer to the actual result list for user u or query q, according to the test set used for evaluation; Q is the set of all queries, U the set of all users

Metric	Formula	Description
Average precision	$\frac{1}{\lvert T_u \rvert}\sum_{i\in 1}^{\lvert L_u \rvert} rel(i)\cdot P@i$ $\frac{1}{\lvert T_q \rvert}\sum_{i\in 1}^{\lvert L_q \rvert} rel(i)\cdot P@i$	Average precision is an extension of precision that is often used in ranking settings. It considers precision at different result list sizes ($P@i$, $i = 1 \dots N$), weighting precision values according to whether the item at position i in result set L_u or L_q is relevant or not, as given by the indicator function $rel(i)$. It is commonly denoted as $AP@N$.
Mean average precision	$\frac{1}{\lvert U \rvert}\sum_{u\in U} AP@N$ $\frac{1}{\lvert Q \rvert}\sum_{q\in Q} AP@N$	MAP quantifies the accuracy of a RS as the arithmetic mean over the $AP@N$ values for all users $u \in U$; accordingly, MAP for a retrieval system is the mean of the $AP@N$ values realized over all queries $q \in Q$.
Mean reciprocal rank	$\min_i \frac{1}{\{i : L_u[i] \in T_u\}}$ $\min_i \frac{1}{\{i : L_q[i] \in T_q\}}$	MRR is the inverse of the ranking position at which the top-ranked relevant item for a user u or query q occurs; $L_q[i]$ and $L_u[i]$ denote the document retrieved for query q at position i and item recommended to user u at position i, respectively.
Discounted cumulative gain	$\sum_{i=1}^{N} \frac{rel(i)}{log_2(i+1)}$	DCG aggregates the relevance information for all items or documents in the result list of size N, weighting each by its logarithmically scaled inverse ranking position; $rel(i)$ is the indicator function (1 if the item at position i is relevant, 0 otherwise).
Normalized discounted cumulative gain	$\frac{DCG}{IDCG}$	NDCG scales the DCG to the range $[0, 1]$ by dividing it by the ideal DCG, which is obtained when ranking documents or items perfectly, i.e., in decreasing order of their relevance. It is, therefore, more interpretable than the raw *DCG* values.

Table 1.2: Common *rank-aware accuracy metrics* to evaluate IRRSs. Notation: L_u and L_q represent, respectively, the result list for a user u or query q created by the IRRS; T_u and T_q, respectively, refer to the actual result list for user u or query q, according to the test set used for system evaluation; Q denotes the set of all queries, U the set of all users

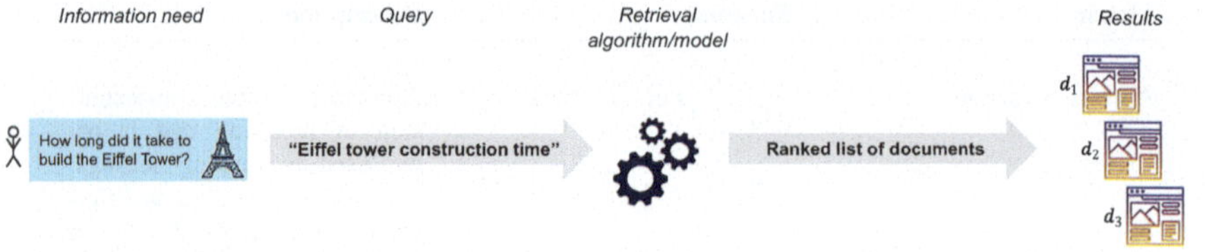

Fig. 1.1: Simplified overview of the traditional pipeline of a retrieval system used for Web search

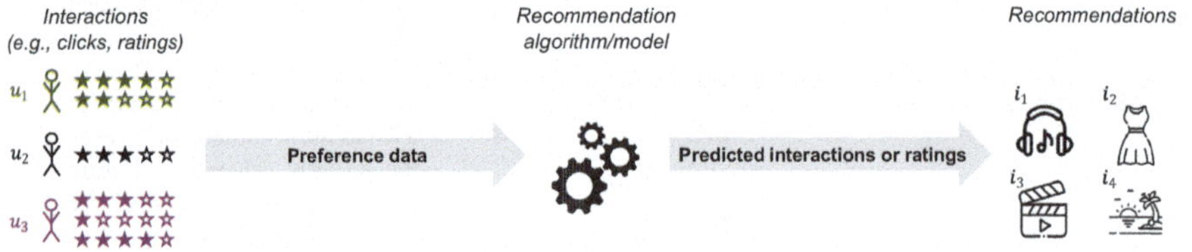

Fig. 1.2: Simplified overview of the traditional pipeline of a recommender system

1.3 Stakeholders

Various stakeholders are involved in the design, development, deployment, maintenance, and use of IRRSs as well as in related research activities [3, 338, 420]. While the vast majority of research focuses on the *end users* of IRRSs, who are also referred to as *content consumers* in the literature, other stakeholders are at least equally important, depending on the perspective taken, e.g., business, law, or psychology. The most prominent stakeholders beyond end users include content creators, service providers, and policymakers. *Content creators*, also referred to as *content producers*, are domain-dependent. For instance, in a music RS, these include music artists, producers, and record labels. In a candidate RS for recruiting, these include the different actors in the companies or institutions that are looking for employees. *Service providers* refer to the maintainers of IRRSs that connect content consumers and creators. Most often, these are big tech companies such as Amazon, Spotify, or Alphabet/Google. *Policymakers* include political institutions and non-governmental organizations (NGOs).

These stakeholders have various goals and objectives, some of which are in line and some are conflicting. For instance, end users are commonly interested in receiving relevant or suited results from a retrieval or recommender system. Often, they also crave novel or diverse content. Content producers, in contrast, typically strive for high exposure of their content, i.e., they want to be included in as many result lists as possible. Platform providers aim to maximize their revenue or create advantages over their competitors. Policymakers, on the other hand, may want to realize some societal benefit or protect certain groups or cultures, often by imposing limitations on retrieved or recommended content. This can be achieved, for instance, by introducing quotas for recommendations of local music artists, as done by France's *Conseil supérieur de l'audiovisuel* [3] to protect national content creators.

1.4 Exemplary Use Cases

Throughout this book, we will refer to three specific use cases to exemplify and illustrate the concepts and methods presented in the subsequent chapters. Moreover, we will discuss the real-world impact that some of the presented technical solutions have on these use cases.

Use Case 1: Music Information Retrieval
The music business represents one of the biggest sectors of the entertainment industry. Therefore, it does not come as a surprise that music information retrieval (MIR) has become an important research area [335], both in academia and industry. MIR technology has paved the way for high-performance *audio fingerprinting* and *music identification* solutions [400] (e.g., Shazam or SoundHound), *music recommender systems* [337] that empower users to discover new music in today's massive catalogs of songs (e.g., Spotify, Deezer, or Apple Music), and *score following* [172], often found in applications to learn or practice an instrument (e.g., Yousician or Simply Piano). This use case connects well to the three major dimensions of trustworthy IRRSs that we target in the book, for instance, ensuring an unbiased exposure of artists in recommendation lists regardless of their gender or previous popularity (*fairness*), recommendations that can be explained to the end user (*transparency*), and measures to ensure that third parties cannot misuse users' data, such as recorded audio for music identification or interactions with songs in a RS (*privacy*).

Use Case 2: Recruitment-Related Recommender Systems
Recommender systems in the context of recruiting [107, 364] have become important tools for job seekers and human resource departments alike. They can be categorized into candidate recommenders and job recommenders. The former create a list of candidates that may be suited for a given job advertisement and are, therefore, commonly used by recruiters. The latter are used by job seekers to find suitable vacancies based on their professional profile, curriculum vitae (CV), or biography. The recruitment domain is a particularly sensitive area in which decisions can have negative effects on the lives of individuals. For instance, *job recommenders* that systematically offer worse-paid

[3] https://www.csa.fr

jobs to female users and better-paid jobs to males contribute to increasing the gender pay gap [210]. Such algorithmic behavior can even be discriminatory in a legal sense. Recruiting decisions made or supported by hiring algorithms in *candidate recommenders* can exhibit similar behavior [105]. Both examples obviously connect to the trustworthiness dimension of *fairness*. Such undesirable algorithmic behavior is very hard to detect for job seekers because they do not know which (perhaps better-paid) jobs are *not* recommended to them. Consequently, this calls for a high level of *transparency* in such systems to explain their decision-making processes. In addition, since CVs and biographies may contain personal information, protecting this information against leakage to attackers or other third parties is crucial. Ensuring *privacy* is, therefore, a strongly desired property of recruitment-related RSs.

Use Case 3: Health-Related Search and Retrieval

Search and retrieval systems have become essential tools in the healthcare industry, facilitating access to vast amounts of medical information and data. By doing so, they enhance the ability of healthcare professionals to make informed decisions, support clinical research, and improve patients' health [175]. Patients, researchers, and medical experts are among the users interested in medical information retrieval. Patients search for information on medical issues and therapies. Researchers aim to identify medical data and recent literature to fuel their research and experiments. Clinicians and general practitioners search for relevant information regarding diagnoses and treatments. Medical information is typically shared through various channels, such as online platforms that provide access to vast amounts of scientific medical literature, or electronic health records (EHRs) and medical databases within healthcare institutions [158]. However, the domain of health and medicine is highly sensitive, and the use of advanced techniques to facilitate information access in healthcare raises questions about bias, fairness, and transparency of algorithms [313]. For example, patients present in an EHR system might not be representative of a more general population [60], leading to biased search results when searching for patient records or other medical information and connecting to the dimension of *fairness*. Furthermore, *privacy* protection is critical due to the sensitive nature of health-related information, involving protecting sensitive health information from unauthorized access, use, or disclosure in compliance with legal and ethical standards.

1.5 Scope and Content

The ongoing debate revolving around regulating AI technology and making it trustworthy considers AI in a broad sense and involves many dimensions of trustworthiness, often adopting vague or even contradicting definitions of key trustworthiness concepts. Notwithstanding the importance of other areas and applications of AI, in this book, we put the focus on algorithms and systems that provide end users with ranked lists of items, either as a result of a query (IR) or a user profile (RS). In terms of trustworthiness dimensions, we narrow the scope of our discussion to the three aspects of fairness, transparency, and privacy (and closely related topics) since these are among the most frequently discussed and impactful aspects in the realm of IRRSs.

The subsequent chapters of the book are organized as follows. We start by providing an overview of recent initiatives and already operational policies to regulate AI technology and discuss them in the context of IRRSs in Chap. 2. Since the European Union is at the forefront of elaborating guidelines and regulations for ethical and trustworthy AI, here, we foremost take a European perspective. Notwithstanding, we also review initiatives outside of Europe, in particular in the USA and China. Chapter 3 presents a categorization of various biases in IRRSs along different axes and discusses their relation to fairness and non-discrimination, taking a multidisciplinary perspective. It further introduces methods to uncover and quantify harmful biases and presents approaches to mitigate them. After that, Chap. 4 introduces major facets of transparency, including explainability, traceability, and auditability. It discusses common strategies to achieve explainability in IRRSs together with concrete methods to generate explanations. The chapter also provides an introduction to algorithmic auditing with a particular focus on auditing algorithms for biased, discriminatory, and harmful behavior of IRRSs. Chapter 5 introduces the privacy and security aspects of IRRSs. It explores regulations around data protection in various regions (Europe, the USA, and China) and then dives into technical approaches to mitigating privacy risks, including anonymization techniques and encryption methods. The chapter continues delving into security threats like adversarial attacks and potential defenses against them. Finally, Chap. 6 rounds the book off and provides an outlook on the grand challenges we identified for the community of researchers and practitioners in IRRSs, as related to the multidisciplinary subject matters of the book. These challenges include dealing with discrepancies between attempts to quantify the fairness of a IRRS, its human perception, and regulatory frameworks; understanding the capabilities and limitations of existing solutions in terms of fairness, transparency, and privacy; and adopting a multistakeholder perspective when developing solutions for fair, transparent, and privacy-preserving IR and RS technology.

1.6 Further Reading

This book provides a solid introduction to regulations and technological approaches related to major trustworthiness aspects of AI technology. It discusses their relevance for IRRSs, also in a legal and societal context. Notwithstanding, we would like to point the interested reader to additional resources that offer insights from other perspectives or a more detailed treatment.

Section 1.1 already pointed to some high-quality and comprehensive resources on the topics of IR [41, 267] and RSs [16, 222, 321]. Specific trustworthiness dimensions in the context of IRRSs are addressed in further literature. For instance, Fan et al. [131] cover in their survey six dimensions of trustworthiness in RSs, namely, the three addressed in the book at hand and, additionally, safety and robustness, environmental well-being, and accountability. Ge et al. [154] provide a detailed and up-to-date review of the current research landscape of RSs addressing explainability, fairness, privacy, robustness, and controllability. The authors also shed light on the combination of these aspects, e.g., they also present research on controllable privacy.

Even more specific resources concerning each of the three dimensions covered in the book at hand (bias, fairness, and non-discrimination; transparency and explainability; privacy and security) can be found in separate sections of the corresponding chapters, respectively, Sects. 3.7, 4.10, and 5.6.

Chapter 2
Regulatory Initiatives

The widespread adoption of IRRSs and their wide-reaching impact on individuals and society as a whole have amplified the need for regulation, particularly concerning *transparency, exposure diversity, more user choice in recommender systems, and unbundling of hosting and content curation.*[1] In the Western Hemisphere, the European Union has been spearheading initiatives and policies to regulate IRRSs and, more generally, computer systems that are based on AI technologies. Therefore, we devote a major part of our investigation of regulatory activities and policies to those happening in the European Union (Sect. 2.1). Nevertheless, recently, the USA has made efforts toward (mildly) regulating and imposing certain requirements on AI technologies. Therefore, we present initiatives and planned regulations also for the USA (Sect. 2.2). Considering its highly different cultural and political background, at the same time, its unprecedentedly spiraling investment in AI technology, we also take a look at China (Sect. 2.3), where regulation of AI has quite different aims than in the Western world.

2.1 European Union

The European Union (EU) has recently adopted comprehensive initiatives to regulate AI technology, most notably with the *Artificial Intelligence Act (AI Act)*,[2] the *Digital Services Act (DSA)* [311], the *Digital Markets Act (DMA)* [310], and the *General Data Protection Regulation (GDPR)* [309]. In this section, we first review the main requirements defined for trustworthy artificial intelligence, which also directly relate to the subsequent chapters of this book (Sect. 2.1.1). Thereafter, the most important

[1] https://www.article19.org/resources/eu-regulation-of-recommender-systems-in-the-digital-services-act

[2] https://artificialintelligenceact.eu/the-act

M. Schedl et al., *Technical and Regulatory Perspectives on Information Retrieval and Recommender Systems*, The Information Retrieval Series 50,
https://doi.org/10.1007/978-3-031-69978-8_2

and relevant regulation, the AI Act, is introduced (Sect. 2.1.2). Finally, additional regulations that are relevant to RSSs are summarized (Sect. 2.1.3).

2.1.1 Ethics Guidelines for Trustworthy AI

Already in 2019, the independent High-Level Expert Group on AI (HLEG), appointed by the European Commission (EC), proposed seven key requirements AI technology should fulfill to be considered trustworthy [176], as illustrated in Fig. 2.1 and explained in the following in the context of IRRSs.[3]

KR1: Human agency and oversight. AI systems should *empower humans*, allowing them to make informed decisions, foster their fundamental rights, and respect their dignity and personal autonomy. Proper *oversight mechanisms* need to be ensured, which can be achieved through human-in-the-loop. For instance, IRRSs should not act as autonomous content filtering systems that give their user no control over the results.

KR2: Technical robustness and safety. AI systems need to be *resilient* and *secure*. They need to be *safe*, ensuring a fallback plan in case something goes wrong. They need to be *robust* to withstand unintended errors (e.g., noise) or intended problems (e.g., attacks). For instance, IRRSs should withstand adversarial cyberattacks that aim at maliciously promoting certain contents.

KR3: Privacy and data governance. AI systems need to ensure full respect for *privacy* and *data protection*, e.g., protection of personal data, data minimization, and anonymization. They need to offer *data governance* mechanisms, taking into account the quality and integrity of the data. It should also be clearly defined how to collect, process, audit, and monitor the data. For instance, IRRS providers should take safety measures to avoid data leakage of sensitive user information to third parties.

KR4: Transparency. The data, system, and business models linked to AI should be *transparent*. AI systems and their decisions should be *explained* in a manner adapted to their stakeholders. Humans need to be *aware* that they are interacting with an AI system and must be informed of the system's capabilities and limitations. For instance, an IRRS user should be able to request and receive an explanation from the system about why certain items have been retrieved or recommended.

KR5: Diversity, non-discrimination, and fairness. AI systems should be inclusive of *diverse stakeholders* and should promote equal access, gender equality, and cultural diversity. *Unfair bias* must be avoided, as it could have multiple negative implications, from the marginalization of vulnerable groups to the exacerbation of *prejudice* and *discrimination*. Fostering *diversity*, AI systems should be accessible to all, regardless of any disability, and involve relevant stakeholders throughout their entire life cycle. For instance, RSs should recommend items of similar quality to male, female, and non-binary users.

[3] https://digital-strategy.ec.europa.eu/en/library/ethics-guidelines-trustworthy-ai

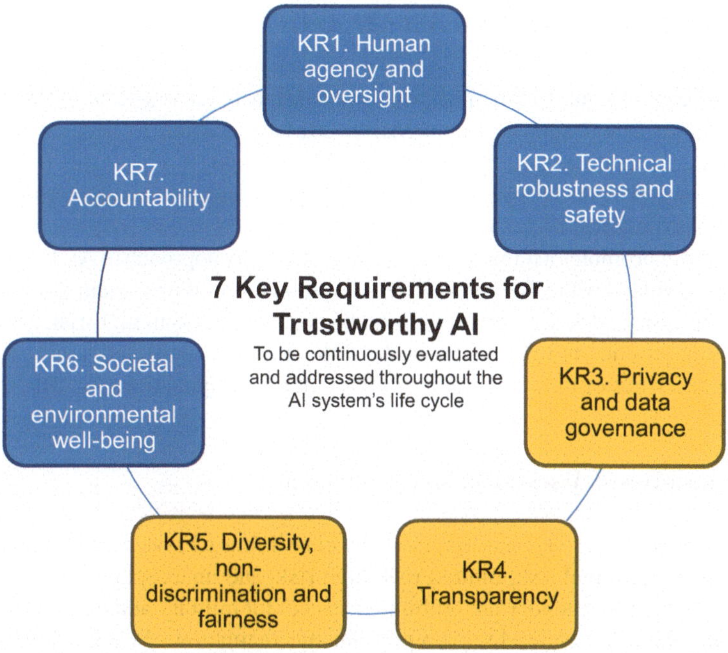

Fig. 2.1: The 7 key requirements for trustworthy artificial intelligence, as laid down in the European Union's *Ethics Guidelines for Trustworthy AI* [176] The three requirements particularly addressed in this book are colored in yellow: KR3 addressed in Chap. 3, KR4 addressed in Chap. 4, and KR5 addressed in Chap. 5

KR6: Societal and environmental well-being. AI systems should *benefit all human beings*, including future generations. It must be ensured that they are sustainable and *environment-friendly*. They should take into account the environment, including *other living beings* such as animals. Their social and societal impact should be carefully considered. For instance, energy consumption during model training and inference should be taken into account when developing IRRSs.

KR7: Accountability. Mechanisms should be put in place to ensure *responsibility* and *accountability* for AI systems and their outcomes. *Auditability* enables the assessment of algorithms, data, and design processes, especially in critical applications. *Reproducibility*, e.g., via open data and code, is a key component in this context. For instance, IRRSs should provide means to assess the origins of the problem (training data, algorithm, etc.) in case they cause harm, such as preventing certain users from realizing opportunities.

While not legally binding, these key requirements are also reflected in the AI Act discussed next.

2.1.2 Artificial Intelligence Act (AI Act)

In December 2023, the EU member states unanimously endorsed the AI Act.[4] The European Parliament approved it in March 2024. It is about to become the most important regulation regarding the use of AI technology within the EU. In the following, we provide an overview of its key parts and discuss their foreseeable implications on IRRSs.

The AI Act promotes a human-centric and trustworthy approach to AI. It lays down harmonized rules for the deployment of AI systems, prohibits certain applications, imposes specific restrictions and requirements for AI systems in high-risk areas, and defines transparency requirements. In the following, we distill and summarize the key characteristics of the AI Act and discuss potential implications for IRRSs.

2.1.2.1 Risk-Based Assessment and Regulation

The AI Act follows a risk-based approach by classifying AI systems into one of four categories: no/minimal risk, limited risk, high risk, and unacceptable risk. Systems that fall into the last category are prohibited, except for military and national security purposes, which are generally exempt from the regulation. AI applications with *minimal* risk include spam filters and bots in video games. There are no specific legally binding rules for them. Systems posing a *limited* risk include generative AI technologies for chatbots as well as deepfake generators. In this case, certain transparency criteria must be fulfilled. In particular, their users must be informed that they are interacting with an AI, and providers need to ensure that AI-generated content is identifiable as such.

Much stricter rules apply to *high*-risk AI systems and general-purpose AI. These regulations will be detailed in Sect. 2.1.2.3. Examples of such high-risk systems include applications used in the context of *employment and work* (e.g., to make decisions about hiring, firing, or promotion), *education* (e.g., to determine admission to educational institutions, to evaluate learning outcomes, or to detect prohibited behavior of students during exams), *law enforcement* (e.g., to predict the risk of a person to become a victim or offender or to evaluate the reliability of evidence when investigating or prosecuting criminal offenses), *immigration and border control* (e.g., to assess eligibility or risk in applications for asylum, visa, and residence permits), and in *safety components* of products or *critical infrastructure* (e.g., to ensure the safety of power and water supply).

AI applications with an *unacceptable* risk are prohibited by the AI Act. These include facial recognition systems used for mass surveillance, emotion recognition systems, social scoring systems that classify persons based on their social behavior (e.g., via social media mining), and systems to infer personal or personality char-

[4] https://artificialintelligenceact.eu/the-act

acteristics.[5] Note that this regulation will likely affect some psychology-informed RSs that leverage emotion or personality information of their users to personalize recommendations [220], at least when this information is automatically acquired through ML or DL technology. Also, the use of AI for commercial practices leading to economic or financial harm to consumers is prohibited.

2.1.2.2 Regulation of Use Cases

An interesting observation is that regulations in the AI Act revolve around *use cases* of AI rather than particular technologies.[6] This makes it hard to generally categorize IRRSs into one of the four risk classes because their classification will strongly depend on the domain in which the IRRS under consideration is applied. Even though no jurisdiction is available because the AI Act has not come into force at the time of writing, we provide our opinion about the likely categorization of systems belonging to our three use cases.

Use Case 1: Music Information Retrieval
Retrieval and recommender systems adopted in entertainment domains, such as music, movies, or books, will probably fall under *minimal* or *limited* risk.

Use Case 2: Recruitment-Related Recommender Systems
Recruitment-related search and recommendation systems will likely belong to the *high-risk* class since AI-powered tools used for employment are explicitly mentioned in the AI Act for this risk class.

Use Case 3: Health-Related Search and Retrieval
Since ensuring a high level of protection of health, safety, and fundamental rights is one of the major goals of the AI Act, AI-powered search engines and RSs in this area will likely be classified as *high risk*.

---

[5] Please note that the AI Act defines exceptions, even for some of these unacceptably high-risk applications. A detailed discussion, however, is beyond the scope of this book.

[6] A notable exception is the part about general-purpose AIs that even specifically addresses "large generative AI models with at least a billion of parameters and trained with a large amount of data using self-supervision at scale."

2.1.2.3 Requirements for High-Risk Systems

The AI Act lays down several requirements for AI systems classified as high risk. Since many IRRSs will likely fall under this category (see Sect. 2.1.2.2), we summarize these requirements in the following:

- *Risk management systems* must be established, implemented, documented, and maintained throughout the entire life cycle of the AI system. It aims at identifying and mitigating the relevant risks of the system regarding health, safety, and fundamental rights, in light of its intended purpose and reasonably foreseeable misuse. The risk management system should also be regularly reviewed and updated.
- *Data and data governance measures* must be installed, in particular for training, validation, and test data. They need to make transparent the relevant design choices, data collection processes, and data processing steps; assess the availability, quantity, and suitability of the data; examine possible biases that may affect the health, safety, or fundamental rights of people and elaborate appropriate measures to prevent or mitigate such biases; and ensure that the used datasets are relevant, representative, error-free, and complete with respect to their intended purpose.
- *Technical documentation* has to be ensured and kept up to date. It must contain all information necessary to assess the compliance of the system with the relevant requirements, e.g., information about the general characteristics, capabilities, and limitations of the system, algorithms, data, training, testing, and validation procedures. It must be written in a clear and comprehensive form.
- *Record keeping* is important to ensure a certain level of traceability of the system's functioning. This means that the system must be capable of automatically logging events throughout its lifetime. Minimum requirements of the logging capabilities include the period of use of the system, input data provided to the system, and persons involved in the verification of system output.
- *Transparency* requirements should ensure clear, concise, correct, and complete instructions for the use of the system and should enable interpretation of its output. These instructions must include details about the system provider; the characteristics, capabilities, and limitations of the system; the system's expected lifetime; the level of accuracy and robustness against which it has been tested; known or foreseeable potential for misuse; system performance estimates for the intended user groups; specifications for the input data; and requirements for computational resources and necessary maintenance measures.
- *Human oversight* must be possible, e.g., by equipping the AI system with human-machine interfaces, so that it can be overseen by humans. These oversight measures must further enable users to understand the capabilities and limitations of the system, to correctly interpret the system's output, to decide not to use the system, or to manually override its output. They should also raise awareness of the possibility that users may automatically rely on the system's output. In addition, users must be provided an option to intervene or interrupt the system's operation, bringing it to a halt in a safe state, e.g., through a "stop" button.

- *Accuracy, robustness, and cybersecurity* must be achieved and maintained at a high and consistent level within the AI system. The system must be resilient against errors, faults, and inconsistencies, as well as against malicious attempts to modify their use, outputs, or performance by exploiting vulnerabilities. One regulation that is especially important in the context of IRRSs requires that high-risk systems that *continue to learn* during their operation should be able to eliminate or reduce the risk of biased outputs influencing the input of future operations. This means that harmful feedback loops should be avoided.

Finally, we would like to provide two further remarks concerning the AI Act. First, the AI Act affects not only IRRS providers in the EU but, more generally, also regulates providers outside of Europe that deploy their systems within the EU. Second, some provisions are particularly important for the scientific community and academic researchers. The AI Act explicitly excludes from its regulatory scope AI systems and models specifically developed and put into service for the sole purpose of scientific research and development. Also, AI systems provided under an open-source license are exempt from the regulations of the AI Act unless they belong to the class of high-risk or prohibited AI.

2.1.3 Other Relevant EU Regulations

There also exist further regulations that are relevant to IRRSs, beyond the AI Act. We discuss the most important ones in the following.

Digital Services Act (DSA): The DSA[7] establishes a legal framework for how online platforms and services should operate [311]. In 2023, it came into effect for very large online platforms, search engines, and RSs and then one year later for all providers of such services. The DSA's focus is on transparency, accountability, and prevention of harmful content. It lays down different obligations, depending on the size and number of users of the platform, where stricter rules apply for larger platforms.

Next to obligations for *all online platforms* regarding the sale of illegal products and services, as well as concerning the provision of access to illegal content, the DSA aims at protecting minors by prohibiting all platforms from using targeted advertising based on the use of their personal data. More generally, it imposes limitations on advertising, especially the use of sensitive personal data (e.g., gender, race, and religion) for targeted advertising. Stricter rules apply for *very large online platforms and search engines*, defined by having at least 45 million monthly active users. Among others, they must offer their users a system for recommending content that is not based on profiling. In addition, they must identify, analyze, and mitigate the systemic risks they create, especially potential negative effects on fundamental rights. As of April 2023, the EC identified 17 very large online platforms (Alibaba AliExpress, Amazon Store, Apple AppStore, Booking.com, Facebook, Google Play,

[7] https://www.eu-digital-services-act.com

Google Maps, Google Shopping, Instagram, LinkedIn, Pinterest, Snapchat, TikTok, Twitter, Wikipedia, YouTube, and Zalando) and 2 very large online search engines (Bing and Google Search). Additional important regulations that affect IRRSs include the following:

- Platforms using RSs must *disclose the main parameters* used to determine how items are ranked.
- Users have the right to *obtain clear information on why* they are recommended certain items or information.
- Users have the right to *opt out from RSs based on profiling*.
- Platforms need to put in place identification and mitigation measures to *counteract certain risks*, for instance, the spread of misinformation.
- Service providers are obliged to *provide clear explanations of how and why content is removed*. This is relevant for RSs that might exclude certain items based on risk assessments.
- Providers need to *publish repositories of all the advertisements* served on their platforms.
- Notably, providers have to give *access to publicly available data* to researchers. A special mechanism for vetted researchers will be established later.[8]

An overview of how the DSA could create conflicts between the liabilities it imposes on platform and service providers and fundamental rights is provided by Frosio and Geiger in [147]. They study these issues from multiple perspectives: the users (both consumers and creators of content), platforms, regulators, and other stakeholders.

Digital Markets Act (DMA): The DMA[9] aims at making the digital online markets fairer and more contestable [310]. By entering into force in 2022 and becoming applicable in 2023, the DMA was one of the first regulatory tools to comprehensively regulate the gatekeeper power of the largest digital companies, including those providing online search engines, app stores, and messenger services. It lays down obligations and prohibitions for these gatekeepers. In particular, in the context of IRRSs, the DMA prevents these gatekeepers from engaging in anti-competitive practices that limit consumers' choices and from restricting competitors that rely on their platforms. This prevents the gatekeepers from attaining an unfair advantage for their own services or products, e.g., by overrepresenting them in search results or recommendations.

General Data Protection Regulation (GDPR): The GDPR[10] is a regulation that lays down rules for the processing of personal data of humans within the EU [309].

[8] In our opinion, the former requirement could be a rather weak one given it concerns data that is already publicly available; plus, it does not specify in which way the data needs to be provided to researchers. The latter is vaguely defined, and we will have to see how these "special mechanisms" will take form. On the other hand, there already exist several reports by human rights organization AlgorithmWatch about researchers who were either denied access to larger datasets by major companies or were given only incomplete data (see https://algorithmwatch.org/en/left-on-read-facebook-data-access).

[9] https://digital-markets-act.ec.europa.eu

[10] https://gdpr-info.eu

It was implemented in May 2018 and is considered one of the strictest privacy and security laws around the globe, ensuring the right to the protection of personal data. At the same time, it includes regulations to ensure the free movement of personal data within the EU. The most important provisions in the context of IRRSs include the following:

- Processing of personal data (e.g., names, email addresses, data about location, ethnicity, gender, religious beliefs, and political opinions) must be *lawful, fair, and transparent* to the user. This means that IRRS providers must have a legitimate reason to collect and use personal data (e.g., the user's consent).
- Data must be collected for *specific and explicitly stated purposes* and not used for other purposes without additional consent.
- Only data that is absolutely necessary for the stated purpose must be collected, i.e., the principle of *data minimization* applies.
- Users must receive clear and *transparent privacy information* that explain what of their data is collected, why it is collected, and how it will be used.
- Users may request and must be given access to their data held by providers (*right to access*).
- Users can request their data to be deleted (*right to be forgotten*).

Charter of Fundamental Rights: Next to the more CS- and AI-specific regulations discussed above, at a more fundamental level, the Charter of Fundamental Rights[11] contains some titles that strongly relate to the trustworthiness aspects addressed in this book [76]. In particular, its second title ("Freedoms") covers liberty, privacy, protection of personal data, marriage, thought, religion, expression, assembly, education, work, property, and asylum. Its third title ("Equality") covers equality before the law, prohibition of all discrimination, including discrimination based on disability, age, sexual orientation, cultural, religious, and linguistic diversity, as well as the rights of children and the elderly.

Relevant in the context of IRRSs, Article 8 ensures individuals' *right to privacy*, including control over their personal data, and transparency about data collection practices of IRRSs. Articles 10 and 11 refer to the *freedom of expression and information*. Since IRRSs impact which information their users see, they may also limit their exposure to diverse viewpoints. Article 21 guarantees *freedom from discrimination* based on traits such as gender, race, religion, or sexual orientation. It, therefore, requires RSS providers to strive for non-discrimination and fairness.

2.2 USA

In the USA, several regulatory initiatives have been taken to harness the power of AI while mitigating its potential risks. The US government's recent **Executive Order**

[11] https://commission.europa.eu/aid-development-cooperation-fundamental-rights/your-rights-eu/eu-charter-fundamental-rights_en

(EO) on Artificial Intelligence[12] lays a foundation for responsible AI development and use. The EO establishes eight guiding principles for AI development in the USA. These principles encompass:

- *Safety and security*: AI systems should operate reliably and avoid causing harm.
- *Responsible innovation*: AI systems should promote public trust by being transparent and accountable in AI development.
- *Supporting American workers*: During development, the potential impact of AI on jobs and the workforce should be considered.
- *Equity and civil rights*: It should be ensured that AI systems are fair and unbiased and do not discriminate.
- *Consumer protection*: Consumers should be protected from AI-driven products and services that could be deceptive or harmful.
- *Privacy and civil liberties*: Personal privacy should be respected throughout the AI development and deployment life cycle.
- *Managing risks from government use of AI*: Safeguards for AI use in government applications should be implemented.
- *Global leadership*: International collaboration on responsible AI development and use should be promoted.

The EO expands beyond theoretical principles, articulating tangible steps for their implementation. It targets several critical domains: In the area of *AI safety and security*, government agencies will establish guidelines and best practices, focusing particularly on generative AI and foundational models. These measures aim to address concerns surrounding the robustness, explainability, and controllability of AI systems. *Addressing bias and ensuring fairness* in AI systems is a key priority. Efforts will be made to identify and mitigate biases, thereby guaranteeing equitable treatment for all users. *Transparency and accountability* will be enforced, requiring agencies involved in AI development or usage to provide detailed reports on their activities. This heightened transparency seeks to cultivate public trust and facilitate independent assessment of AI systems. Regulatory frameworks will be developed to *mitigate risks* associated with large AI models that are vulnerable to misuse. Potential measures include the establishment of registries or mandates for companies to disclose their AI model capabilities. Cloud service providers may also be compelled to report on large AI models hosted on their platforms. It is important to note that the specific details of the reporting requirements might not be fully fleshed out in the EO itself. In detail, the EO mentions that the information to be reported includes the types, sizes, and capabilities of AI models being developed and deployed. This knowledge helps assess potential risks and benefits associated with these models. Further guidance documents or regulations from the National Institute of Standards and Technology[13] (NIST) are likely to provide more specifics on what information cloud providers need to report and how the reporting process will work. Addition-

[12] https://www.whitehouse.gov/briefing-room/presidential-actions/2023/10/30/executive-order-on-the-safe-secure-and-trustworthy-development-and-use-of-artificial-intelligence/

[13] https://www.nist.gov

ally, foreign resellers of US cloud services might be subject to regulations requiring customer identity verification. These measures aim to prevent malicious actors from accessing or deploying harmful AI.

The EO establishes a timeframe for some actions. For instance, the NIST has 270 days, starting from the issuing date (October 30th, 2023), to develop the initial guidelines for safe and secure AI. However, NIST and the White House Office of Science and Technology Policy (OSTP)[14] publish updates and draft documents for public comment as the process unfolds. Previously, NIST published the **AI Risk Management Framework (RMF)**,[15] which provides voluntary guidelines for organizations to manage risks throughout the life cycle of an AI system. The AI RMF is a voluntary framework designed to equip organizations with a structured approach to managing risks associated with AI systems. It emphasizes the importance of trustworthiness throughout the AI system life cycle, from design and development to deployment and use. Several functional aspects are described. First, the "Govern" function establishes clear roles, responsibilities, and policies for AI development and use. Then, "Map" focuses on understanding the AI system itself, its purpose, data usage, and potential risks. "Measure" involves assessing the severity of these risks, while "Manage" tackles implementing controls to mitigate them. These controls can range from technical safeguards to training programs, ensuring the AI system functions as intended and minimizes potential harm.

Beyond federal laws and regulations, several states also have some relevant legislation and initiatives that touch on specific aspects of AI use.

California has implemented a legislation that significantly impacts various aspects of data collection, privacy rights, and workforce classification. The **California Consumer Privacy Act (CCPA)**[16] underwent modifications through the **California Privacy Rights Act (CPRA)**,[17] which collectively regulate practices concerning data gathering and utilization. Although not directly tailored toward AI, these laws exert considerable influence on the development and deployment of AI technologies. Together, these laws act as a powerful duo regulating how businesses collect and use consumer data. The CCPA and CPRA indirectly influence the development and deployment of AI technologies in California. Since these laws empower consumers with control over their data, AI developers and businesses must tread carefully when gathering information to train and operate AI systems. This ensures that AI development in California aligns with consumer privacy expectations and fosters a more responsible approach to this powerful technology. The CCPA and the CPRA can significantly impact how IRRSs collect and use user data. These systems might need to be more transparent about data collection practices and offer users more control over their information. Additionally, regulations might restrict the use of certain sensitive data, such as the output of facial recognition systems, for personalization purposes. Moreover, the **California Assembly Bill 5 (AB 5)** primarily addresses

[14] https://www.whitehouse.gov/ostp

[15] https://www.nist.gov/artificial-intelligence

[16] https://oag.ca.gov/privacy/ccpa

[17] https://cppa.ca.gov/regulations

the classification of workers, particularly in the gig economy (i.e., the economy involving temporary or freelance work arrangements). Despite its main focus on labor classification, AB 5 holds implications for the integration of AI-powered automation within the workforce. If AI automates tasks that meet the ABC test[18] (controlled, directed, core business),[19], the workers previously classified as independent contractors might be reclassified as employees. This could significantly increase costs for companies due to employee benefits and payroll taxes. The act could have several implications. Companies might choose to directly employ workers for tasks that AI cannot fully automate to avoid AB 5 implications. This could lead to a decrease in the number of independent contractor positions in California. Companies might seek out AI solutions that can handle tasks with a higher degree of autonomy, ensuring workers meet the requirements for true independent contractor classification under AB 5. Finally, businesses might explore hybrid models where AI handles routine tasks while human workers oversee the process or handle complex situations requiring judgment or creativity. Detailed information regarding these legislative measures can be accessed through the California Attorney General's Web site[20] for CCPA and CPRA and the California Legislature Web site[21] for AB 5.

In New York City, legislative measures have been implemented to address concerns regarding the use of algorithmic tools in employment decisions. One significant regulation is the **New York City Local Law 144**,[22] which prohibits the use of algorithmic tools for employment purposes without first undergoing a bias audit (see Sect. 4.8 for a brief discussion of algorithmic auditing). This law is tailored specifically to the hiring process, aiming to ensure fairness and transparency in employment practices.

Use Case 2: Recruitment-Related Recommender Systems
Recruitment-related search and recommendation systems will be impacted by the New York City Local Law since those systems have to undergo a bias audit before being made available.

Additionally, in 2023, a series of bills were introduced in New York aiming to regulate the use of automated employment decision tools further. These proposed bills seek to establish clear criteria for the implementation of AI tools in hiring processes, with a focus on promoting fairness and transparency. While these bills have not yet been enacted into law, they provide insight into the potential future direction of regulations regarding AI in employment. Updates on the progress of these

[18] https://www.labor.ca.gov/employmentstatus/abctest

[19] According to the ABC test, a worker is considered an employee and not an independent contractor unless the hiring entity satisfies several conditions.

[20] https://oag.ca.gov/privacy

[21] https://leginfo.legislature.ca.gov/faces/billTextClient.xhtml?bill_id=201920200AB5

[22] https://www.nixonpeabody.com/insights/alerts/2023/11/13/complying-with-new-york-city-bias-audit-law

bills can be tracked through the New York State Senate Web site.[23] While New York City's Local Law does not directly regulate IRRSs, it signifies a growing movement toward addressing algorithmic bias. This awareness might indirectly influence how IRRSs are developed and deployed in the future, potentially leading to fairer and more transparent experiences for users in New York City.

The **New Jersey Disclosure and Accountability Transparency Act (NJ DATA)** represents a pending piece of legislation aimed at addressing data privacy concerns within the state. This proposed act seeks to introduce regulations concerning the disclosure and handling of personal information utilized by AI systems. Although it has not been enacted into law, its existence underscores New Jersey's proactive approach to overseeing the influence of AI on data management practices. For the latest information and updates regarding NJ DATA, the interested reader can refer to the New Jersey Office of Legislative Services Web site.[24] The NJ DATA, while still awaiting enactment (as of June 2024), has the potential to significantly impact IRRSs operating in the state. NJ DATA, if enacted, represents a step toward greater user control and transparency in data practices. This could lead to IRRSs becoming more accountable, collecting less data, and offering fairer recommendations and search results for New Jersey residents.

Overall, it is important to remember that AI regulations in the USA are still under development. The specific ways they might impact IRRSs will depend on their final form. As the legal landscape evolves, we can expect a more nuanced approach to AI governance, shaping the future of IRRSs in the USA.

2.3 China

AI-based technology in China, including IRRSs, is subject to strict regulations to align with the objectives of the Chinese government, including maintaining state control and social stability through AI governance [433]. These regulations specifically aim to ensure the security and authenticity of information. Additionally, they enforce the promotion of content that aligns with government values and aim to prevent the dissemination of harmful or sensitive content, always in line with governmental policies [351].

The **Cybersecurity Law of the People's Republic of China (CLPRC)** [387, 388], introduced in June 2017, requires online service providers to implement measures to ensure the security and authenticity of information, including guidelines on content filtering, censorship, and promoting content that aligns with the Chinese government values [350]. It contains a wide range of regulatory measures aimed at enhancing national security and social stability while also promoting the development of China's digital economy and information society [304]. At the same time, public bodies in China are granted extensive powers to monitor and control online ac-

[23] https://www.nysenate.gov

[24] https://www.njleg.state.nj.us

tivities. Concretely, the CLPRC addresses the following points, which are elaborated in more detail in the translation of the law given in [388]:

- *Cybersecurity:* The law defines a framework to monitor, prevent, and deal with cybersecurity risks from within and outside of the country. Network operators are mandated to ensure the security and stability of their networks.
- *Critical infrastructure:* According to the CLPRC, critical information infrastructure must be protected against malicious attacks and intrusions.
- *Data localization and security assessments:* Certain data has to be stored in China. In the case of cross-border transfer of personal data or critical information, specific security assessments need to be conducted.
- *Cooperation with authorities:* All providers need to cooperate with public bodies. Public bodies can demand access to data and communication to conduct investigations and for security purposes.
- *Content regulation:* The law demands that IRRSs promote core socialist values and controls for content that could violate such values or promote behavior that could violate them.

Failure to comply with regulations can result in penalties such as fines, restrictions of operations, or even shutdowns of services or organizations.

Approximately 1 month after the CLPRC was introduced, China issued a comprehensive strategy for the development of AI, which outlines a roadmap for AI development until 2023 in key domains such as deep learning, natural language processing, or computer vision [419]. This **New Generation Artificial Intelligence Development Plan (AIDP)** aims to ensure that the development of any AI algorithms, including, for example, IRRSs, generative AI, or facial recognition techniques, align with China's broader geopolitical, fiscal, legal, and ethical objectives [323]. While the AIDP describes legal and regulatory standards related to data security, privacy, and the ethical use of a broad range of AI technologies, it also recognizes the importance of ethical guidelines for AI development, including transparency, fairness, and accountability. Nevertheless, it underscores the need for AI technologies to align with predefined social norms and values [178].

As another part of China's strategic efforts to regulate AI and related technologies, the **Data Security Law** came into effect in 2021. It regulates data processing activities with a focus on data security and sovereignty [83]. Here, data is categorized based on its importance to national security and public interest, whereas stricter regulations apply for handling sensitive and critical data. While it does not directly affect IRRSs, it has implications on how IRRSs can handle and process user data. For instance, if IRRSs process sensitive or critical data, they are subject to stricter regulations.

Also in 2021, another law that is relevant in the context of IRRSs, the **Personal Information Protection Law (PIPL)** [99], was introduced. It regulates the collection, use, and processing of personal information. This includes obtaining consent for the use of sensitive personal information [65], the right to transparency in automatic decision-making [230], privacy, and users' control over their data [99]. It has similarities to the GDPR (see Sect. 2.1.3 for more details) as both aim to protect user privacy and data. However, they differ in that the PIPL prioritizes state control and social stability, which means that governmental bodies are not limited with respect to access to data [99], while the GDPR emphasizes users' control over their data, and thus, also authorities fall under the GDPR [65].

In 2022, specific provisions were put into effect that regulate algorithm-powered IRRSs in China [406, 425]. These **Provisions on the Administration of Algorithm-generated Recommendations for Internet Information Services** [302] focus on issues such as content filtering, censorship, and promoting content that aligns with core government values. Some even regard it as the first approach of a national regulator to control for potential misuse of decisions made by algorithms [395]. Notably, the provisions reflect several principles of trustworthy AI, including transparency, fairness, and accountability [353]. In the following, we discuss the provisions in more detail.

Article 1 defines the aims of the Provisions on the Administration of Algorithm-generated Recommendations for Internet Information Services as

> To regulate algorithm recommendation activities of Internet information services, promote the core socialist values, safeguard national security and social public interests, protect the legitimate rights and interests of citizens, legal persons and other organizations, and promote the healthy and orderly development of Internet information services. [302]

In other words, the provisions regulate online information services that feature IRRSs as part of their service and that operate in mainland China.

Chapter I, Article 2, General Provisions, defines algorithm recommendation technologies as:

> Technologies such as generation and synthesis, personalized push, sorting and selection, retrieval and filtering, and scheduling and decision-making to provide information to users. [302]

Use Case 2: Recruitment-Related Recommender Systems

Recruitment-related RSs are impacted by the Provisions on the Administration of Algorithm-generated Recommendations for Internet Information Services since they select potential candidates for job offers, filter unsuited candidates, and provide decision-making information to recruiters or other stakeholders.

Chapter II of the provisions defines a set of information service standards (Articles 6 to 15), which mandate service providers to prevent the spreading of harmful content via content filtering or censorship measures (Article 6), ensure that the IRRSs are secure and data and user privacy is not infringed upon (Articles 7 and 9), conduct regular reviews and verification measures to ensure that algorithms align with regulations and ethical standards so that users do not become addicted to the services (Article 8), or improve

> the transparency and explainability of retrieval, sorting, selection, push, and display rules to avoid adverse effects on users and prevent and reduce disputes.

Furthermore, content providers must ensure that interaction data, recommended or retrieved content, or user accounts are not faked or manipulated (Article 14). For more details on the articles, please refer to [302].

Notably, the law features a whole chapter on user rights protection (Chapter III). It regulates users' rights to understand under which circumstances they are offered IRRSs outputs, how the underlying algorithms operate, and their intended goals and outcomes (Article 16). Also, users must be allowed to opt out of personalization and be provided with explanations if the use of the IRRS could influence their rights (Article 17). Furthermore, it regulates the need to protect minors and has safeguards for seniors (Articles 18 and 19) or workers (Article 19). Interestingly, the law also mandates service providers to enable users to submit complaints and reports about their services, to which the providers need to respond swiftly (Article 22). Again, please refer to [302] for more details on the respective passages of the law.

Use Case 3: Health-Related Search and Retrieval
A health-related search or recommendation system is designed to provide users with personalized health information and recommendations based on their current health status and medical history. We assume a user using the system to search for information on managing diabetes. A system complying with regulations as outlined in the Provisions on the Administration of Algorithm-generated Recommendations for Internet Information Services must provide information on how the underlying algorithms function and how it arrived at its results. Hence, the system displays explanations detailing that the recommendations are based on the user's search history and the personal data the user has entered into the system. It also includes a link to detailed information on how the algorithm operates, its goals, and its intended outcomes. The user can opt out of personalized recommendations by selecting a clear and accessible option in the settings menu. Then, the system shows general health information on managing diabetes not tailored to the user's specific data.

According to the law, public governmental bodies are mandated to classify service providers based on the service's impact on public opinion, social mobilization capabilities, content types, user scale, data importance, and the extent of user behavior intervention (Article 23). Any service provider whose service could influence public opinion or result in social mobilization must register their service within a short period (i.e., ten working days), provide detailed information about the service, and perform a predefined canceling procedure in case of termination (Article 24). Such service providers are also required to publish information about their service online (Article 26), conduct specific security assessments (Article 27), and facilitate regular inspections by governmental bodies (Article 28). Such security assessments are confidential (Article 29). Violations of the regulations can be reported to the relevant bodies (as described in Article 29). Again, please refer to [302] for more details on the respective passages of the law, and there, please also refer to Chapter V (Articles 31 to 33) for all legal liability aspects.

Recent regulatory efforts in China are mostly concerned with deep synthesis and generative AI. Early 2023, China's **Deep Synthesis Provisions** [288], which regulates AI techniques that can generate synthetic data (e.g., deepfakes), went into effect and later in 2023, interim measures on generative AI [350]. How IRRSs will be affected by these regulations remains unclear to date.

In summary, the Chinese regulatory frameworks for IRRSs have substantial implications. They are designed to guide the development and deployment of IRRSs in a manner that aligns with national security, ethical standards, and governmental policies. As these regulations evolve and adapt to new technological advancements, they will likely continue to shape the strategic landscape in China. Their implications on the design of IRRSs worldwide are yet to be understood.

Chapter 3
Biases, Fairness, and Non-discrimination

The fear of AI threatening humankind has been the topic of countless novels and movies, ranging back at least to *WarGames* and *The Terminator*. These are just fictional stories and nothing more, of course—or as AI pioneer Yoshua Bengio states: "We are very far from super-intelligent AI systems, and there may even be fundamental obstacles to get much beyond human intelligence."[1] In contrast, other world-famous scientists such as Stephen Hawking have warned that "AI will be extremely good at accomplishing its goals, and if those goals aren't aligned with ours, we're in trouble."[2,3]

3.1 Introduction and Context

Although the elimination of humankind by AI looks pretty far-fetched, there is a genuine risk of algorithmic decision-making systems, such as IRRSs, powered by ML and DL technology, to systematically discriminate against certain individuals or groups in favor of others [40, 145], as we will see in this chapter. What appears much less harmful than super-intelligent AI, therefore, still has substantial negative impacts

[1] https://www.bbc.com/news/technology-50166357

[2] https://www.independent.co.uk/tech/stephen-hawking-ai-could-be-the-end-of-humanity-9898320.html

[3] https://www.independent.co.uk/tech/stephen-hawking-artificial-intelligence-could-wipe-out-humanity-when-it-gets-too-clever-as-humans-could-become-like-ants-being-stepped-on-a6686496.html

M. Schedl et al., *Technical and Regulatory Perspectives on Information Retrieval and Recommender Systems*, The Information Retrieval Series 50,
https://doi.org/10.1007/978-3-031-69978-8_3

on our society. In particular, discrimination against certain groups of individuals has been shown to create or amplify:

- *economic inequalities* that may result in individual economic instability but also perpetuate systemic poverty within certain communities [291],
- *educational disparities* that limit career opportunities and contribute to social exclusion [305],
- *mental and physical health issues*, such as increased risks of anxiety, depression, cardiovascular diseases, hypertension, and stress-related disorders [295, 413],
- *mistrust in institutions*, including the legal system, education system, law enforcement, and healthcare, which can hamper citizens' participation in societal processes [389].

While these consequences have been researched predominantly in the context of discrimination by humans against humans, some directly translate to discrimination by algorithmic decision-making systems such as IRRSs, for instance, the detrimental effect of algorithmic discrimination on the trustworthiness of IRRSs.

The scientific literature on unfairness and discrimination of algorithms against humans dates back to the late 1990s [145]. In the last few years, though, the widespread adoption of IRRSs and, lately, generative AI tools leveraging large language models (LLMs) has brought the discussion to the forefront of societal attention and markedly fueled the public debate.

Example: AMS Berufsinfomat/Occupational Information System
When Austria's Public Employment Service (AMS) introduced a chatbot to answer occupational questions,[4] based on a customized ChatGPT instance, it was quickly found to give stereotypical and even sexist suggestions to job seekers [89, 411]. For instance, if its user indicated to be female, the system frequently recommended jobs in the health or beauty sector or the creative industries. In contrast, a male user with otherwise same attributes received recommendations for software developers, retailers, or storekeepers.

In the remainder of this chapter, we briefly review existing regulations on discrimination (Sect. 3.2), provide a multifaceted categorization of biases and fairness criteria as we as various stakeholders (Sect. 3.3), discuss techniques to measure popularity and demographic biases (Sect. 3.4), and present methods to mitigate harmful biases (Sect. 3.5). We conclude by reflecting on open challenges (Sect. 3.6) and point the reader to further literature (Sect. 3.7).

[4] https://www.ams.at/arbeitsuchende/aus-und-weiterbildung/berufsinformationen/berufsinformation/berufsinfomat

3.2 Regulatory Aspects

Regulations targeting the fairness of IRRSs can be found at the European level in the European Union's *Ethics Guidelines for Trustworthy AI*[5] [176] and the *AI Act*,[6] both highlighting the importance of fairness and non-discrimination of AI systems. More precisely:

> Diversity, non-discrimination and fairness means that AI systems are developed and used in a way that includes diverse actors and promotes equal access, gender equality and cultural diversity, while avoiding discriminatory impacts and unfair biases that are prohibited by Union or national law.

For IRRSs, this implies that unfair bias should be avoided at all stages of their creation and use because it can have negative consequences, including the marginalization of vulnerable groups or the exacerbation of prejudice and discrimination. Instead, IRRSs should be accessible to all, regardless of gender, race, or any disability. The process should also involve all relevant stakeholders (see Sect. 3.3.4) throughout the system's entire life cycle.

On a more fundamental level, the topic of non-discrimination even connects to Fundamental Rights and Human Rights, in particular when it comes to employment and labor. For instance, the United Nations' *Universal Declaration of Human Rights*[7] from 1948 states in Article 23:

> Everyone, without any discrimination, has the right to equal pay for equal work.

Similarly, in the USA, the *Civil Rights Act of 1964*[8] prohibits labor market discrimination based on protected human characteristics, for instance, stating:

> It shall be an unlawful employment practice for an employer [...] to fail or refuse to hire or to discharge any individual, or otherwise to discriminate against any individual with respect to his compensation, terms, conditions, or privileges of employment, because of such individual's race, color, religion, sex, or national origin.

Taking a look back at Europe, the *EU Charter of Fundamental Rights*,[9] declared in 2000, in Article 21 forbids

> Discrimination on grounds of sex, race, colour, ethnic or social origin, genetic features, language, religion or other belief, political opinion, membership of a national minority, property, birth, disability, age or sexual orientation.

---

[5] https://digital-strategy.ec.europa.eu/en/library/ethics-guidelines-trustworthy-ai

[6] https://artificialintelligenceact.eu/the-act

[7] https://www.un.org/en/about-us/universal-declaration-of-human-rights

[8] https://www.archives.gov/milestone-documents/civil-rights-act

[9] https://commission.europa.eu/aid-development-cooperation-fundamental-rights/your-rights-eu/eu-charter-fundamental-rights_en

Example: Discrimination in Digital Recruiting/Candidate Recommendation

According to many national and international laws, discrimination in terms of treating one person in a less favorable way than another based on protected grounds such as gender, age, sexual orientation, civil status, religion, race, or disability is prohibited. However, personal differences that are used as the basis for employment decisions are typically not regarded as discriminatory under the law. These include educational requirements or job performance. Another popular example is *affirmative action* (in US law) or *positive action* (in EU law), which refer to policies that are intended as countermeasures to address historical inequalities, such as an underrepresentation of certain groups of employees in certain industries.

One example of such action in digital recruiting is to re-rank candidates for a given job to achieve parity for groups according to certain protected traits, for instance, ensuring that a job advertisement is shown to the same number of male and female job seekers. However, suppose a candidate recommender would strictly enforce in its results a fixed fairness definition, neglecting the actual suitability of the candidates for the job under consideration. In that case, such a system will likely conflict with the requirements of positive or affirmative action. Notwithstanding, in both the EU and US legal frameworks, it is possible to address and mitigate harmful biases present in society (societal biases) and datasets (statistical biases) in recruitment RSs, provided these actions are taken prior to their application in real-world scenarios [207]. Therefore, from a system implementation perspective, the preferred approach to ensuring legal compliance is, for instance, through data pre-processing before training the recommendation model rather than fine-tuning recommendations afterward.

Another legal aspect of discrimination by job RSs is the challenge individuals face in providing evidence that they have been discriminated against. This is because the individual job seeker does not see which jobs were *not* recommended to them. A possible solution could be recommendation algorithms and explanation mechanisms that adopt counterfactual inference, thereby indicating how the recommendations would change if the user had a different trait (e.g., gender or race). While such approaches have recently started to emerge, they have not found their way into commercial systems. One likely reason for system providers' reluctance is their concern over revealing any algorithmic unfairness of their services.

It is important to highlight a significant distinction in terms of the intended recipients of these regulations. The European AI Act and the American Civil Rights Act specifically set forth requirements for companies and employers. In contrast, the Universal Declaration of Human Rights and the EU Charter of Fundamental Rights establish obligations that are directed at entire nations. This difference underscores the varying scopes and targets of these documents, ranging from individual organizations to broader national commitments.

3.3 Categorization of Biases and Fairness Criteria

Issues of unfairness and discrimination caused by—or related to—IRRSs are commonly the result of different biases that the entire life cycle of such systems is exposed to. In technical AI and ML literature, the term "bias" has traditionally been used to refer to the prediction error of a learned model, e.g., the overall discrepancy between a classifier's predictions and the true values of the data instances (according to some "ground truth") [396]. A high bias in this sense commonly leads to a simple model that represents the training data poorly and is therefore said to "underfit."

In contrast to this technical definition of bias, the term is also commonly used in psychology and sociology. In the former discipline, it more generally refers to an individual's systematic deviation from rationality and objectivity in perception, cognition, judgment, or decision-making, which often happens unconsciously (cf. cognitive bias) [103, 119]. In sociology, bias typically refers to collective prejudices of a society that favor one group's values, norms, and traditions over others (cf. cultural and social bias) [56, 123]. Notwithstanding their predominantly negative connotations or implications, certain human biases can also have positive effects, for instance, by improving the efficiency of human learning through heuristics [156].

In this section, we discuss bias from different perspectives by introducing various kinds of biases according to different categorizations. Section 3.3.1 takes a high-level view in distinguishing societal from statistical bias. In Sect. 3.3.2, we focus on biases related particularly to IRRSs and discuss their origins at different stages of the system development and usage processes. Section 3.3.3 then discusses to which extent detrimental biases pose a risk to the fairness of IRRSs and may even result in discriminatory algorithmic behavior. In Sect. 3.3.4, we finally explore the bidirectional relationship between bias and different stakeholders in IRRSs, analyzing how bias affects stakeholders and how stakeholder characteristics and behavior shape bias.

3.3.1 *Societal Bias and Statistical Bias*

Our world is full of biases. Some of them are important—even helpful—for us to navigate through everyday life, e.g., creating stereotypes as part of the human cognitive process. Others can have negative consequences for society and its different actors. In any case, it is vital to be aware of the various kinds of biases we encounter in our lives and, more specifically within the scope of this book, in the context of creating and interacting with IRRS technology.

When it comes to biases in ML- or DL-powered computer systems, we can distinguish from a high-level perspective societal bias and statistical bias. Both are relative concepts that relate to an idealized world or the actual world as it is.

Concretely, *societal bias* refers to the divergence between how the world should be and how it is in reality [126, 266]. However, the crux lies already in this very definition because it raises the question of who defines what an ideal world should look like. In reality, it is cultural values, norms, and traditions that shape societies. And these are not homogeneous around the globe, even though they have been affected by globalization to some extent [196, 249, 344]. Furthermore, in addition to cultural norms, there are also individual differences at play when it comes to defining an ideal world. In fact, while the cultural background of a person shapes their perception of an ideal world, also individual variations play a significant role. What complicates things even more is that the pervasiveness and intensity of such individual differences vary between cultures, as indicated, for instance, by the axis of individualism vs. collectivism that forms one distinctive property in the popular Hofstede's cultural dimensions theory [180]. Correspondingly, we will barely find a universal agreement on the characteristics of an ideal world. In this chapter, we will therefore resort to the guidelines, declarations, and charters introduced in Sect. 3.2, especially considering equality and non-discrimination.

Different from societal bias, *statistical bias* refers to the discrepancy between how the world is and how it is represented in the computer system under consideration [126, 266]. In the case of IRRSs, statistical bias is commonly the result of insufficiently representative data that is leveraged during the training process of the underlying learning to rank (LTR) algorithm, which causes the retrieval or recommendation model to pick up and sometimes even amplify the pre-existing bias in the data [116, 338]. Most often, this is caused by *sampling bias*, e.g., when the data instances used by the ranking model (e.g., Web pages in a retrieval system or products in a recommender system) are missing-not-at-random. For instance, this occurs when users are more likely to consume or interact with popular content even if they do not have a sincere interest in it, and these interactions are used to train or update the recommendation model [329].

To make societal and statistical biases more graspable, we provide the following illustrations to exemplify the concepts.

Example: Societal and Statistical Biases in the Music Industry
Women have been historically underrepresented in the music industry, both as performers and producers [127, 173, 366]. Females comprise only one-fifth to one-fourth of all music artists [366]. This disparity exists despite greater female representation among the highly successful superstars [127, 365]. However, substantial differences can be found between genres. For instance, an analysis by Epps-Darling et al. has shown that 95% of Spotify streams belonging to the genre rap involve male-only artists. Less than 1% of streams to metal music involve female-only performers; 7% are made up of mixed-gender bands [127].

Let us now assume that we aim for a world of equal representation of male and female artists in all genres. We further assume that, in reality, 10% of metal music performers involve female artists.[10] An MIR system that is queried to return metal music may include only 10% of metal songs by female artists in its results, reflecting existing *societal bias* in the world. In this case, the system would not introduce *statistical bias* in its results. In contrast, if such a system would return 50% female and 50% male artists, ignoring for simplicity non-binary genders, the *societal bias* in the results of our retrieval system would be nullified, according to our definition of an ideal world. On the other hand, in this case, one could argue that male metal artists would have to give up quite a large part of their exposure, yielding to a substantial underrepresentation with respect to their true prevalence in metal music. This indicates a *statistical bias* in the retrieval results as they no longer reflect the world as it is.

From a practical perspective, when aiming at debiasing IRRSs—at the data, algorithm, or result level—researchers, system designers, and engineers often need to make a choice: try to make the world fairer by reducing societal bias or model the world with its existing biases as accurately as possible, i.e., reducing statistical bias.

3.3.2 *Origins of Bias*

Biases in IRRSs have been discussed from various angles and (their origins) have been categorized using different taxonomies, e.g., [82, 126, 283]. For instance, Chen et al. focus on biases in *data*, *model*, and *results* [82], while Ekstrand et al. further discuss biases as a result of *evaluation* procedures and of *human responses* to the system's output [126]. Di Noia et al. additionally highlight *cognitive biases* originating from mental processes of the users [283]. In this chapter, we adopt and extend Di Noia et al.'s categorization of the origins of bias, adding some more specific examples from [82, 126] and our own considerations. We also connect them to the different stakeholders and provide an illustration in Fig. 3.1.

3.3.2.1 Data Bias

Data in the context of IRRSs can be broadly categorized into system-provided and user-generated data. The former refers to data included in the catalog the system provides access to (e.g., Web pages in a Web search engine, documents in a scholarly article retrieval system, or products offered by an e-commerce platform). While this kind of data originates from the content creator, the platform provider (also influenced

[10] These percentages are different from the ones reported above from the study in [127] because Epps-Darling et al.'s results are based on streams, not individual artists.

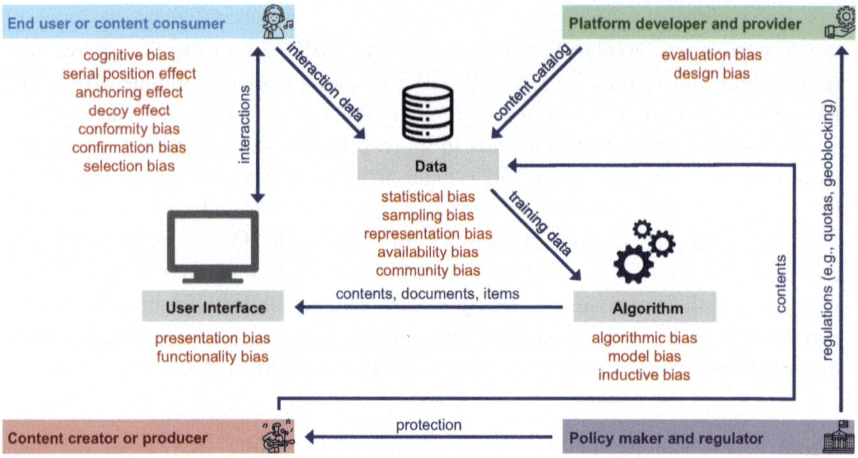

Fig. 3.1: Overview of important biases (red font), their main sources (gray boxes), and their relation to important stakeholders (boxes at the corners)

by other stakeholders, such as record labels in case of a music RS) decides which contents to include in their catalog.[11]

The second kind of data that is important for IRRSs is of user-generated nature. In IR systems, these most commonly comprise queries to the search engine and information on which content is accessed by the user, i.e., which links to documents provided on the result page are followed by the user. In RSs, the user-generated feedback to the system is often more nuanced. While the core information again comprises interactions, these can come in different forms in a RS, including explicit ratings of items or signals of different strengths, e.g., clicking, viewing the details of an item, or purchasing it.

Both system-provided and user-generated data are prone to data biases. Most of these can be described as *statistical bias* (see Sect. 3.3.1), meaning that the data is not representative of the world from a high-level perspective. In the context of IRRSs, this lack of representativeness is commonly caused by *sampling bias* (or similarly *representation bias*), which refers to the way data is collected and fed into the system [254, 371]. For instance, this issue occurs if the data (e.g., Web pages or products in the catalog; queries or purchasing histories) is obtained in a way that leads to an under- or overrepresentation of certain topics (e.g., in news), languages, or limited diversity in the users' population (e.g., concerning gender, age, geography, or culture). In this context, also *availability bias* is noteworthy, which refers to the fact that some data is harder (or even impossible to obtain) than others. For example, in some parts of the world, the use of analog audio cassettes to listen to music still accounts for a substantial share of music consumption, which is not

[11] Notwithstanding that the choice what content to include in the catalog is often made (semi-) automatically, for instance, with the help of a Web crawler in case of a Web search engine.

reflected in any music RS. Another example is Web pages in the deep Web that are not indexed by standard Web search engines and are therefore not retrievable by them [10, 412]. A related bias, which is foremost relevant in RSs, is *community bias*. It refers to distortions in the data caused by the non-representativeness of the users of a certain service, product, or platform for the population at large. An often-found example in the music domain is a systematic underrepresentation of classical music listeners in the community of Last.fm and of Twitter users [339]. Analogously, an overrepresentation of rap music listeners among users of Apple's iTunes platform has been uncovered [336].

3.3.2.2 Algorithmic or Model Bias

The data, which is commonly already biased, as just discussed, is then used by the retrieval or recommendation algorithm. Nowadays, these algorithms most often involve training—and continuously updating or refining—a DL-based ranking model. Training requires some kind of representation of the items in the catalog or repository, along with interactions or queries provided by users, depending on the specific algorithm.

During the creation of a ranking model, the algorithm used for training the model or the resulting learned model itself can pick up and even amplify pre-existing biases in the data (see Sect. 3.3.2.1). This has been evidenced, for instance, in retrieval scenarios in [312] and for recommendation in [257]. These kinds of biases are commonly referred to as *algorithmic bias* or *model bias*, depending on where they manifest.

In contrast to these mostly negative biases, *inductive bias* helps the ranking model to generalize to unseen data, which is particularly important in recommendation scenarios with a highly sparse user-item interaction matrix. High sparsity commonly occurs when catalogs are large (e.g., user-generated videos or music songs) or users are barely active. Concretely, this kind of bias refers to assumptions made by the RS about patterns in data, with the aim to avoid overfitting the model to the (biased) training data and to offer recommendations in sparse settings.

3.3.2.3 Presentation Bias

Biases can also originate from the way retrieved or recommended items are presented to the users of the system. While some research defines *presentation bias* in a more narrow sense, e.g., [40, 126, 254], restricting the notion to whether items are presented to the user at all, we argue here along the lines of [116, 338] that presentation bias is a more comprehensive concept, which also relates to research in human-computer interaction (HCI), user interface design, and information visualization [171]. Concretely, it is not only the presence (or absence) of an item in a result list that strongly influences whether users view or rate it but also many visual attributes of its presentation. For instance, the position in the ranking that determines where on the screen an item shows up (*position bias*), its color, font, and size are all determinants of the likelihood of interaction with the item and ultimately its success [91, 286]. The influence of the ranking position is strongly connected to the serial position effect discussed in Sect. 3.3.2.4.

A related bias originates from the availability or unavailability of certain functionalities in the IRRS's user interface. Such a *functionality bias* has a significant influence on user engagement and user experience, as identified in the context of RSs in [202, 303], which also propose frameworks for a user-centric assessment of RSs. Examples include the various content interaction mechanisms RSs can provide users with, such as slate recommendations [109, 125], clustering-based browsing [201, 255], and automatic playlist generation [57, 385, 430]. The availability of these functionalities directly impacts the types and semantics of user interactions, ultimately influencing the recommendation model when this interaction data drives subsequent model updates.

It is important to note that the decisions leading to (or alleviating) presentation bias are made, first and foremost, by the system designers.

3.3.2.4 Cognitive Bias

Psychological, mental, and neurological processes and characteristics of humans, e.g., the way humans perceive, process, store, and retrieve information, reveal another source of bias that is commonly subsumed under the class of *cognitive bias*. While all humans are prone to cognitive bias, in the context of IRRSs, it is foremost the end user's cognition that is of interest. Research, foremost conducted in psychology and economics, has unveiled countless cognitive biases [103, 119], not all of which are relevant in an IRRS context though. Most relevant and notable biases in this category include the *serial position effect*, which refers to the phenomenon that humans remember the first and last items better than the ones in the middle when presented with a list of items [101, 108]. In the broader context of IRRSs, this also translates to clicking behavior [97, 275], i.e., users are more likely to click on top-ranked items (primacy effect) and on the last items shown in a result list (recency effect).

Another prominent example of a cognitive bias is the *anchoring effect*, which refers to the overemphasis of the first piece of information ("anchor") a human sees when making a decision [75, 268]. It has been shown that this can have a negative impact on decision-making for the user [268] but can at the same time serve as a tool for system providers to offer a hook to the user to set a reference. For instance, if an e-commerce platform shows the user a highly priced item on top of the result list, the user is likely to form the expectation that also other items will be expensive. If the user then encounters, further down in the list, items that are still overpriced, they will experience them as cheap. This particular variant of the bias is referred to as *decoy effect* or *context effect*, where the expensive item serves as a decoy to push sales of a (much cheaper but still overpriced) target product [184, 297]. Leveraging this effect is common business practice. In a RS context, it can impact rating behavior, as evidenced, for instance, in [13]: In CF-based recommenders, artificially generated ratings can act as anchors. When users are shown these ratings before providing their own, their ratings tend to be closer to the artificial ones compared to a setting where no anchor is presented [13]. The same holds when artificial ratings are replaced by the average of the item's ratings provided by other users. This latter effect is also known as *conformity bias*, meaning that users tend to act similarly to other users in a group to avoid sticking out, even when doing so involves making decisions against their true preferences. This effect occurs not only when users are presented with an anchor before their initial rating but also when new information is introduced after they have already rated an item, influencing their subsequent re-evaluation of the item [238, 407]. This conformity effect obviously introduces bias in user interaction and feedback data, both in explicit ratings [216] and implicit feedback, e.g., users are more likely to click on an item if they see that many others have done so too [443].

A further cognitive bias that has been well studied in psychology is *confirmation bias* [280]. It denotes the effect that users are more likely to interact with content that is in line with their opinions and beliefs and more reluctant to choose content that contradicts them. Such effects are particularly evident in IRRSs for news [214, 231, 276] and health-related information [372, 440], in social networks [137], as well as in educational settings [343]. This reinforces recommendations of content that is in line with one's beliefs or originates from like-minded users, potentially isolating them within filter bubbles.

Another bias that relates to cognitive processes when humans make decisions is *selection bias*. This refers to the fact that humans do not choose the items they rate randomly from the list of all items, not even from those presented by the IRRS. Instead, they are more likely to rate content they like or content they deem particularly good or bad [248, 369]. This results in interaction and rating data in which instances are *missing-not-at-random* (MNAR), which in turn means that the observed distribution of ratings is not representative of the true rating distribution.

More information on cognitive biases can be found for recommendation in a survey by Lex et al. [220] and for retrieval in works by Gomroki et al. [159] and by Azzopardi [38].

Importantly, the various biases discussed so far do not exist in isolation. Instead, they influence each other through a *feedback loop* between the actors and components of the IRRSs. For instance, position bias (as a form of presentation bias) together with the serial position effect (cognitive bias) influence the likelihood of the user clicking on an item, which affects the data used by the system and therefore introduces data bias, and in turn, may again result in a biased model if the algorithm used to train the ranking model is sensitive to data bias.

3.3.3 Individual Fairness and Group Fairness

Having been exposed to different kinds, categorizations, and definitions of bias, the reader may now wonder about their relationship to fairness. While more details are provided in Sect. 3.4, we would like to offer here a high-level distinction similar to what we provided for societal versus statistical bias.

First, it is important to highlight that some biases are needed if we want to build an IRRS that is *personalized*, which is a core requirement, at least for recommender systems [321]. Failing to reflect the user's preferences in the recommendations will likely lead to the system's rapid disappearance from the market. These preferences are, however, full of biases themselves, for example, an inclination for popular items (otherwise, they would not be popular). Additionally, users commonly prefer content that aligns with their existing beliefs, representing a form of cognitive bias, more precisely, confirmation bias.

Despite their benefits for personalization, some biases have unintended or even harmful effects on the fairness of IRRSs, potentially leading to discrimination against certain stakeholders. Accordingly, unfairness is defined as *systematically* discriminating against certain individuals or groups of individuals in favor of others [145, 283]. In this context, it is common practice to distinguish between individual fairness and group fairness.

The concept of *individual fairness* means that similar individuals are treated similarly by the IRRS. For instance, similar users should have similar experiences or receive results of similar quality from the system.

Example: Individual Fairness in Job Recommendation
Job seekers with similar skills, education, and professional experience are recommended vacancies for jobs that offer comparable salaries.

Example: Individual Fairness in Music Recommendation
Consider a music-streaming service that offers music recommendations to its users. Music listeners with similar tastes and interaction behavior should receive recommendations of comparable quality or utility to them.

On the other hand, *group fairness* focuses on ensuring that different groups, defined by protected attributes like gender, age, race, or religion, receive equal treatment from the RSS. These attributes commonly align closely with the categories protected under non-discrimination laws (see Sect. 3.2).

Example: Group Fairness in Health-Related Web Search
Male patients seeking online guidance on a health-related issue receive documents containing information or advice of comparable quality to what their female counterparts receive.

Example: Group Fairness for Artists in Music Recommendation
Let us take the perspective of content contributors instead of the system's end users. In a music recommendation scenario, a band from a developing country should have the same opportunity for exposure through the RS as an artist from a developed country. Therefore, the artist's country of origin should not influence the likelihood that the artist is recommended.

3.3.4 The Role of Different Stakeholders

The development, maintenance, and usage of IRRSs involve various stakeholders, as already described in Sect. 1.3 and discussed in detail, for instance, in [2, 62, 338, 402]. They include end users, content creators, system developers and providers, and policymakers. These different stakeholders are, in different ways and to different extents, involved in and affected by the various biases discussed so far. More precisely, the relationship between biases and stakeholders' behavior (e.g., interaction with the system by end users and content producers; creation of the system by programmers, ML experts, and data scientists) is a bidirectional one. Noteworthy, the stakeholders also differ in their goals and whether they are aligned or in conflict with the goals of other stakeholders. We discuss these aspects in the following, for the major stakeholders involved in IRRSs. We refer the reader again to Fig. 3.1 for an overview of biases, their sources, and interactions between stakeholders and system components that produce biases or are affected by them.

3.3.4.1 End Users or Content Consumers

The end user of an IRRS is usually the person who is looking for content that satisfies their information or entertainment needs by interacting with some of the retrieved or recommended items, e.g., purchasing a product, watching a movie, applying to an open position, listening to a song, reading a news article or posting on social media, etc. End users are the actors of an IRRS that have been most thoroughly targeted in research on bias and fairness of IRRS [338]. While their goals may differ between individuals and also depend on the context of the search or recommendation process (e.g., based on intents or activities), most frequently, they can be categorized into *exploitation* or *exploration* scenarios. In the former, the user's primary aim is to obtain relevant results, which commonly means the algorithm should optimize some measure of accuracy such as NDCG or MRR. In contrast, the latter describes a scenario where the user is foremost interested in discovering something new or unexpected to broaden their horizon. In this case, users are often looking for characteristics such as diversity, novelty, or serendipity in the results provided by the IRRS. Corresponding metrics are referred to as *beyond-*

accuracy metrics. Many computational measures have been proposed to quantify such beyond-accuracy aspects, an overview of which is provided in [193, 242, 340]. We summarize a few popular choices in Table 3.1.

Concerning biases of the user, the most relevant ones are cognitive biases (see Sect. 3.3.2.4). They have a strong impact on the way users interact with items, which results in a feedback loop when the interaction data is fed back into the IRRS algorithm. Also, selection bias (together with others) can result in over-personalization of retrieved or recommended contents, which may lead to "echo chambers" or "cocoons" of homogeneous contents and viewpoints, hindering users' ability to encounter diverse items or perspectives [299].

3.3.4.2 Content Creators or Producers

This group of stakeholders encompasses everyone who contributes to the creation of the content that is made available through the retrieval or recommender system. The creation or production of corresponding content is usually done as part of a professional routine. However, content creation and sharing can also be a leisure activity without involving a particular commercial interest. In this case, the resulting items are commonly referred to as user-generated content. Who the content creators and producers are varies strongly, depending on the system's application area. To give some examples, in the case of a movie RS, creators include directors, screenwriters, producers, actors and actresses, and many more. In a search engine for high-quality photographs, the group of creators will foremost be composed of professional photographers. In a music RS, this stakeholder group will include composers, songwriters, performers, producers, publishers, and record labels.

While the composition and roles of the members of this stakeholder group are diverse, their main goal in the ecosystem of IRRS commonly revolves around increasing the *exposure* of the contents they contribute to the system, sometimes, also increasing their own fame and reputation [104, 296, 421]. If their contents occur in the result list for many queries or are recommended to many consumers, users are more likely to interact with them, increasing their exposure. In turn, *item exposure* is commonly related to the uniformity with which items are exposed to users [110]. Sometimes, this definition extends to groups of items that are exposed to groups of users. More concretely, exposure can be defined according to a weak or strict notion. In the former, an item is already exposed if it occurs in the result list for a query or user. The latter notion requires that users actually pay attention to the item, i.e., interact with it. When this strict notion is applied, exposure strongly depends on the item's ranking position in the result list and is therefore influenced by presentation bias, in particular, position bias (see Sect. 3.3.2).

Metric	Formula	Description
Novelty (Global)	$\frac{1}{\lvert U\rvert}\sum_{u\in U}\sum_{i\in L_u}\frac{-\log_2 pop(i)}{N}$ $\frac{1}{\lvert Q\rvert}\sum_{q\in Q}\sum_{d\in L_q}\frac{-\log_2 pop(d)}{N}$	Global novelty of an item i or document d is proportional to the inverse of its overall popularity $pop(i)$ or $pop(d)$, expressed as percentage of users who interacted with i or d in the result list of size N.
Novelty (User)	$\frac{1}{\lvert L_u\rvert}\ \lvert\{i : i \in L_u \wedge i \notin \mathcal{L}_u \setminus L_u\}\rvert$	User-specific novelty of a result list L_u is the average number of unseen items or documents i in L_u provided to user u, considering the appearance of i in all result lists $\mathcal{L}_u$ that have been presented to u in the past.
Diversity	$\frac{1}{\lvert L_u\rvert\cdot(\lvert L_u\rvert-1)}\sum_{i\in L_u}\sum_{j\in L_u\setminus\{i\}} dist(i,j)$ $\frac{1}{\lvert L_q\rvert\cdot(\lvert L_q\rvert-1)}\sum_{i\in L_q}\sum_{j\in L_q\setminus\{i\}} dist(i,j)$	Diversity can be computed as the average pairwise distance between all items in the result list L_u or L_q, where $dist(i, j)$ is some distance metric defined between items or documents i and j, and commonly considers item properties (e.g., inverse overlap coefficient or Jaccard similarity between genres or tags assigned to movies i and j; inverse cosine similarity between embedding representations of two texts or images i and j). This variant of diversity is also referred to as intra-list diversity.
Item coverage	$\frac{1}{\lvert I\rvert}\ \lvert\{i : i \in L_u \in \mathcal{L}\}\rvert$ $\frac{1}{\lvert D\rvert}\ \lvert\{d : d \in L_q \in \mathcal{L}\}\rvert$	Item coverage denotes how many items from the catalog the system can retrieve or recommend, expressed as a fraction of the catalog size.
User coverage	$\frac{1}{\lvert U\rvert}\ \lvert\{u : u \in U \wedge \mathcal{L}_u \neq \emptyset\}\rvert$	User coverage denotes the fraction of users, for which a result list can be generated.

Table 3.1: Common choices to measure *beyond-accuracy* aspects in IRRSs. Notation: L_u and L_q represent, respectively, the result list for a user u or query q; $\mathcal{L}_u$ denotes all recommendation lists ever presented by the system to user u; $\mathcal{L}$ denotes all result lists that can be generated by the ranking model of the IRRS under investigation

3.3.4.3 System Providers and Developers

Providers of recommendation platforms and search engines, such as Google, Netflix, Spotify, Amazon, or Meta, constitute another vital group of stakeholders. Their goals are commonly driven by economic objectives, such as increasing revenue, the number of (paying) customers, customer loyalty, sponsored content, or similar aspects. To achieve this, companies regularly seek competitive advantages, e.g., through unique system functionalities designed to enhance the user experience with their IRRSs. This is where system designers and developers play a vital role since they are directly involved in creating and implementing such functionality.

System designers and developers are both influenced by existing biases and can introduce new ones. The most noteworthy ones are design bias and evaluation bias. *Design bias* refers to choices made during the development of IRRSs that influence how end users will (be able to) interact with the system. Even personal factors of the developers might come into play here. Unconscious biases may shape their assumptions about what makes a good recommendation or how users will interact with the system. For example, a developer's own music preferences could subtly influence the design of a music RS. In addition, *evaluation bias* arises whenever the system's performance is assessed. For instance, choices about experimental design (e.g., online versus offline study or A/B testing), evaluation metric, and, more fundamentally, how a "successful" system output is defined significantly impact the results of evaluation experiments.

3.3.4.4 Policymakers and Regulators

Data and algorithmic biases may result in unfair treatment of certain groups of individuals, as briefly touched upon in Sect. 3.3.3 and discussed in more detail in Sect. 3.4.2. Most commonly, end users or content creators are affected in this case. For instance, a RS could systematically deliver worse recommendations to people of color, while another could systematically limit exposure of content created by males. To counteract the adverse effects of such discriminating system behavior, which is regarded as socially unacceptable in many societies, institutions like the *European Commission* or national governments have come up with solutions, commonly taking the form of regulations. Some of the regulatory frameworks and concrete policies have already been presented in Chap. 2. To give one specific example, such regulations can impose minimum quotas on the exposure of items from national content creators. A prominent example is France, whose *Conseil supérieur de l'audiovisuel*[12] requires French radio stations and streaming services to provide at least a certain share of music by French artists to their listeners.

The different interests and goals of the discussed stakeholders highlight the need for multistakeholder IRRSs, including a particularly sensitive handling of unfairness issues arising from harmful biases. While promising initial research on multistakeholder fairness has emerged, e.g., [78, 403], it is crucial to recognize that optimizing fairness for one stakeholder can have negative consequences for others.

[12] https://www.csa.fr

3.4 Identifying and Measuring Harmful Biases

As we have discussed, there exist countless biases, originating from different sources, affecting different stakeholders in different ways, and impacting the fairness of IRRSs to varying degrees. In the next two sections, we focus on *popularity bias* and *demographic bias* because they have wide-reaching effects and are already well studied. We describe them in detail and present common measures for their quantification.

3.4.1 Popularity Bias

Popularity bias is a phenomenon that has predominantly been studied in the context of RSs. It refers to the frequently observable effect that recommendation lists are often dominated by popular items. As a result, already popular contents are shown to many users, increasing their chance of being consumed or interacted with even more. This can lead to a feedback loop when this new interaction data is used to update the model, ultimately resulting in a "rich get richer" behavior, also known as the Matthew effect. This is particularly worrisome since the popularity of items in the catalog oftentimes follows a long-tail or power-law distribution, as shown in Fig. 3.2 for the LFM-2b dataset of music listening events from the Last.fm platform [257, 334]. This long-tail distribution of item popularity, coupled with popularity bias in the recommendations, means that the vast majority of items rarely, if ever, get the chance to be selected by the RS.

Example: Music Recommendation
In the entertainment domain, popularity bias is a particularly pertinent phenomenon. For instance, music consumption frequencies over songs or artists follow a power-law distribution, meaning that a small number of songs (or artists) accumulates the vast majority of music-listening activities, while the vast majority of songs (or artists) is consumed very infrequently [74]. As a consequence, much more interaction data for already popular music is available for training the music RSs, which often results in more frequent recommendations of such popular music. Consequently, this yields more frequent listening activities involving already popular music, producing even more interaction data. Such a vicious cycle often leads to an amplification effect that leaves little room for lesser-known songs or artists in recommendation lists if no countermeasures are taken.

Popularity bias can be harmful for many stakeholders, in particular system end users, content creators, and service providers. Users risk becoming trapped in filter bubbles of popular content within their broader preferences, which hinders them in discovering novel content and diversifying their taste. More severely, lesser-known

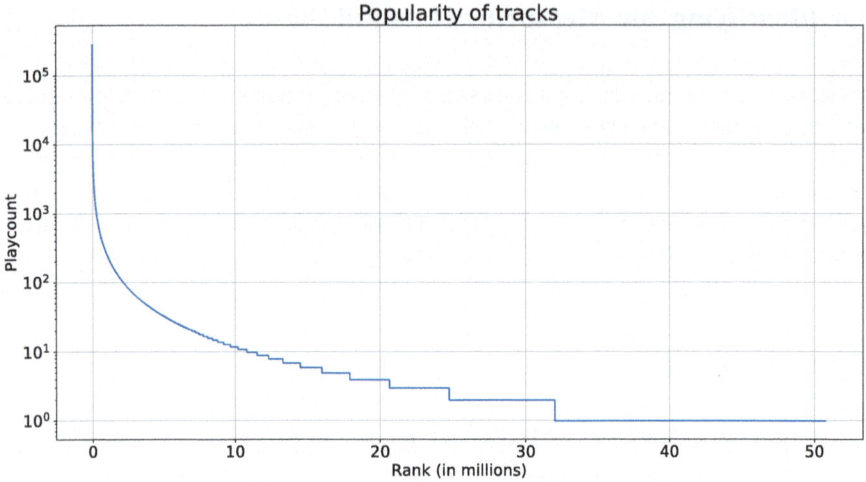

Fig. 3.2: Distribution of track popularity in the LFM-2b dataset for music recommendation. Note that the y-axis is logarithmically scaled. It clearly shows a heavy long-tail distribution of playcount values, i.e., listening interactions with songs

content creators forego the chance of being recommended because the recommendation lists are already filled with popular items, leaving no space for less popular ones. Also, popularity bias can have negative economic consequences for service providers because it severely limits their ability to sell long-tail items while potentially recommending items the user would have purchased anyway.

Due to these wide-reaching consequences of popularity bias, much research has been devoted to measuring its various aspects as a vital first step toward mitigation. We next review the most common metrics used to quantify popularity bias. We generally provide the formulas at the user level, i.e., denoting popularity bias for a given user u. To obtain a system-level quantification of popularity bias, the individual values are averaged over all users U. Strategies to alleviate this bias will be discussed in Sect. 3.5.1. For a more detailed investigation of popularity bias, we refer the reader to the survey by Klimashevskaia et al. [200]. Please note that most of the following metrics have been proposed for RSs. Nevertheless, many can be easily adapted to IR scenarios.

Average recommendation popularity (ARP) of a user u is defined as the average popularity of items in u's recommendation list L_u, as shown in Eq. 3.1. The popularity of an item $\phi(i)$ can be measured, for instance, as the total number of interactions or ratings for i in the training data [199].[13] Alternatively, $\phi(i)$ can be defined as

[13] Other proxies for item popularity can be used, too. For instance, in the case of a music RS, song popularity can be defined through their position in the Billboard charts or other regional music charts, record sales, or number of plays on radio stations.

the fraction of users that already interacted with i, again computed on the training data [274]: $\phi(i) = \frac{|U_i|}{|U|}$ with U_i denoting the set of users that interacted with i.

$$ARP(u) = \frac{1}{|L_u|} \sum_{i \in L_u} \phi(i) \tag{3.1}$$

Average percentage of tail items (APT) measures the contribution of items from the long tail to a user's recommendation list [5, 199], as shown in Eq. 3.2. It requires the definition of a set of long tail items Γ, which is commonly done by selecting a percentage of the least popular items according to the interaction or rating data in the training set. Due to the long-tail distribution of item popularity (see Fig. 3.2), a common choice is to select the 80% of items with the lowest amount of interactions [4].

$$APT(u) = \sum_{i \in L_u} \frac{|\{i : i \in L_u \cap \Gamma\}|}{|L_u|} \tag{3.2}$$

Popularity miscalibration assumes that users prefer recommendations whose popularity matches the popularity of the items they typically consume. Therefore, corresponding metrics quantify the discrepancy in terms of popularity between a user u's interaction history H_u and recommendation list L_u. Several ways exist to quantify this discrepancy, most notably, delta metrics and comparing popularity distributions [219]. *Delta metrics* (or *%$\Delta\xi$ metrics*) can be defined according to Eq. 3.3, where $\xi(\cdot)$ represents a statistical aggregation function such as mean, median, variance, or higher statistical moments and $\phi(L_u)$ denotes a popularity measurement function that maps each element in L_u to its popularity score. Analogously, $\phi(H_u)$ refers to the set of popularity values of all items in H_u. Considering the mean for ξ, the formula intuitively measures the relative difference between the average popularity of items in u's history and u's recommendation list. Positive values indicate an overrepresentation of items that are more popular than what u commonly prefers or interacts with.

$$\%\Delta\xi(u) = \frac{\xi(\phi(L_u)) - \xi(\phi(H_u))}{\xi(\phi(H_u))} \tag{3.3}$$

Comparing the results of statistical aggregation functions applied to popularity values, however, does not consider the entire distribution of item popularities and can be prone to outliers (e.g., when using the mean). Therefore, another class of popularity miscalibration metrics is distribution-based. Most prominently, the *Kullback-Leibler divergence* or its preferable symmetric variant *Jensen-Shannon divergence (JSD)* is used, e.g., in [203, 217]. JSD measures the extent to which the two popularity distributions differ in terms of the information they convey (relative entropy). Intuitively, if they are very similar, their JSD will be low, indicating low popularity bias. Equation 3.4 shows the computation, where $\widehat{H_u(c)}$ and $\widehat{L_u(c)}$ represent the (normalized) number of items in $c \in C$ popularity bins,[14] respectively, in the interaction history and the recommendation list of u.

$$JSD(\widehat{H_u}, \widehat{L_u}) = \frac{1}{2}\left(\sum_{c \in C} \widehat{H_u(c)} log_2 \frac{2\widehat{H_u(c)}}{\widehat{H_u(c)} + \widehat{L_u(c)}} + \sum_{c} \widehat{L_u(c)} log_2 \frac{2\widehat{L_u(c)}}{\widehat{H_u(c)} + \widehat{L_u(c)}}\right) \tag{3.4}$$

Furthermore, rank-order correlation measures, such as *Spearman's* ρ or *Kendall's* τ, can be used to estimate popularity miscalibration based on concordant and discordant pairs of item rankings in H_u and L_u, e.g., [219].

Example: Popularity Miscalibration in Music Recommendation Algorithms

In their investigation of popularity miscalibration among popular music recommendation algorithms, Lesota et al. [219] discovered that state-of-the-art algorithms, such as `MultVAE`, recommend up to four times more popular items than those found in the users' listening history, on average ($\%\Delta Mean > 300$). For comparison, a non-personalized recommender that always predicts the overall most popular songs scored $\%\Delta Mean \sim 430$. Out of the five studied personalized recommendation algorithms, only one (`ItemKNN`) showed a low popularity bias ($\%\Delta Mean < 10$).

Popularity lift (PL) addresses the fact that popularity bias varies between different groups of users, for instance, according to gender [219] or their preference for popular or niche items [204], which is also referred to as "mainstreaminess" [47]. For example, users who prefer less popular items face a greater degree of popularity bias than those who prefer mainstream content [6, 204]. Therefore, the popularity lift quantifies popularity bias for distinct user groups [7, 8, 203], which can subsequently be compared to uncover differences between groups that may indicate fairness issues. While slightly different formulations of PL exist, they all relate a user group U_g's average popularity of recommendations (see ARP above) to the group's average popularity of items in its members' interaction history. Groups can be defined based on characteristics such as gender, age, ethnicity, country, or mainstreaminess. Formally, this can be expressed by Eq. 3.5, where the *group average popularity (GAP)* indicated in Eq. 3.6 measures the average popularity of items consumed by members of group U_g, again, according to some measure of item popularity $\phi(i)$.

$$PL(U_g) = \frac{\frac{1}{|U_g|} \sum_{u \in U_g} ARP(u) - GAP(U_g)}{GAP(U_g)} \tag{3.5}$$

[14] For instance, [219] quantizes all items' popularity values into 10 bins $c \in C$. $\widehat{H_u}$ and $\widehat{L_u}$ can, therefore, also be interpreted as ten-dimensional vectors over these 10 popularity bins.

$$GAP(U_g) = \frac{1}{|U_g|} \sum_{u \in U_g} \frac{1}{|H_u|} \sum_{i \in H_u} \phi(i) \tag{3.6}$$

While popularity bias has foremost been studied in recommendation scenarios, generally, most metrics can be easily adapted to fit an IR context. However, in IR settings, a notable problem arises for metrics that compare the popularity of items in users' interaction histories with the popularity of recommended items. While the popularity of documents can be approximated by their occurrence in interaction logs or in retrieved document lists, information on the popularity of queries is usually much harder to obtain, especially for researchers in the academic world, because common open datasets rarely contain such information.

3.4.2 Demographic Bias

Generally speaking, demographic bias refers to any systematic difference in algorithmic treatment between two or more groups of users, depending on some demographic characteristics, such as age, gender, or country. This is problematic because it can easily lead to favoring one group over the other, in turn to discrimination of the disfavored group. The behavior of IRRSs for which demographic bias is studied can be defined in various ways. For instance, based on performance metrics of the system, such as accuracy or beyond-accuracy metrics, or even popularity bias as just discussed in Sect. 3.4.1. Alternatively, it can also be assessed based on characteristics of the retrieved or recommended items, e.g., salary paid by the jobs recommended by a job RS. Similar to popularity bias, demographic bias can be viewed from the perspective of various stakeholders. The end user's viewpoint is often concerned with receiving worse results than users of another demographic group. Content creators, on the other hand, may experience different exposure of their items or documents by the IRRS.

In the following, we review the most commonly used metrics to quantify different kinds of demographic bias. Approaches to mitigate them are presented in Sect. 3.5.2.

Many approaches to measuring demographic biases are based on comparing the retrieval or recommendation performance of the IRRS between different groups, either of end users or of content creators, depending on which stakeholder's perspective is taken. In this context, *performance gap* is a direct way to quantify the discrepancy of the system's output between two or more user groups belonging to different demographic cohorts or groups defined based on other protected attributes.

RecGap is one metric to investigate performance gaps, proposed by Melchiorre et al. [258]. It is shown in Eq. 3.7 and quantifies the average pairwise discrepancy in terms of some performance metric μ between user groups. RecGap considers a RS as fair if it performs equally well across all user groups, with respect to μ, which can be any accuracy or beyond-accuracy metric (examples provided in Tables 1.1, 1.2, and 3.1).[15] More precisely, as shown in Eq. 3.7, the *RecGap* bias with respect to the evaluation metric μ is defined as the mean of the absolute differences between the average evaluation performance for users in each pair of groups.

$$RecGap^{\mu} = \frac{\sum_{\langle g,g'\rangle \in G^{pair}} \left| \frac{\sum_{u \in U_g} \mu(u)}{|U_g|} - \frac{\sum_{u' \in U_{g'}} \mu(u')}{|U_{g'}|} \right|}{|G^{pair}|} \tag{3.7}$$

Formally, G^{pair} is the set of all tuples of user groups, i.e., $G^{pair} = \{\langle g, g'\rangle \mid g, g' \in G \text{ and } g \neq g'\}$, U_g denotes the users in group g, and $\mu(u)$ is the performance of the system under evaluation for user u according to μ. If *RecGap* is zero, the system performs equally well for all user groups G; therefore, the equal opportunity criterion is fulfilled with respect to μ and the attribute according to which groups are defined.

Example: Demographic Performance Gap in Music Recommendation
The *RecGap* metric can be used to assess performance gaps between genders (male and female users) in a music recommendation setting, as done by Melchiorre et al. [258]. The authors measured a *RecGap* of up to 0.063 in terms of NDCG@10 (see Table 1.2), for personalized recommendation algorithms. This translates to a 16.7% worse performance for female users compared to male users. *RecGap* with respect to item coverage at 10 recommended songs (see Table 3.1) was 0.084, translating into a 62.2% worse catalog coverage for female than for male users.

Such measures may also consider properties of documents or items beyond relevance. For instance, a gap between user groups that may lead to unfair system behavior can also emerge if a job RS recommends jobs paying lower salaries to a certain demographic group irrespective of their skills. Such a behavior can be uncovered by the *user group fairness (UGF)* metric, here adapted from [227]. It is a reduced and slightly modified version of Eq. 3.7 and is provided in Eq. 3.8, where μ is an aggregation function for the property under investigation in the result list of an IRRS. For instance, $\mu(L_u)$ could be the average salary paid by recommended jobs in list L_u for a job-seeking user u that belongs to either group U_g or $U_{g'}$.

$$UGF(U_g, U_{g'}) = \left| \frac{1}{|U_g|} \sum_{u \in U_g} \mu(L_u) - \frac{1}{|U_{g'}|} \sum_{u \in U_{g'}} \mu(L_u) \right| \tag{3.8}$$

[15] RecGap is conceptually related to the *equal opportunity* metric for classification tasks in ML [167], which considers a predictor as fair if its probability of a positive prediction for data samples of the positive class (i.e., true-positive rate) is independent of the value of the protected attribute that defines the user groups.

Another group of demographic bias metrics focuses solely on the lists of recommended or retrieved items, disregarding their characteristics (unlike UGF) as well as their relevance to the user or query (unlike RecGap in most variants):

Set difference rate (SDR) measures the discrepancy in recommendation lists between users belonging to two distinct groups U_g and U_g' [436]. Intuitively, SDR computes the fraction of items that are exclusively recommended to users in group U_g or exclusively to users in group U_g'. Formally, this is illustrated in Eq. 3.9 using set operations, i.e., the number of items in the intersection between all items recommended to users $u_g \in U_g$ and $u_{g'} \in U_{g'}$ is subtracted from the total number of items recommended to all users, regardless of their protected attribute.

$$SDR(U_g, U_{g'}) = |L_U| - \left|L_{U_g} \bigcap L_{U_{g'}}\right|$$
$$L_U = \bigcup_{u \in U} L_u, \quad L_{U_g} = \bigcup_{u_g \in U_g} L_{u_g}, \quad L_{U_{g'}} = \bigcup_{u_{g'} \in U_{g'}} L_{u_{g'}} \tag{3.9}$$

List difference rate (LDR) similarly compares the item lists recommended to users in groups U_g and $U_{g'}$ [436]. In contrast to SDR, which solely considers the occurrence of identical items in L_{u_g} and $L_{u_{g'}}$, LDR further requires that the ranks of the items in both lists align to be considered equivalent, therefore, the underlying IRRS unbiased. Formally, this is shown in Eq. 3.10, where $\gamma\left(L_{u_g}, L_{u_{g'}}, j\right) = 1$ if the jth-ranked items in L_{u_g} and $L_{u_{g'}}$ are identical, and 0 otherwise; $|L_{u_g}| = |L_{u_{g'}}| = N$.

$$LDR(L_{u_g}, L_{u_{g'}}) = \frac{\sum_{j=1}^{|L_u|} \gamma\left(L_{u_g}, L_{u_{g'}}, j\right)}{|L_u|} \tag{3.10}$$

Example: Set Difference Rate and List Difference Rate in Job Recommendation

Zhang studied *SDR* and *LDR* on job recommendation platforms [436]. In total, 2,240 artificial profiles of job seekers were created on four job boards, which received 319,974 recommendations. In terms of *SDR*, Zhang found that ~10% of jobs were exclusively recommended to either men or women, even with identical profiles except for gender. Regarding the stricter *LDR* measure, which requires both items and their ranks to match, Zhang discovered that ~75% of recommendation lists differed between male and female job seekers.

While the metrics discussed above measure discrepancies in a system's performance or result lists between end users belonging to different groups, demographic biases can also be studied from a content creator's or item's perspective. Corresponding metrics can reveal unfairness concerning equal opportunities and include the following.

True-positive rate parity (TPRP), also referred to as *true-positive rate gap* or *sourcing bias*, is defined on a protected attribute of the documents' or items' creators, respectively, in a retrieval or recommendation task [111, 190]. For instance, in a RS, TPRP with respect to a given binary protected attribute of items according to which two item groups I_g and $I_{g'}$ are defined is given in Eq. 3.11 for a user u with recommendation list L_u. Here, $\rho(u, i) = 1$ implies that an item i is suitable or relevant for user u; $\mathcal{P}$ denotes probability. $TPRP = 0$ implies that equal opportunity is achieved. In simple words, TPRP assumes a value of zero if suited items have equal chances of being recommended to user u regardless of the value of their protected attribute, i.e., their belonging to either I_g or $I_{g'}$.

$$TPRP(u) = \left|\mathcal{P}(i \in L_u \,|\, i \in I_g, \rho(u,i) = 1) - \mathcal{P}(i \in L_u \,|\, i \in I_{g'}, \rho(u,i) = 1)\right| \quad (3.11)$$

Note that true-positive rate (TPR) is equivalent to recall (see Table 1.1). Therefore, Eq. 3.11 can be rewritten as shown in Eq. 3.12 for a recommendation scenario, where T_u^g and $T_u^{g'}$ denote the items belonging to group I_g and $I_{g'}$, respectively, for which interactions exist in the test set.

$$TPRP(u) = \left| \frac{|L_u \cap T_u^g|}{|T_u^g|} - \frac{|L_u \cap T_u^{g'}|}{|T_u^{g'}|} \right| \quad (3.12)$$

Analogously, for a retrieval scenario, Eq. 3.13 shows the rewritten formula, replacing users $u \in U$ by queries $q \in Q$.

$$TPRP(q) = \left| \frac{|L_q \cap T_q^g|}{|T_q^g|} - \frac{|L_q \cap T_q^{g'}|}{|T_q^{g'}|} \right| \quad (3.13)$$

Example: True-Positive Rate Parity in Job Recommendation
Investigating datasets of 322,337 biographies and 2,775 job advertisements covering 24 different job categories, Kumar et al. [206] computed a *TPRP* of 0.326 between male and female applicants when using a cross-encoder architecture and a Transformer-based language model for job-candidate matching.

Adverse impact ratio (AIR) is highly related to TPRP but computes the ratio between the group-specific TPR (recall) values instead of their absolute differences [61], as shown in Eq. 3.14.

$$AIR(u) = \frac{\mathcal{P}(i \in L_u \,|\, i \in I_g, \rho(u,i) = 1)}{\mathcal{P}(i \in L_u \,|\, i \in I_{g'}, \rho(u,i) = 1)} \quad (3.14)$$

3.4.3 Ecological Validity of Bias and Fairness Metrics

One important but unfortunately heavily underresearched topic when studying biases is the ecological validity of the numerous metrics that have been proposed to quantify them. The underlying question is whether mathematically well-defined measures of bias that are often used to quantify the fairness of IRRSs translate to actually perceived disparities.

Addressing this question for *popularity bias*, first steps have been taken in [141], where Ferwerda et al. conduct a user study to investigate the extent to which popularity bias is perceived by users of RSs powered by different algorithms (`ItemKNN`, `SLIM`, and `MultVAE`). These algorithms produce highly different levels of popularity bias in their results, i.e., songs in this study. Surprisingly, study participants did not perceive significant differences between the algorithms, neither in terms of the popularity of recommended items nor in the overall fairness of the entire recommendation lists. Furthermore, no significant correlations between participants' perceived popularity and computational popularity bias metrics such as $\%\Delta Mean$ (see Sect. 3.4.1) could be found. A shortcoming of Ferwerda et al.'s study is that users were asked to rate popularity in absolute terms, i.e., questions of the form "Do you think the song is popular?" or "Do you think the songs in the recommended playlist contains a balanced representation of popular and unpopular songs?" were asked.

Assuming that the perception of popularity and popularity bias is subjective, Lesota et al. investigate in a follow-up study how users of RSs perceive popularity bias when they are given an anchor [218]. More precisely, Lesota et al. adopt the concept of miscalibration (see Sect. 3.4.1) to model popularity bias, by computing JSD between the item popularity distribution of a user's interacted items and the popularity distribution computed on the items recommended to the user (see Sect. 3.4). The authors analyze the same three algorithms as done in [141] but additionally investigate simple personalized baselines that produce extreme values of popularity bias. In fact, algorithms `Genre-MostPop` and `Genre-LeastPop` recommend items selected from the user's preferred genres in a way that only the most popular and least popular songs (computed across all users) are included, respectively. In a questionnaire-based study, Lesota et al. asked users to rate whether the recommendations were too popular, too unpopular, or just right compared to their usual listening habits in terms of popularity preference. Unsurprisingly, recommendations made by `Genre-MostPop` and `Genre-LeastPop` were perceived as too popular and too unpopular, respectively. More surprisingly, recommendation lists created by `MultVAE` were perceived as even more popularity-biased than those made by `Genre-MostPop`. The authors, furthermore, found a highly significant correlation between the JSD bias values and the participants' indications of popularity miscalibration.

In sum, the studies [141, 218] indicate that users indeed do perceive popularity bias in terms of popularity miscalibration (i.e., when they are asked to judge bias by relating the popularity of recommended items to their usual popularity preferences). In contrast, users barely perceive popularity bias in recommendations when asked to judge the popularity of items in absolute terms (i.e., whether they think an item is popular or not).

Concerning *demographic bias*, there is also a significant lack of studies that investigate the relationship between computational bias assessments and human judgments of perceived fairness in the context of RSSs. A notable exception is the study of recommendation fairness, acceptance, and gender conformity carried out by Wang et al. [401]. The authors investigate a career recommender; more precisely, they build a RS for college majors, using profiles of Facebook users. They base their recommender on a neural collaborative filtering (NCF) [170] architecture trained on user-item interactions (Facebook "Likes") from 16,619 users (60% males and 40% females) with 1,380 unique college majors. To create a gender-debiased variant of the RS, Wang et al. correct the user embeddings by subtracting a gender bias vector derived from the average representation of male and female users. Evaluating both variants of the RS (original and gender-debiased), the authors unsurprisingly found a slightly lower bias for the latter variant according to the *non-parity unfairness (NPU)* metric, which measures the absolute difference of the average predicted ratings between male and female users across all items I. This is formalized in Eqs. 3.15 and 3.16, where $\hat{r}_{u,i}$ refers to the predicted interaction or rating score of user u with item i, $\mu^g(i)$ denotes the average of this score for item i among all users in a certain group g (which can be male or female users in this case), and NPU gives the finale non-parity unfairness score.

$$NPU = \frac{1}{|I|} \sum_{i \in I} \left| \mu^{female}(i) - \mu^{male}(i) \right| \tag{3.15}$$

$$\mu^g(i) = \frac{1}{|U_g|} \sum_{u \in U_g} \hat{r}_{u,i} \tag{3.16}$$

While NPU was slightly lower (fairer) for the debiased RS variant (1.119 vs. 1.145), in a user study with 202 participants, Wang et al. discovered that users nevertheless preferred the recommendations of the original RS over those of the debiased RS. Concretely, the mean acceptance score of recommendations was 0.372 and 0.279, respectively, for the original and debiased system variants.[16] This result raises the question of whether users actually do prefer debiased and non-stereotypical recommendations at all. Finally, the authors found that the perceived gender conformity associated with a career influences the acceptance of the career recommendation. For instance, female users rather accepted recommendations for stereotypical female careers than for male-dominated careers.

In summary, existing studies, though limited, reveal a complex relationship between computational bias metrics, how users perceive fairness, and their willingness to accept recommendations. Computational bias metrics, therefore, seem to have only limited expressiveness.

[16] Participants were shown the top 3 recommendations made by each system and had to rate them as suited (scoring 1), unsuited (scoring 0), or unsure (scoring 0.5) for a future career choice. The mean acceptance score was then computed as the average over all these scores among all users of a given system.

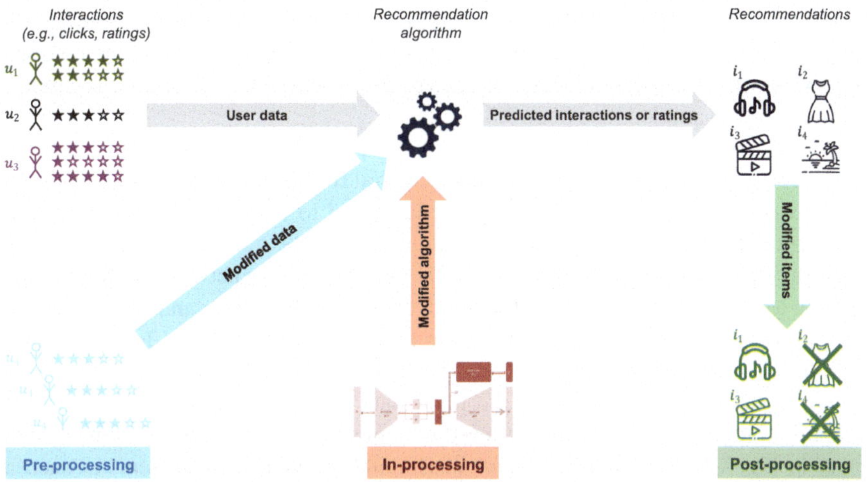

Fig. 3.3: Categories of debiasing approaches for RSs. The gray part depicts the standard pipeline of a recommender system: The algorithm is trained on interaction data created by users and predicts which items the target user might like. The blue part illustrates the pre-processing strategy for debiasing, which modifies the input data the algorithm is trained on, to achieve a better balance of training data with respect to some user or item characteristics. The red part visualizes the functioning of in-processing techniques, which directly alter the recommendation algorithm to make unbiased predictions. The green part delineates post-processing approaches, which keep input and algorithm untouched but adapt the recommendation list by removing or reordering its items

3.5 Mitigating Harmful Bias

Once we have identified the presence of harmful biases in IRRSs using, for instance, the measures presented in Sect. 3.4, we commonly want to mitigate them to avoid unfair or even discriminatory treatment of content consumers or producers.

Depending on the stage in the retrieval or recommendation pipeline at which the mitigation of harmful biases takes place, it is common to distinguish between *pre-processing*, *in-processing*, and *post-processing* debiasing techniques. Figure 3.3 illustrates these three strategies for a recommendation setting. For retrieval, the figure can be read accordingly, replacing the user's explicit or implicit rating data with the query and the predicted interactions or ratings with the list of retrieved documents.

Pre-processing methods adapt the input data that is used to train the ranking model, aiming at encouraging or discouraging a certain behavior of the learned model (blue parts in Fig. 3.3). This is commonly achieved by making the distribution of the training data more representative of the real world (see statistical bias in Sect. 3.3.1) or closer to an idealized world (see societal bias in Sect. 3.3.1). For instance, interactions of users belonging to certain under- or overrepresented groups can be upsampled (duplicated) or downsampled (dropped), respectively, if mitigation targets demographic bias (see Sect. 3.5.2). In case of popularity bias, interactions with items from overly popular creators can be downsampled; those from less popular ones can be upsampled (see Sect. 3.5.1).

In-processing methods alter the retrieval or recommendation algorithm at its core (red parts in Fig. 3.3). In the case of modern neural IRRSs, this often means changing the network architecture or training procedure used to learn the document or item ranking model. Common approaches include adapting the training objective, such as the loss function in a neural network architecture, to penalize network configurations leading to a biased model. Alternatively, adversarial architectures and corresponding training regimes can be adopted to unlearn protected user attributes during training or from a pre-trained model.

Post-processing methods keep the input data and the algorithm untouched but adapt the output, i.e., the list of retrieved documents or recommended items (green parts in Fig. 3.3). Commonly, this entails reranking documents or items in such a way that a certain bias or fairness metric is improved. For instance, by downranking documents containing already overrepresented content or upranking documents featuring underrepresented content, e.g., for a query about parental leave, one may want to give more weight to documents containing information specific to fathers and less weight to information specific to mothers, if the latter information is overrepresented in the original results.

In the following, we present selected debiasing approaches in more detail, again for popularity bias (Sect. 3.5.1) and demographic bias (Sect. 3.5.2), organized according to pre-, in-, and post-processing strategies.

3.5.1 Popularity Bias

3.5.1.1 Pre-processing Methods

Literature that exclusively applies pre-processing techniques to mitigate popularity bias is scarce, possibly due to the modest improvements they offer and the generally questionable practice of altering input data. The latter often involves discarding potentially valuable information that could otherwise help achieve a higher accuracy (e.g., in terms of NDCG). The most common pre-processing approaches include *upsampling*, *downsampling*, or otherwise *removing or augmenting parts of the interaction data* before it is fed into the retrieval or recommendation algorithm.

For instance, Seki and Maehara address popularity bias in the news domain by *sampling interactions uniformly* from each of a set of categories (e.g., politics, entertainment, or sports) [345]. By doing so, the same number of items are sampled from unpopular and popular categories, which ensures a more balanced representation of interactions. Cremonesi et al. conducted a simulation study on a hotel recommendation task, in which one variant was created by *excluding the most popular items* from the catalog [100]. A more sophisticated pre-processing approach is integrated into the popularity bias mitigation framework proposed by Boratto et al. [58]. The authors use a *popularity-aware sampling* and augmentation method to create the training data for their ranking model. Concretely, their approach augments observed interactions and creates unobserved interactions—used as negative samples for training—by selecting items that fall above or below a certain popularity threshold. Boratto et al. investigate their framework in the movie and the e-learning domain and find that combining the proposed sampling (pre-processing) and regularization (in-processing) leads to less popularity bias than applying them separately.

3.5.1.2 In-processing Methods

Approaches that change the retrieval or recommendation algorithm, or the architecture or process for learning the ranking model, to reduce popularity bias are referred to as in-processing bias mitigation methods. They represent a common alternative to pre-processing methods and frequently rely on integrating a popularity-related objective into the optimization process (for instance, through adapting the loss function in the training process of the ranking model), on leveraging additional side information (such as interaction context, user properties, or item descriptors), or on adapting the internal user or item representation of the model to achieve a specific objective (e.g., making the embeddings of highly popular items indistinguishable from those of lesser popular ones).

Approaches that change the *optimization objective* of the ranking model to encourage less popularity-biased models regularly integrate a *regularization* term into the loss function. Doing so steers the training process by giving more weight to less popular items or reducing the influence of overly popular items. For instance, Abdollahpouri et al. [4] approach the problem by adapting traditional matrix factorization (MF), i.e., decomposing the user-item interaction matrix into lower-dimensional embeddings that project both users and items into a joint latent space, in which rating or interaction prediction can be performed efficiently. They use the alternating least squares (ALS) technique to perform MF and define an optimization objective composed of two components: a standard pairwise ranking loss and a diversity component. The latter is computed over item popularity groups defined as regions in the popularity distribution (see Fig. 3.2). This approach effectively performs regularization because it penalizes low diversity in the results, i.e., cases where only items with similar (high) popularity are recommended. Vice versa, this popularity-based diversity objective is achieved if the recommended items are perfectly balanced over the popularity groups. The authors show in the movie domain (using the MovieLens-1M dataset [168]) and in the e-commerce domain (using the Epinions dataset of product ratings [251]) that their approach substantially increases the number and percentage of long-tail items in recommendations (see APT in Sect. 3.4.1) at the expense of a reduction in NDCG.

More recently, Li et al. propose to integrate a popularity regularization term into the objective function of a BPR-based RS [226]. BPR is a Bayesian personalized ranking model and a popular choice to solve the MF problem in RSs. It aims to build a model that preserves the ranking of item pairs for each user, i.e., the information which of two items is preferred over the other by the given user. The authors evaluate their approach on MovieLens datasets [168] and demonstrate a substantial reduction in the correlation between the popularity of items and their ranks in the recommendation lists, a metric which Li et al. introduce to quantify popularity bias.[17] Concretely, compared to a standard non-debiased BPR model, the proposed debiased variant reduces the popularity-rank correlation of items from more than 0.90 to less than 0.25, marking a substantial drop in popularity bias according to this metric.

Regarding in-processing methods that *leverage side information*, their main motivation is that popularity bias results from a scarcity of interaction data for less popular items. Such methods assume that this problem can be mitigated by leveraging side information associated with items or users or interaction contexts, such as content descriptors (e.g., tags) of items, social connections (e.g., friends) of users, or the timestamp of interaction, respectively. For instance, Rahmani et al. approach the problem of point of interest (POI) recommendation [306]. The authors introduce a fusion model for various context information based on linear regression and integrate it into popular POI recommendation models to overcome data sparsity issues. On two popular POI datasets, Gowalla and Yelp [239], Rahmani et al. show that their approach is less susceptible to popularity bias than common CF-based methods.

In-processing strategies based on *adapting the internal user or item representation* include Liu et al.'s framework for a "fairness-centric model that adaptively mitigates the popularity bias in both users and items for recommendation" (FAiR) [241]. The framework's main components are *adaptive fairness filters* and *adversarial fairness discriminators*. The former aim to mitigate popularity bias by modifying user and item embeddings through scaling and shifting operators. These are learned using feature-wise linear modulation (FiLM) [298] and a multilayer perceptron (MLP), a simple neural network architecture. FiLM enables the learning of parameters that can dynamically adapt to the varying degrees of bias mitigation required for different users or items. To investigate whether the learned fairness filters effectively reduce popularity bias, Liu et al.'s FAiR framework also contains different fairness discriminators that predict whether a user or item belongs to the high-popularity or low-popularity group, defined by their frequency of interactions. Three components of the FAiR architecture, i.e., fairness filters, fairness discriminators, and base recommendation model, are trained jointly.[18] Concretely, an *adversarial training* procedure is used to alternatingly optimize (1) the accuracy of the base recommendation model and of the fairness filters that act as generators and (2) the classification accuracy of the adversary that aims to uncover the popularity group to which users and items belong. Liu et al. evaluate FAiR on the tasks of product, friend, and movie recommendation, using datasets from Amazon [181], Twitter [35], and MovieLens [168],

[17] The authors define this popularity-rank correlation for items as the average Spearman's rank-order correlation between each item's popularity and its average rank in users' recommendation lists.

[18] For the sake of simplicity, we omit here the implicit fairness discriminator. For details, please refer to [241].

respectively. Experiments show that FAiR improves UGF and other fairness metrics on all datasets, though at the expense of recommendation precision and recall.

3.5.1.3 Post-processing Methods

Post-processing approaches operate only on the list of suggested items or documents that are output by a regular non-debiased IR or RS algorithm. They commonly perform some kind of score adjustment (reweighting items) or rank adjustment (reranking items).

For instance, Yalcin and Bilge propose a *score adjustment* approach via *reweighting* ratings based on the concept of "blockbuster score" (see B_i in Eq. 3.17 that shows the formulas used for score reweighting). Items are considered "blockbusters" if they are both overly popular and highly rated. Popularity is referred to as p_i in Eq. 3.17 and is defined as the number of users who rated item i. $\hat{r}_i$ denotes the average rating of item i. Their method penalizes items with high B_i values in the recommendation list by reformulating the rating prediction score $\hat{r}_{u,i}^{debiased}$ as a linear combination of the normalized predicted ratings $\hat{r}_{u,i}$ given by any CF algorithm and the inverse blockbuster score w_i, controlled by a sensitivity parameter α.

$$\hat{r}_{u,i}^{debiased} = (1 - \alpha) \cdot \hat{r}_{u,i} + \alpha \cdot w_i, \quad w_i = (1 + B_i)^{-1}, \quad B_i = \frac{\hat{r}_i + p_i}{2} \tag{3.17}$$

Yalcin and Bilge show that their approach increases APT (see Sect. 3.4.1) and user-specific novelty scores (see Table 3.1), using MF and nearest neighbor approaches (`ItemKNN` and `UserKNN`) on several datasets, including MovieLens-1M [168].

An example of a *rank adjustment* or *reranking* approach is the work by Abdollahpouri et al. [5], which proposes a probabilistic approach to create a new, reranked recommendation list L'_u that considers both the probability of the target user u being interested in item i of the original list L_u (the output of the used base RS) and the probability of u being interested in a candidate item from L_u that is not yet included in the reranked list L'_u. The latter probability is defined based on the diversity over item popularity categories, thereby rewarding the inclusion of more diverse items in L'_u, in terms of their popularity. The authors show on MovieLens-1M [168] and Epinions [251] datasets that their approach leads to a substantial decrease in ARP while APT increases, indicating less popularity bias in results, though at the expense of a drop in NDCG.

Other reranking approaches are based on the concept of *calibrated popularity* [9] (see Sect. 3.4.1), i.e., they assume that users prefer results of similar popularity than what they consumed in the past. Therefore, ideally, the popularity of the items the system outputs should mimic the popularity of already consumed items. For instance, Lesota et al. [217] approach calibrated popularity [9] as a simple item reranking strategy. Given an initial recommendation list L_u created by any backend RS, a new recommendation list L'_u of reranked items is generated by solving the optimization problem given in Eq. 3.18,[19] where $rel(L_u)$ refers to the sum of predicted relevance scores or ratings for all items in L_u; $\widehat{H_u}$ and $\widehat{L_u}$ denote the distribution of items over popularity bins, respectively, in the historic interactions of u and in u's original recommendation list (cf. Eq. 3.4). The parameter λ controls the balance between accuracy/relevance and strength of bias mitigation.

$$L'_u = \underset{L_u}{\operatorname{argmax}}\ (1-\lambda)\cdot rel(L_u) - \lambda \cdot JSD(\widehat{H_u}, \widehat{L_u}) \tag{3.18}$$

Lesota et al. also identify optimal λ values for different user groups (e.g., defined according to gender or inclination toward mainstream content), optimizing the harmonic mean of NDCG and the (inverse) JSD. They evaluate their strategy for music and movie recommendation scenarios, using the LFM-2b [257, 334] and MovieLens-1M [168] datasets, respectively. Using a graph-based recommendation model (`LightGCN`) on LFM-2b, the trade-off between NDCG/JSD ranges from 0.155/0.23 (for $\lambda = 0.0$, i.e., recommendations are only optimized for relevance) to 0.05/0.13 (for $\lambda = 0.9$) [217].

3.5.2 Demographic Bias

3.5.2.1 Pre-processing Methods

These methods address bias mitigation (in this case, demographic bias; see Sect. 3.4.2) before data is inputted into the IRRS. In Fig. 3.3, their operation is illustrated in blue. Pre-processing in this context typically involves modifying the interaction data used to train a model to achieve a more balanced representation of the user or item interactions. One common approach is *data rebalancing*, as discussed in [198, 257]. This can be addressed from either the user's or the creator's (item's) fairness perspective.

As for the user's perspective, *upsampling* involves increasing the amount of training data, i.e., user-item interactions in a RS, from the minority group, while *subsampling* entails reducing the data from the majority group. These user groups are delineated based on the protected attribute targeted for debiasing, e.g., gender, race, age, or religion. Upsampling can be simply realized by duplicating existing interactions of the minority group. Subsampling can be effected by randomly dropping interactions of the majority group. Focusing on the creator's (or item's) perspective, likewise, the training data produced by the minority group of content creators can be augmented, or parts of the interactions with items created by the majority group can be removed. Similar procedures are applicable in retrieval scenarios, for instance, duplicating documents created by the minority group for training purposes.

To illustrate pre-processing approaches in the context of recommendation, let us consider the study by Melchiorre et al. [257], which investigates the effects of

[19] This can be done, for instance, using greedy optimization [9].

upsampling to obtain a balanced representation of different genders in the training data of various recommendation algorithms: `ItemKNN` (item-based k-nearest neighbors) [332] is a traditional CF approach that recommends items that are similar to the items the target user has already interacted with. This item similarity is computed based on the interaction history of users with the items under consideration. `ALS` [182] and `BPR` [315] are MF-based CF approaches. The former uses an iterative, alternating training procedure to factorize the user-item interaction matrix, thereby generating user and item embeddings in a shared vector space. `BPR`, in contrast, adopts a pairwise optimization strategy, trying to maximize the difference between the predicted ratings of items the target user has interacted with (positive examples) and those the target user has not interacted with (negative examples). `SLIM` [282] factorizes the co-occurrence matrix of items and utilizes the identified item coefficients to sparsely aggregate the interactions. `MultVAE` (multinomial variational autoencoder) [228] is a type of neural network that encodes the interactions of each user in a latent space, such that the original interaction vector can be reconstructed with minimal error. Items with the highest scores in the reconstructed vector, but which the user has not interacted with yet, are then recommended.

To investigate the effect of data rebalancing for pre-processing, Melchiorre et al. leverage the LFM-2b music dataset of interactions between users and music tracks from Last.fm [257, 334]. The authors duplicate user-item interaction data from female users (the minority group) in the training set until it matches the number of instances from male users (the majority group). They train the aforementioned recommendation algorithms, once with the original data, once with the upsampled data [257], and measure the performance of all variants in terms of NDCG and beyond-accuracy metrics.

Computing the gender-related $RecGap^{NDCG@10}$ metric (see Sect. 3.4.2) reveals that all aforementioned recommendation algorithms perform worse for female users than for their male counterparts. This holds regardless of whether upsampling is performed. The disparity in performance between genders is found highest for `ALS`. Concretely, NCDG@10 values are 0.251 vs. 0.205 for males vs. females, therefore, $RecGap^{NDCG@10} = 0.046$, or 18.3% when expressed as percentage with respect to the user group that receives better recommendations. `BPR` yields the lowest $RecGap^{NDCG@10}$ disparity of 0.012 (9.3%). In contrast, when applying the described upsampling strategy, $RecGap^{NDCG@10}$ narrows down to 0.044 (17.7%) in case of `ALS` and to 0.008 (6.5%) for `BPR`. Even though this provides evidence that a simple pre-processing method can improve gender disparity, the observed reduction of the gap comes at an overall decrease of NDCG@10 for all genders. For more details, please refer to [257].

Another recent work that falls into this category is [129]. Escobedo et al. jointly address debiasing and privacy objectives by a pre-processing technique that obfuscates parts of the input data to a RS. Based on the proposed stereotypicality measures for users and items (computed, e.g., with respect to gender), the authors present a probabilistic stereotypicality-based obfuscation approach, applied to the interactions used to train the underlying ranking model of the RS. By removing highly stereotypical items from the users' profiles with a certain probability, they reach a better accuracy-privacy trade-off than several baselines, for both music and movie recommendation tasks (respectively, using the LFM2b-DB [257] and MovieLens-1M [168] datasets). At the same time, their approach also reduces the accuracy of an attacker network that aims at predicting the user's gender, thereby approaching demographic bias through the fairness by blindness principle.

3.5.2.2 In-processing Methods

The concept of in-processing is illustrated in the red part of Fig. 3.3. Corresponding approaches most frequently integrate a debiasing objective or component into the model training or optimization procedure. This can be achieved, for example, by extending the loss function used during model training with a bias regularization term or by using adversarial training, as proposed for retrieval in [312] and for recommendation in [149, 417].

One possible use of *adversarial training* in this context is illustrated in Fig. 3.4, adapted from [149]. Ganhör et al. propose an approach that integrates an adversarial block into a `MultVAE` network used for recommendation. This block serves to debias the latent representation of users [149]. Concretely, the architecture, coined `Adv-MultVAE`, is composed of a main recommendation component, realized as an autoencoder [139, 228], and an adversarial network realized as a simple feed-forwarMost often, this is caused byd neural network. The multinomial variational autoencoder `MultVAE`, depicted in gray in Fig. 3.4, aims at learning a latent representation z of its input x such that x can be reconstructed from z at the network's output x'. The discrepancy between the original x and reconstructed x' is minimized as a training objective. In the recommendation scenario, x represents the item interaction vector of a given user, whose dimensionality corresponds to the number of items in the catalog. The latent user representation z is learned by an encoder network $f(\cdot)$, the reconstruction x' by a decoder network $g(\cdot)$.[20]

Complementing the `MultVAE`-based recommendation component, the adversarial block is responsible for bias mitigation. Concretely, it enables the unlearning of the protected attribute y from the latent user representation z by trying to predict the former (resulting in prediction y') from the latter. The sensitive attribute is commonly modeled as a one-hot-encoded categorical value. This adversarial part is depicted in petrol color in Fig. 3.4. The intuition of this architecture is that the protected attribute should not be considered in the process of learning the user's representation z and, in turn, should not affect the created recommendations. Both networks (main recommender and adversary) are trained jointly. Their objective is to maximize the performance for their respective tasks: reconstructing x and predicting y. The loss function for training is therefore composed of the recommendation loss (input reconstruction error) and the loss of the adversary (cross-entropy loss between the predicted and the true value of the protected attribute). The interested

[20] To be precise, in a variational autoencoder, the encoder is not directly used to infer z, but the z's are sampled from a Gaussian distribution whose parameters (mean μ and standard deviation σ) are learned during training.

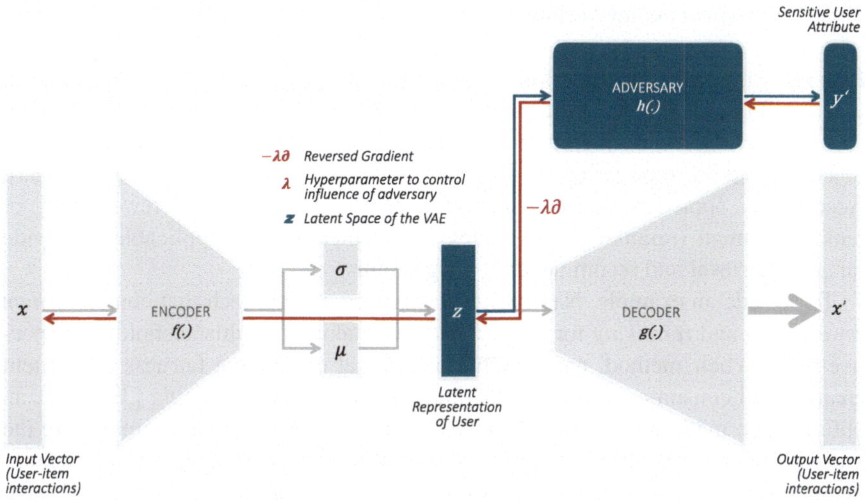

Fig. 3.4: Architecture of adversarial multinomial variational autoencoders (`Adv-MultVAE`), according to [149]

reader is referred to [149] for details. `Adv-MultVAE` has been evaluated on two datasets: MovieLens-1M [168]) (movies) and LFM2b-DB [257] (music). Ganhör et al. demonstrate a substantial reduction of the predictability of gender from z, from about 70% balanced accuracy in `MultVAE` to 57% (MovieLens-1M) and 61% (LFM2b-DB) when using `Adv-MultVAE`. This results in only a marginal decrease in NDCG@10 (from 0.621 to 0.593 for ML-1M and from 0.211 to 0.206 for LFM2b-DB).

Similar to recommendation, adversarial training can also be used for in-processing bias mitigation in retrieval settings, notably, to mitigate gender bias in search results. For instance, Rekabsaz et al. propose a network architecture for unlearning gender-biased information from embeddings of query-document interactions [312]. They extend the popular Transformer-based language model `BERT` [115], which is adapted for document ranking. Their proposed architecture, coined `AdvBERT`, comprises the main scoring component that estimates a relevance score for each query-document pair. For this purpose, Rekabsaz et al. add an adversarial feed-forward network that predicts the protected attribute. This attribute is defined as the *document neutrality* score and derived from the occurrence of male and female words appearing in the query-document pairs. Rekabsaz et al. demonstrate, on the popular passage retrieval dataset MS MARCO [96, 279, 314], that `AdvBERT` can substantially increase document neutrality of retrieved documents. However, they also point out a significant trade-off between neutrality and utility in terms of NDCG. For details, please refer to [312].

3.5.2.3 Post-processing Methods

Bias mitigation methods that follow a post-processing procedure are illustrated in green in Fig. 3.3. They adjust the scores or ranks of items (in recommendation scenarios) or documents (in retrieval scenarios) in the result list to enforce a debiasing objective without modifying the ranking algorithm or model itself [73, 277, 432]. Accordingly, approaches can be categorized into score adjustment (reweighting) or rank adjustment (reranking) techniques. These methods are applicable to a wide range of retrieval and recommendation algorithms.

To provide an example, Naghiaei et al. propose an approach that combines *item reweighting* and *reranking* for recommendation, taking a multistakeholder perspective [277]. Their method, named `CPFair`, aims at optimizing fairness for content creators and consumers alike. For this purpose, linear programming [390], i.e., an optimization method for linear objective functions, is used to jointly maximize the utility of recommendations for end users and minimize the discrepancies of recommendations in terms of fairness notions for both creators and consumers. For the former, the fairness notion that is optimized for is exposure parity (see Sect. 3.3.4.2). Concretely, this means that each item should be recommended to a similar number of users, irrespective of any item property, such as popularity or its creator's gender. The user-side fairness notion is defined via parity of recommendation utility (NDCG) regardless of any user characteristic, such as their activity level or gender. Therefore, intuitively, all content creators should have equal chances to appear in recommendation lists. And all recommendation lists should be of comparable utility for their users, on average. `CPFair` first creates top N recommendations by solving a linear programming task that is composed of a linear combination of the underlying (biased) recommendation algorithm's prediction and the parity notions for users and items. In a second step, items are reweighted according to actual expose and utility in the final recommendation list, and the top items are ultimately recommended. Naghiaei et al. show on eight datasets including MovieLens-1M [168] and Epinions [251], and for various recommendation algorithms including neural matrix factorization (`NeuMF` [170]) and variational autoencoders (`MultVAE` [228]), that `CPFair` can effectively mitigate the unfairness for creators and consumers while largely maintaining the utility of recommendations in terms of NDCG. Detailed results can be found in [277].

As an example of a simple *reranking* strategy targeting fairness from a content creator's perspective, Ferraro et al. address the problem of an unequal gender distribution of music artists in recommendation lists [140]. Concretely, the authors first analyze the demographics of artists in (song) recommendations made by the popular `ALS` algorithm for CF [182], They perform training on two datasets from Last.fm (LFM-1b [333] and Last.fm 360K [74]) and identify the average position of the highest-ranked track by a female and by a male artist in the ranked recommendation list. The former is found between ranks 8 and 9 while the latter between ranks 1 and 2, on average.[21] To mitigate this gender bias, Ferraro et al. propose a reranking strategy that simply downranks all tracks created by male artists by a certain number of ranks defined via a parameter λ, aiming at achieving a balanced gender distribution in the recommendation list. To study the long-term effects of this approach, the authors further conduct a simulation study in which users are assumed to listen to all recommended tracks in each iteration of the simulation. These simulated interactions are then used to retrain the ALS model. The study demonstrates that stable, gender-balanced results can be achieved when setting $\lambda = 7$, i.e., the λ value that closes the ranking gap between male and female artists identified beforehand (see the aforementioned discrepancies in ranks). However, closing this gap also reduces NDCG@10 by 5% for $\lambda = 7$, marking a significant trade-off between recommendation utility for users and a gender-balanced representation of content creators in recommendations.

As a concluding remark on bias mitigation, from a legal perspective, according to both EU and US jurisdictions, post-processing techniques are perhaps the most problematic ones since they are closest to real-world application [207]. Since they directly up- or downrank certain documents or items, this may result in (other) discrimination actions. In contrast, using algorithms to mitigate biases in datasets or society is generally allowed.

3.6 Summary and Open Challenges

This chapter provided an introduction to (harmful) biases occurring in IRRSs, their origins, their effects on different stakeholders, and their relation to the fairness of RSSs. We connected them to relevant regulations, especially to those on non-discrimination. Addressing two common and well-studied kinds of biases in IRRSs, namely, popularity bias and demographic bias, we also discussed computational methods to quantify them. Additionally, we provided a critical review of the capacity of formal metrics to reflect the human perception of these notions. Finally, we presented a selection of approaches to mitigate harmful biases in an effort to reduce the algorithmic unfairness of IRRSs.

While great achievements have already been accomplished to make IRRSs less prone to harmful biases and, in turn, increase their fairness, this is a very active field of research, and many open questions and challenges remain. A personal selection of the authors includes the following:

- **How should we address the trade-off between accuracy and fairness?** As already discussed in Sect. 3.3, a certain amount of bias toward the preferences of a user is required, especially in RSs, to personalize the results presented to the user. The level of personalization is typically reflected in the accuracy of these results,

[21] These results should be contextualized considering the overall underrepresentation of female artists in music recommendation datasets and generally in the music industry. In fact, only 23% of artists in both datasets are women.

meaning results that are better tailored to the user are assigned more relevance, value, utility, or gain. On the other hand, over-personalization results in filter bubbles, impairs content diversity, and may lead to disparate treatment of content creators as well as content consumers. We believe researchers and developers of IRRSs should ensure that their systems are transparent about this trade-off, being able to communicate it to their different stakeholders, and providing means to carefully balance and adjust this trade-off.

- **How should the requirements and goals of various stakeholders be accounted for?** In Sects. 1.3 and 3.3.4, we identified various stakeholders of IRRSs and discussed their roles, goals, and different biases they are prone to but also create themselves. These stakeholders include content creators, content consumers, service and platform providers, IRRS developers, advertisers, policymakers, regulators, lobbyists, non-governmental organizations, and many more. The overarching challenge in this context is how we, as a society, prioritize and reconcile the (conflicting) objectives and intentions of stakeholders, recognizing the deep interdependence of their actions and influences.
- **Do computational bias and fairness metrics capture how these aspects are perceived?** Extensive research has been devoted to uncovering and measuring bias in IRRSs by computational means, i.e., through formulas whose proponents claim that they capture fairness aspects. However, the ecological validity of these formulas remains poorly understood. In other words, we lack decent knowledge about how these mathematical definitions align with individuals' actual perceptions of bias and fairness. This is still a strongly underresearched area, despite some initial works (see Sect. 3.4.3). Further complicating the issue, different stakeholders likely have varying perceptions or priorities when it comes to bias and fairness.
- **How to address fairness in the era of large language models?** The spiraling success of LLMs, and in particular their widespread application as generative language models in chatbots, such as OpenAI's ChatGPT,[22] Microsoft's Copilot,[23] or Google's Gemini,[24] has raised many concerns about issues such as hallucination (reasonably sounding but incorrect answers) as well as biased or stereotypical results. Please refer, for instance, to the example in Sect. 3.1 and the survey by Gallegos et al. [148]. These concerns are important also in the context of IRRSs because generative LLMs are frequently used for recommendation and retrieval tasks by end users. Vice versa, much research is being devoted to integrating LLMs into retrieval [85, 250, 325] and recommendation [11, 183] systems. In this case, again, issues of unfairness and discrimination have been revealed [423, 435].
  While enriching the capabilities of generative LLMs and reducing hallucination has been addressed by recently emerging retrieval-augmented generation (RAG) methods, e.g., [64, 87, 117, 152, 189], research that explicitly aims at debiasing LLMs is still scarce, e.g., [112, 133], despite its urgent need. However, some

[22] https://chat.openai.com

[23] https://copilot.microsoft.com

[24] https://gemini.google.com

researchers even claim that it is impossible to build fair LLMs [37]. We believe that elaborating powerful debiasing solutions for LLMs as well as IRRSs that make use of their output will be one of the major challenges in the years to come.

3.7 Further Reading

Since this chapter could only give a brief introduction to the vast field of research revolving around the topics of bias and fairness in IRRSs, we would like to point the reader to the following additional resources, which provide a much deeper treatment.

Addressing bias and fairness from a general ML and DL perspective, Mehrabi et al. [254] review biases in data, algorithms, and user experiences and provide real-world applications where these biases matter. They further create a taxonomy of fairness definitions and outline methods for fair representation learning and natural language processing. Mitchell et al. [266] offer a consistent categorization of fairness definitions from literature and discuss the choices and assumptions made in the design of algorithmic decision-making systems powered by ML.

Particularly tailored to IR and RSs, Ekstrand et al. [126] provide a highly accessible introduction and contextualization of biases and fairness in information access systems, also discussing how these are different compared to other ML applications. The authors organize their deliberation along categories of algorithmic harm, sources of bias, involved stakeholders (especially focusing on consumers and providers), time scale, and mitigation strategies for unfairness. Focusing exclusively on RSs, Jannach et al. [187] review harmful biases and algorithmic countermeasures for their mitigation. Chen et al. [82] provide a survey about various kinds of biases that affect RSs and discuss strategies for debiasing RSs. Klimashevskaia et al. [200] focus their survey on popularity bias and provide an in-depth review of relevant works. Finally, Amigó et al. [21] organize and classify commonly used fairness measures in RSs literature according to five dimensions: benefit, stakeholder, partition granularity, exposure scheme, and fairness criterion. They also provide a new fairness framework based on information theory.

Chapter 4
Transparency

In today's digital landscape, IRRSs are fundamental tools that influence what information we consume and what choices we make. With their increased adoption, concerns about their transparency have become increasingly prominent [174]. Albert Einstein famously said, "Any fool can know. The point is to understand." This statement underscores the fundamental challenge in AI-driven systems: knowledge of their existence is on the rise, but understanding their inner workings and decision-making processes is, in many cases, still limited, in particular when the corresponding systems are black boxes. Critically, transparency in IRRSs is not just about providing abstract information about technical details but corresponds to making their functionality and decision-making processes more understandable to human users. As Carl Sagan once remarked:

> It is far better to grasp the universe as it really is than to persist in delusion, however satisfying and reassuring. [328]

Pioneering scientists and thinkers like Sagan or Einstein provide a philosophical foundation for the importance of transparency in IRRSs. Their thinking encourages us to question and shed light on the opaque algorithms that recommend, retrieve, and rank the content we see online. By doing so, we, as the users of these systems, can ensure they serve our needs and not provide us with biased or misleading information, leading to trust and informed decision-making.

4.1 Introduction and Problem Description

Improving the transparency of IRRSs is essential for providing various stakeholders, including users, system developers, and policymakers, with insights into the rationale behind the retrieved or recommended documents or items they receive. Such an understanding enables stakeholders to evaluate the relevance and accuracy of IRRSs' results, fostering trust and enhancing user satisfaction and engagement in the

M. Schedl et al., *Technical and Regulatory Perspectives on Information Retrieval and Recommender Systems*, The Information Retrieval Series 50,
https://doi.org/10.1007/978-3-031-69978-8_4

system [95, 384, 438]. Critically, a lack of transparency in IRRSs can lead to adverse effects, such as the spread of biased or inaccurate information [367].

The motivation for more transparency aligns with a broader trend toward ensuring the trustworthiness and accountability of AI-based technologies [379]. This trend is particularly pronounced in high-risk application domains such as healthcare or employment [161], where algorithmic decisions may have serious consequences [161]. For example, in the recruitment domain, IRRSs might be used for screening job applicants, where biases in the algorithms could lead to unfair hiring practices (see Sect. 3.2 for a more detailed description of a use case related to digital hiring practices). Similarly, in healthcare, an IRRS could influence diagnostic and treatment decisions, thus affecting patient outcomes directly.

Example: Healthcare Recommender Systems
Transparency in health RSs is a critical factor that influences user trust, system credibility, and the overall quality of healthcare services [124]. It involves clear communication, access to information, and the ability to understand and evaluate the processes behind medical data handling and decision-making [368]. Health-related platforms such as Ada Health [12] incorporate transparency into their systems by explaining their recommendations. They disclose the data sources used, the algorithms employed, and the reasoning behind specific recommendations. In this way, platforms like Ada Health help users understand why a particular medical condition is suggested based on their self-reported symptoms, supported by pointers to relevant medical literature.

In high-risk domains like our healthcare example, transparency plays a crucial role in auditing IRRSs to detect and mitigate potential biases or adverse outcomes, such as false inferences made by an IRRS about a user [383]. It also enables users of the corresponding systems to adapt their behavior or adjust the data they share with the system. Additionally, transparency supports system designers in identifying and addressing shortcomings in their systems.

Moreover, transparency has become a critical factor in meeting regulatory requirements, including data protection regulations or recent regulations put forward by, e.g., the EU, as is discussed in Sect. 4.2. Regulatory requirements related to transparency increasingly affect various fields and domains.

For example, in the recruitment domain, job seekers frequently utilize digital recruitment platforms to discover potential employment opportunities. Such platforms and networks have become essential tools for companies to post job vacancies and actively search for candidates while users have the opportunity to present themselves to potential employers [54]. They typically incorporate complex algorithms to deliver personalized job recommendations and content feeds, which raises specific challenges related to privacy, fairness, and transparency [285].

Example: Regulatory Demands in Digital Recruiting/Candidate Recommendation
Let us consider a scenario where a RS deployed in a digital recruitment platform inadvertently prioritizes candidates from a specific demographic because of biased algorithmic training data. As a consequence, the RS leads to discriminatory results, which are not only unethical but also prohibited under anti-discrimination laws (please refer to Sect. 3.2 for an overview of related regulations in Europe, the USA, and China). Due to the opaque nature of the leveraged RS, the respective candidates, human resources professionals, and regulators find it difficult to understand how the RS came to its results and why it recommended specific jobs to only a particular demographic.

A lack of transparency could diminish user trust and perceived fairness and potentially damage the reputation of the platform, thereby affecting the overall effectiveness of the recruitment process [213]. Critically, the importance of incorporating transparency in IRRSs extends beyond ethical concerns; it also addresses legal requirements. For instance, in the EU, regulations such as the GDPR and the AI Act (see Sect. 2.1) impose strict guidelines on automated decision-making, granting individuals the right to a meaningful explanation of the decisions made by algorithms [309]. Hence, IRRSs should be designed to ensure that their decision-making processes are explainable to candidates and fully compliant with regulatory standards. That entails comprehensive documentation of the systems and incorporating mechanisms that allow candidates to review and challenge automatically generated decisions.

In the remainder of this chapter, we discuss recent regulatory and ethical aspects of transparency (Sect. 4.2), clarify the relevant terminology, and highlight the benefits of challenges and barriers to transparency in IRRSs. We then discuss enhancing transparency in IRRSs via either interpretable IRRSs or post hoc interpretability techniques. A part of this chapter is devoted to explanations, which are a critical tool to achieve transparency in IRRSs, whereas we discuss data sources for explanations and highlight the most common explanation styles. Furthermore, we outline how transparency can be evaluated and how to achieve transparency via documentation, and we present how algorithmic auditing helps improve the transparency of IRRSs. We conclude the chapter by highlighting open challenges and further related work.

4.2 Regulatory Aspects

The discourse on transparency and explainability in AI and algorithmic systems has grown significantly in recent years [42]. Stakeholders worldwide, including governments, policymakers, and industry leaders, have become increasingly aware of the substantial impacts that IRRSs can have on user behavior, access to information and services, public opinion, and content distribution. This is exemplified by the 2023 US Senate Judiciary Committee Subcommittee on Privacy, Technology, and the

Law hearing on *Oversight of AI: Rules for Artificial Intelligence*,[1] where politicians, industry representatives, and researchers came together to discuss how to implement human oversight measures into AI development. Quoting Gary Marcus, Professor Emeritus of the New York University, who was asked for comments during the hearing:

> Transparency is absolutely critical here to understand the political ramifications, the bias ramifications, and so forth. We need transparency about the data. We need to know more about how the models work. We need to have scientists have access to them.[2]

In a similar fashion, signatures from the European Federation of Journalists have urged EU policymakers in the preparation of the AI Act:

> To prioritise maximum transparency on training data and artificially generated content to provide guarantees to citizens, authors and performers that their rights are respected: transparency is a prerequisite for both innovation and creation to continue to grow for the benefit of all.[3]

In response to such discussions and remarks, policies and regulations have been put forward already in several regions of the world to ensure that the decision-making processes and data usage within IRRSs are transparent, comprehensible, and subject to scrutiny by entities such as independent bodies, integrating ethical considerations into the deployment and governance of IRRSs. In the following, we review relevant regulatory efforts in Europe, the USA and China.

4.2.1 Regulating for Transparency in Europe

In the EU, transparency is a central principle outlined in the *General Data Protection Regulation (GDPR)* [309] and the *Digital Services Act (DSA)* [311].

The GDPR, introduced in 2016, has significantly shaped transparency standards and requirements, particularly concerning data privacy and users' rights related to their personal data collected in digital platforms. It mandates that organizations processing personal data uphold transparency by providing clear information to data subjects about the purpose and legal basis of data processing and any data-sharing arrangements (GDPR Articles 13 and 14). Individuals have rights under the GDPR to access, rectify, and erase their personal data (GDPR Articles 15-17). Furthermore, organizations must disclose the criteria for generating recommendations or rankings and implement privacy-preserving techniques such as data anonymization or encryption.

---

[1] https://www.techpolicy.press/transcript-senate-judiciary-subcommittee-hearing-on-oversight-of-ai

[2] https://www.techpolicy.press/transparency-wont-be-enough-for-ai-accountability

[3] https://composeralliance.org/news/2023/11/joint-statement-europe-s-creative-community-urges-eu-policymakers-to-put-transparency-back-at-the-heart-of-the-eu-ai-act

The recently adopted *Digital Services Act (DSA)* represents another landmark piece of legislation defining obligations for transparency for algorithmic systems. While the GDPR was introduced to address data protection of individuals on a general level, the DSA specifically addresses digital services, and thus, also IRRSs, which are defined in Article 3 [311] as follows:

> 'Online search engine' means an intermediary service that allows users to input queries in order to perform searches of, in principle, all Web sites, or all Web sites in a particular language, on the basis of a query on any subject in the form of a keyword, voice request, phrase or other input, and returns results in any format in which information related to the requested content can be found;

and

> 'Recommender system' means a fully or partially automated system used by an online platform to suggest in its online interface specific information to recipients of the service or prioritize that information, including as a result of a search initiated by the recipient of the service or otherwise determining the relative order or prominence of the information displayed

Put simply, providers of IRRSs are mandated to explain their main targeting criteria and information about the parameters used for personalization. Critically, the DSA imposes transparency requirements currently only on providers of very large online platforms (see Sect. 2.1): according to Article 27 of the DSA, online platforms are mandated to provide clear and understandable explanations of how their systems work, allowing users to understand and influence what content they see. For platforms that rank or prioritize content, users must be able to choose how they want information presented [130].

Example: Recommending Therapy Programs
A user with a history of anxiety uses a mental health app [392]. The app analyzes the user's self-reported symptoms and mobile phone habits. Based on this data, the app recommends a specific online therapy program focusing on cognitive behavioral therapy (CBT). However, the app does not explain its criteria for recommendations nor disclose that certain therapeutic approaches could sometimes worsen the condition. The user follows the app's recommendations and starts with the suggested therapy program. Unfortunately, the program uses a very intense form of CBT that is not suitable for the user's specific condition, and hence, the user's condition worsens. Since the app did not disclose that, in some cases, the recommended therapy can worsen anxiety, it could be seen as negligent.

In our example, a user following the app's recommendations experienced worsened anxiety due to unsuitable therapy, highlighting the consequences of a lack of transparency in the used RS. This example highlights the critical need for mental health apps to incorporate high standards in their IRRSs. Transparency must be enhanced not only to meet ethical and legal obligations but also to ensure user safety. The app should provide detailed explanations of its inner workings, especially when recommending interventions that could carry significant risks. Additionally, offering users options to customize or influence the selection process and accessible information about potential risks associated with various therapies could prevent adverse outcomes. Such measures would support users to make informed decisions aligned with their personal health needs.

4.2.2 Regulating for Transparency in the USA

In the USA, regulatory efforts regarding IRRSs and their transparency are still evolving. At the time of writing this book, some efforts are underway to address transparency issues of IRRSs, even though they are currently less extensive than those of the EU.

The *California Consumer Privacy Act (CCPA)* and its successor, the *California Privacy Rights Act (CPRA)*, are two examples of such efforts, which require businesses to provide users with transparency regarding collecting, using, and sharing their personal information [114]. The CCPA is a law in California that safeguards the privacy of consumers by granting them various privacy rights. It went into effect in 2020 and focuses on transparency and grants users various rights, including the ability to view, delete, and opt out of their personal information being sold [66, 72]. Businesses in California that fulfill certain criteria, including an annual gross venue of more than 25 million dollars or collecting, buying, or selling the data of more than 50,000 users, fall under this CCPA. The CPRA [381], which went into effect in January 2023, builds upon the CCPA and expands the privacy rights of California consumers. It also established a specific enforcement agency called the *California Privacy Protection Agency* [67] to ensure that the law is enforced and that breaches are penalized. Both laws are designed to protect the data privacy rights of California residents and provide them with more transparency and control over their personal information.

At the federal level, the proposed *Algorithmic Accountability Act (AAA)* [380] is another effort toward regulating AI technologies. If passed, this act would mandate transparency of AI and algorithmic systems, potentially impacting IRRSs by requiring transparency about the inner workings of algorithms and data usage. Although this act primarily focuses on automated decision-making processes used by large companies, it could also affect IRRSs that shape a user's access to opportunities, such as job RSs. In such cases, companies may be required to provide more transparency about the inner logic of the system, its parameters, and underlying data.

4.2.3 Regulating for Transparency in China

The Chinese government's efforts to regulate IRRS with respect to transparency include requirements for transparency in data processing activities, respect for intellectual property rights, obtaining consent for the use of personal information, and maximizing the accuracy, objectivity, and diversity of training data [142].

In this vein, the *Personal Information Protection Law (PIPL)* [388], which came into effect in 2021 and is designed to protect personal information rights and interests, defines how personal information should be handled and can be used. Here, transparency is a key factor, as PIPL upholds the principles of openness and transparency when it comes to processing personal information. This means that businesses are required to provide individuals with comprehensible information regarding how their personal information is being used [352]. Plus, the law also requires companies to conduct compliance assessments and publish the results of these assessments to enhance transparency and accountability [352].

Also related to transparency are regulations such as the *Algorithm Recommendation Regulation*, the *Provisions on Management of Deep Synthesis in Internet Information Service*, and the *Generative AI Regulation*. These regulations oblige service providers to maintain transparency in AI-related activities by submitting relevant algorithms to the *Cyberspace Administration of China*, providing explanations for algorithm recommendations, and ensuring that the training data is authentic, accurate, objective, and diverse [212].

In general, Chinese regulations of IRRSs are primarily aimed at ensuring compliance with government policies. Unlike some Western countries, China's approach to transparency in IRRSs emphasizes social control, national security, and user experience. Although transparency requirements in China may differ from those in Western jurisdictions due to distinct regulatory frameworks and cultural considerations, there is a growing emphasis on enhancing transparency in IRRSs to align with China's strategic goals and promote responsible AI development. This includes requiring IRRS providers to disclose information about their algorithms, such as the criteria used for ranking or user profiling [355].

4.3 Background

The importance of transparency within IRRSs has increasingly come to the forefront in recent years, even though transparency was already identified as a critical concept in 2000 [14, 174]. Naturally, the aim to improve the transparency of IRRSs is also stimulated by regulations such as the GDPR (see Sect. 2.1.3), which underscores the right of users to understand automated decision-making processes influenced by their digital interactions, including those employed by IRRSs, as discussed in Sect. 4.2.

Transparency in IRRS is a crucial system property that enables making the functioning of IRRSs understandable to the various stakeholders involved in an IRRS process, from end users to system designers [44, 166, 363]. Critical components of transparency are algorithmic disclosure and data transparency. *Algorithmic disclosure* reveals the system's logic, parameters, and policies to generate results or recommendations. At the same time, *data transparency* addresses the need to clarify the types of data utilized, their processing methods, and their impact on the outcomes of IRRSs. [51].

Bernard and Balog highlight that "understanding of a system can occur at several levels" [51]. They categorize such understanding into illustrating "the *how* and *why* of a system" [51]. That is directly related to the different needs and interests of various stakeholders: users are likely more interested in understanding *why* they have received a particular result, while system designers might be more interested in gaining deeper technical insights into the inner logic of an algorithmic system, i.e., understanding *how* the corresponding IRRS functions internally [163].

Discussions around transparency in IRRSs typically revolve around the concepts of explainability, justification, and interoperability. In the following, we differentiate between these concepts, briefly explain their meaning, and discuss the aspect of transparency they cater to.

4.3.1 Explainability, Justification, and Interpretability

Researchers have proposed various approaches to enhance IRRS transparency, primarily through explainability. Explainability aims to answer "the problem of *why*" [438] by providing users with explanations for the results or recommendations they receive. This can help users better understand and accept the IRRSs' results they receive, leading to improved user satisfaction [93] and even persuasion [235] as users feel more informed about the information presented. Research on transparency within IRRS often centers around the intertwined concepts of explainability and justification, with a growing body of literature underscoring their importance [23, 177, 367, 444]. *Explainability* involves breaking down the IRRS's decision-making process into human-understandable explanations highlighting factors influencing the generated outputs. The goal is to make the system's inner workings more transparent, helping users, developers, and other stakeholders understand *why* an IRRS arrived at a particular result. For example, a music RS might explain that it recommends a particular track because similar users have also listened to that track. Conversely, *justification* is more related to building trust and explaining to the user that a retrieval or recommendation result is relevant and valuable. Continuing with the music recommendation example, a justification for a recommended music track might incorporate the information that the track was composed by a user's favorite artist or is published by an independent label from which the user frequently listens to music. While both concepts are closely related, they address different aspects of transparency. An ideal IRRS should cater to both to achieve transparency, as explainability empowers users with understanding, while justification fosters users' trust in the system's capabilities.

Also related to the concept of explainability is *interpretability*. While the two terms are often used interchangeably in discussions about AI and ML, there are nuanced differences that distinguish them. Interpretability emphasizes understanding the internal workings of a model and the relationships between its inputs and outputs [269]. An interpretable model is transparent about the factors that most influence its predictions and how changing them might affect the outcome. Examples of interpretable models include decision trees, rule-based systems, and linear models. In decision trees, for instance, each node represents a decision based on specific features, offering a clear and interpretable path to the retrieval or recommendation outcome. Similarly, rule-based systems provide explicit rules that guide the retrieval or recommendation process, enabling users to understand the rationale behind results and how they align with their preferences. In this way, interpretability is one approach to achieving explainability in IRRSs. However, as this chapter outlines, explainability can also be achieved for non-interpretable models by devising post hoc explanations [438] (see Sect. 4.4.2), which are generated after the IRRS has produced its results and which provide insights into the factors that influenced the decision.

4.3.2 Benefits of Transparency

Transparency in IRRSs goes beyond simply informing the users of the corresponding systems. Enhancing their transparency offers a range of advantages that benefit various stakeholders in the process, such as users, policymakers, regulatory bodies, system designers, platform providers, and the systems themselves.

One advantage of transparency is the enhancement of user trust and engagement [281]. Users who understand why a system recommends certain items become more confident in its reliability [94, 263]. Moreover, transparency can improve the user experience by allowing for more informed decision-making, as well as the perceived quality of documents or items [278], rooted in a clear understanding of how information is relevant to individual needs [363], as well as users feeling more in control about the results they receive [370]. Transparent systems empower users by giving them the knowledge to understand and potentially question or challenge the system's outputs, leading to more user-centric IRRSs [356].

In specific application scenarios such as learning settings supported by a RS, transparency facilitates learning, enhances trust during the learning process for students and faculty, helps identify new research topics [15], and facilitates the evaluation of how personalized learning resource recommendations affect a student's learning process [46]. Transparency can also foster social learning among users of IRRSs; for example, Che and Hörner [79] present a study on how real-world IRRSs balance exploration (i.e., the discovery of new items) and exploitation (i.e., tailoring recommendations based to the users' history). The authors discuss the role of transparency in light of sharing reasons for a particular recommendation result versus a controlled level of non-transparency to encourage users to interact with items different from their typical preferences (i.e., exploration). As the authors also highlight, users have a higher tendency to select recommendations featuring serendipitous items if they understand the underlying recommendation mechanism, i.e., if there is a certain level of transparency.

Example: Transparency in Music Discovery
Music-streaming services can enhance user experience by providing transparency in music discovery and playlist curation. This could be achieved by clearly explaining the reasons behind each music recommendation. For example, if a user frequently listens to jazz music, the system could suggest a Miles Davis track and explain why it is suggested. The explanation could include the user's previous enjoyment of similar jazz subgenres, instrumental use, or tempo. This transparency can help users trust the provided suggestion and encourage them to explore new genres or unfamiliar artists by informing them why particular recommendations are made.

Transparency plays an important role in addressing fairness and bias issues in IRRSs. As highlighted in Chap. 3, IRRSs can inadvertently perpetuate biases in the training data, leading to unfair treatment or biased retrieval or recommendation results. Transparency can support stakeholders in analyzing the systems for fairness, bias, and ethical use of data, thereby promoting more responsible AI practices [151, 179]. Furthermore, transparency enables system developers to evaluate and adapt the underlying algorithms and frameworks as transparency facilitates a more informed analysis of systems' strengths and areas for improvement [98]. Moreover, in the context of the increasing legal and regulatory requirements around data use and algorithmic decision-making, transparency can help comply with corresponding standards to avoid potential legal and reputational risks [341, 410, 441].

Example: Recruitment-Related Recommender Systems
Recruitment departments are increasingly leveraging IRRSs to streamline the hiring process, enhance the accuracy of candidate matches, and improve overall efficiency. For example, a large international company could use a RS to be able to deal with a high volume of job applications for multiple positions in the company. The RS automatically scans the data submitted by the applicants to recommend the top candidates for each job offer. To ensure fair hiring practices, the company has decided to implement transparency measures within its RS. Concretely, the RS includes a feedback mechanism where candidates can inquire about their rankings and the reasons behind them, while recruiters get an explanation of the rationale behind the recommended candidates.

In this example, the leveraged RS could rank candidates based on various criteria, such as educational background, advanced degrees, work experience, skills, experiences in particular markets the company aims to invest in, and so forth. A transparent RS would openly communicate these criteria to both job seekers and recruiters so that both are aware of the rationale behind the recommendation. Such transparency could also help identify biases in the RS outputs. For example, if the RS consistently recommends candidates from specific universities, a particular gender, or other personal attributes, such a bias can be detected. For more details on biases and corresponding mitigation strategies, please refer to Sect. 3.2.

4.3.3 Challenges and Barriers to Transparency

One of the most fundamental challenges to achieving transparency within IRRSs lies in the complexity and opacity of the models used [437]. Contemporary IRRSs heavily rely on complex algorithms and utilize vast data to generate retrieval and recommendation results. Despite their effectiveness, these algorithms frequently are so-called black boxes, meaning their inner workings are so complex that they cannot be interpreted [269]. Consequently, such IRRSs lack transparency in how they arrive at their results. That, in turn, makes it challenging for a human user to assess why particular documents or items are retrieved or recommended to them and how the IRRS decides that the provided outputs are relevant and even reliable. Without any explanation, users might be critical of these systems and perceive a lack of trust when interacting.

Another challenge is that transparency and system performance can be conflicting because if we choose a simpler, transparent model, we might sacrifice predictive performance, as typically, more complex models also achieve higher accuracy [438]. To tackle this issue, the research community has devoted significant efforts in recent years to designing explainable deep models for recommendation [43, 48, 235, 431] and retrieval [244, 292] tasks.

How to effectively communicate essential information about the decision-making capabilities of an IRRS to users who are not experts in ML, search technologies, RSs, or data science presents a significant challenge that must be addressed to enhance transparency and user trust. It is critical to achieve meaningful transparency without overwhelming users [342]. Moreover, the level of detail of the information to be explained presents another challenge in achieving transparency that is helpful for human stakeholders. While some non-expert users might be satisfied with rather abstract justifications for IRRS results, others may require more detailed insights into algorithms, data, and data processing techniques. Achieving meaningful transparency without overwhelming users with complexity is essential.

Furthermore, IRRSs heavily rely on user data, including, for instance, clicks, browsing behavior, demographics, and user preferences, to produce personalized results. Revealing this data, for instance, in the form of explanations, can lead to privacy concerns (see Chap. 5 for a discussion on the role of privacy in IRRSs). Finding the right balance between the need for transparency and the user's right to privacy (see Sects. 4.2 and 5.2 for relevant regulatory efforts related to privacy) requires carefully designed trade-offs and privacy-aware approaches (see Chap. 5 for more details on how to ensure privacy and security in IRRSs).

Finally, navigating diverse regulations and legal frameworks, especially in multinational settings, is challenging. Ensuring algorithmic transparency while protecting intellectual property rights and adhering to legal standards is crucial for the sustainable operation of IRRSs. Operating in multinational settings and diverse regulatory environments, companies, developers, and researchers must ensure compliance with algorithmic transparency regulations. However, most real-world IRRSs are proprietary, and corresponding algorithms, data sources, and data processing steps are treated as business secrets [63]. Facilitating transparency while protecting their intellectual property rights presents a significant challenge for companies. However, failing to comply with regulations can lead to legal and reputational consequences; hence, incorporating meaningful transparency mechanisms will be one of the critical challenges for all future IRRS developments.

Addressing these challenges is pivotal for the development of IRRSs. Balancing transparency, performance, privacy, and regulatory compliance is essential to enhance user trust and ensure the responsible deployment of these systems. Achieving such a balance requires both technical expertise and a strong user focus, as transparent IRRSs should be effective, user-friendly, and engaging.

In the following section, we present strategies and methodologies to enhance the transparency of IRRSs.

4.4 Enhancing Transparency in Retrieval and Recommender Systems

As elaborated earlier in Sect. 4.3, transparency in IRRSs is centered around the concept of explainability, which corresponds to a system's ability to provide human-understandable and human-interpretable reasons for its outcomes and decisions.

In this section, we discuss how explainability in IRRSs can be achieved, which is critical not only to improve transparency and trust in the systems [318], user satisfaction, and engagement but also to help system providers tune their IRRSs, and independent researchers and regulatory bodies assess potential problematic side effects [383].

Research efforts related to improving the explainability of IRRSs are typically categorized into work on *interpretable* IRRSs and *post hoc* approaches [191]. Interpretable IRRSs refer to approaches whose inner workings are explainable by design [121, 247]. Here, the IRRS model is inherently interpretable, allowing users to directly understand the system's functioning. In contrast, post hoc approaches explain the IRRSs' outputs or predictions, justifying the retrieved documents or produced recommendations [121]. Such explanations are derived through external methods such as importance scores, visualization, or surrogate models.

Other categorizations exist as well. For instance, Zhang and Weng [438] provide a detailed differentiation between two fundamental perspectives on explainability in IRRSs, namely, (1) a ML perspective and (2) a human-centered perspective. The ML perspective aims to make the complex algorithms of IRRSs transparent. That is achieved by developing inherently interpretable algorithms or enhancing opaque algorithms with *explainable artificial intelligence (XAI)* techniques to achieve post hoc interpretability [22]. These techniques are further categorized into *model-intrinsic* approaches, built directly into the algorithms, and *model-agnostic* approaches, which can be applied regardless of the nature of the underlying algorithm.

In contrast, the human-centered perspective focuses on how end users perceive and utilize explanations. This approach emphasizes creating meaningful and valuable explanations for the user rather than being technically accurate. It often involves integrating psychological and cognitive insights into the design of the explanation interface, ensuring that the explanations improve user trust, satisfaction, and understanding of the system's decisions.

Although these additional categorizations by Zhang and Weng offer a comprehensive view of explainability, addressing both the technical transparency and user experience aspects, for the remainder of this discussion, we adhere to the first categorization scheme that distinguishes corresponding explainability techniques into *interpretable* IRRSs and *post hoc* approaches due to its simplicity and intuitive scheme.

Before we continue with this chapter, we would like to note that achieving transparency either in the form of interpretable models or post hoc approaches can be linked to psychological theory, which suggests that human decision-making can happen through deliberate, analytical processes or more intuitive, heuristic-based judgments [192]. The first approach is commonly associated with System 2 thinking of the dual-process theory, which involves a conscious and rational examination of choices. In this approach, individuals carefully evaluate evidence, assess likelihoods, and logically decide their subsequent actions. As outlined in the survey on explainable recommendations by Zhang et al. [438], this aligns with methods that provide insights into how recommendations or retrieval results are generated, such as feature importance scores or decision trees. The authors state that the second approach relates to System 1 thinking, characterized by fast, automatic, and emotion-driven judgments. This type of decision-making is influenced by factors such as familiarity, affective responses, and cognitive shortcuts like heuristics. Post hoc approaches that correspond to this thinking typically use narrative or social proof (e.g., "People similar to you have bought this item") as a justification without explaining technical aspects of the IRRS, especially in the case of black box models, whose internal mechanisms are not accessible due to their complexity.

In the following sections, we discuss research devoted to designing interpretable IRRSs and then continue with a selection of post hoc approaches.

4.4.1 Interpretable Retrieval and Recommender Systems

Interpretable IRRSs involve designing IRRS algorithms so that their decisions can be understood directly from their structure and behavior. These systems incorporate transparency directly into the algorithmic framework, facilitating an intuitive understanding of how decisions are made. This inherent clarity allows both users and developers to easily follow and verify the rationale behind each recommendation, enhancing trust and ease of use. Such approaches prioritize simplicity and understandability in the system's architecture, ensuring that the logic driving the recommendations is accessible and straightforward. In the following, we discuss a selection of interpretable approaches.

4.4.1.1 Rule-Based Retrieval and Recommendation

Rule-based systems employ a set of predefined, concise rules to retrieve results or generate recommendations, and their decision-making functionality is, thus, inherently transparent. These systems operate based on predefined rules or logic, typically derived from domain knowledge. Each rule defines the conditions under which particular recommendations or retrieval results are obtained, making the decision-making process highly transparent and verifiable by humans [247].

Examples of rule-based systems include *expert systems*, which are designed to support experts in their decision-making tasks based on predefined rules that are typically provided as *if-then* statements [18]. For example, expert systems have been proposed in the context of healthcare to support medical personnel when diagnosing diseases based on patients' symptoms [234].

Example: Personalized Health Guide
Assume a personalized health guide that delivers personalized health recommendations and information to individuals based on their specific health profiles and relevant medical guidelines. Users input their health data, including age, gender, medical history, current medications, allergies, and lifestyle factors. Health professionals and medical researchers collaborate to define a comprehensive set of rules. These rules are based on clinical guidelines, research findings, and best practices in medicine. Each rule would clearly specify the conditions under which certain health advice should be given. For example, a rule could be: *If age > 50 and smoker, then recommend annual lung cancer screening.* When a user queries the system for health advice or information, the system applies these predefined rules to the user's health profile. This process involves checking which rules are applicable based on the user's data and then retrieving information or generating the appropriate health recommendations. The system presents the retrieved information or recommendations to the user in an understandable format. It also explains why each piece of advice was given, citing the specific rules and medical evidence that apply to the user's situation.

Although rule-based systems are frequently simple from an algorithmic perspective, they play a crucial role in high-stakes domains like healthcare, where users need to understand the basis of a decision-making process to make informed decisions. Here, the authors of [327] even argue to avoid enhancing the transparency of black box models and "use interpretable models instead" and critically reflect on the interpretability/accuracy trade-off that is mentioned frequently across XAI research, echoing also [232]. Furthermore, since the logic is explicitly defined, rule-based systems are easier to audit and adjust to changing regulations or user feedback.

4.4.1.2 Factorization-Based Techniques

Factorization-based techniques, such as matrix factorization (MF), are widely used in RSs to decompose user-item interaction matrices into lower-dimensional latent factors representing users and items. In IR, similar techniques can be used to decompose document-query matrices, helping to reveal how documents are related to queries. These techniques make it easier to interpret how items or documents are recommended or retrieved based on the underlying patterns in user behavior or query contexts. They decompose a large matrix (e.g., user-item interaction matrix) into lower-dimensional matrices representing latent factors associated with users and items.

For example, in a user-item matrix, each user's interactions with various items are distilled into a smaller set of latent preferences, which are matched against item characteristics and reduced to similar latent dimensions. This matching process helps to explain retrieval or recommendation results based on a user's preferences and item attributes.

Similarly, in the context of IR, latent semantic factors can be computed from document-query matrices, leveraging techniques such as *singular value decomposition (SVD)*. These factors can be leveraged to explain how documents are associated with user queries as they describe the relationship between documents and their terms.

One example of an explainable factorization-based technique has been proposed by Melchiorre et al. [256]. The authors introduce a collaborative filtering algorithm designed to enhance the effectiveness and explainability of recommendations in machine learning models by utilizing the concept of *prototypes*. Prototypes in this context correspond to a set of representative similar users or items that capture general consumption patterns within a dataset [165]. These general consumption characteristics are then used to calculate prediction scores based on similarities to these prototypes, leading to accurate and explainable recommendations.

Abdollahi et al. [1] propose an explainability-constrained MF technique that computes the recommendation list from items that are explainable, generating accurate and explainable recommendations. Zhang et al. [439] introduced an *explicit factor model (EFM)* to identify user preferences from user reviews and used these preferences as a basis to explain why a user received a particular result. EFMs are also leveraged by Chen et al. [86] and Wang et al. [404]; however, here, tensor factorization methods are incorporated to extract even more precise justifications from the reviews.

4.4.1.3 Case-Based Reasoning

Case-based reasoning (CBR) utilizes past experiences to make decisions in similar cases. This approach is inherently interpretable as CBR bases its decisions on retrieving and reusing solutions from previous similar cases. Specifically, the reasoning behind each result can be explained by referencing the relevant past cases [153].

For example, when CBR is applied in an IRRS task, CBR involves identifying previous situations that are similar to the current query or user profile and then suggesting solutions that were effective in those past cases [215]. This method allows users to see the reasoning behind each recommendation, as the system can provide explicit examples of past cases that led to the documents or recommendations. Furthermore, CBR systems can adapt and learn over time as they accumulate more cases and outcomes, continuously improving their accuracy and relevance while maintaining a high level of explainability.

Approaches based on CBR have, for instance, been used to explain medical diagnoses [70], recommend medical cancer treatments [211], or generate explanations for hotel recommendations [270].

4.4.2 Post Hoc Interpretability for Retrieval and Recommender Systems

Post hoc interpretability techniques have gained significant importance in IRRSs as they can explain outputs of complex, often black-box IRRSs models without requiring access to their inner workings, which makes them widely applicable across various models and domains. Such model-agnostic techniques explain a model's outputs rather than its internal logic; hence, such techniques also benefit non-expert users who are interested in understanding the model's decisions instead of the complex decision-making processes. Since model-agnostic techniques heavily draw from the field of *explainable artificial intelligence (XAI)*, in the following, we first briefly introduce XAI and then outline a selection of key techniques that can be leveraged to enhance the interpretability of IRRS models.

4.4.2.1 Explainable Artificial Intelligence

XAI [14] is a research field that aims to make AI systems' outputs and inner workings more transparent and understandable to humans. XAI involves explaining or providing insights into systems' decision-making processes, particularly those inherently complex and opaque, like black-box DL models [121]. While XAI can be understood as an umbrella term encompassing various techniques and approaches for making AI models more transparent and interpretable, explainability in IRRSs specifically focuses on RSs and IR systems. In this context, the primary objective is to clarify the recommendation or search process, providing users and stakeholders with explanations of why specific items were recommended or documents were retrieved [14]. The most frequently adopted techniques are *local interpretable model-agnostic explanations (LIME)* [318] and *Shapley additive explanations (SHAP)* [347]. Both techniques are feature importance methods, i.e., they identify and rank the contribution of individual features to a model's predictions [445]. In this way, they enhance a model's transparency as they shed light on what factors most influence a result.

LIME constructs simpler, interpretable models, such as decision trees, to explain the predictions of more complex models. That enables a clearer understanding of why a particular output was generated for an individual instance within the IRRS. To mention two examples, Singh and Anand [362] adapted LIME to create explanations for ranking-based systems, while Wu et al. [422] used LIME to explain medical recommendations.

SHAP employs principles from game theory, particularly Shapley values, to assign importance scores to input features based on their contribution to the model's predictions. By quantifying features' marginal contributions, SHAP offers insights into the relative importance of different factors in shaping the recommendation outcomes. For example, Fernando et al. [138] used the *DeepSHAP* method to generate explanations for the outputs of neural retrieval models. DeepSHAP helps estimate the relative importance of input features and is an adaptation of the *DeepLift* algorithm that utilizes activations in the network for a given image, compared to a reference input, to generate Shapley values.

4.4.2.2 Representation Learning-Based Techniques

Representation learning techniques in IRRSs involve creating DL models that generate interpretable representations of data [235]. In the context of RSs, representation learning techniques create embeddings of users and items in a shared latent space [113]. These embeddings reflect underlying user preferences and item characteristics, and thus, an analysis of the created embedding space can help understand why particular items are recommended to a user. For instance, if items a user has consumed are closely positioned in the embedding space, they likely share attributes that align with the user's preferences.

Representation learning-based techniques have been used, for example, by Bellini et al [48]. The authors utilize an autoencoder to learn latent representations. Autoencoders are unsupervised learning algorithms designed for dimensionality reduction. They transform the input data into a lower-dimensional representation and then aim to reconstruct the output given this representation with a low error [408]. In the work of Bellini et al., autoencoders are combined with knowledge graphs to create meaningful explanations for RSs' outputs.

In another example, Liu et al. [235] propose an explainable recommendation model that enhances the explainability of representation learning for RSs. This model segments latent dimensions into factors corresponding to underlying features that capture different characteristics of users and items (e.g., user preferences or item attributes). Each pair of users/items and factor is assigned a score based on which model quantifies their relationship. This way, the model can explain how a respective factor influences interactions between users and items.

In IR, representation learning can also be utilized to embed documents and queries. This helps in better understanding and visualizing the relationships between them. The embeddings can illustrate how certain documents are related to specific queries based on their similarity in the embedding space. This visualization facilitates a deeper comprehension of why certain documents are retrieved in response to a query, thus making the retrieval process more transparent.

4.4.2.3 Layer-Wise Relevance Propagation

Layer-wise relevance propagation (LRP) is an advanced technique used to interpret the predictions made by DL models by decomposing the output of these models back to the input features that influenced these predictions. This method is highly applicable in both RSs and IR systems.

In RSs, LRP can trace how each feature of the input data (such as user demographic information, previous interactions, and item attributes) contributes to the recommendation. For example, LRP can identify whether the genre of a movie or the past viewing history of a user had more influence on the recommendation of a new movie. In this vein, the work published in [52] uses LRP to explain the outputs of a DL-based RS that uses product images as input. The presented approach is able to identify pixel-level details that contributed to the RS's decision-making in Amazon product datasets.

In IR, LRP can explain why certain documents are retrieved in response to specific queries. By applying LRP, the model can reveal how different aspects of a document (such as keywords, topics, or other metadata) and elements of a query contribute to the relevance score that leads to the retrieval of that document. This is particularly beneficial in complex queries where multiple features might be influencing the retrieval process, and stakeholders need to understand which aspects have the highest impact.

4.4.2.4 Interpretable Knowledge-Aware Systems

Interpretable knowledge-aware IRRSs [209, 409] integrate domain-specific knowledge into the algorithms of IRRSs. In this way, systems can provide contextually enriched explanations that align with user expectations and domain characteristics. For example, in a movie RS, knowledge about genres, directorial styles, and historical reception might be integrated. This allows the system not only to recommend movies based on user preferences but also to explain those recommendations in terms of the integrated domain knowledge (e.g., recommending a film because it fits a user's preference for award-winning directors). The effectiveness of such systems naturally depends on their ability to leverage external knowledge bases. These could include scientific databases, public reports, or clinical guidelines (e.g., in the case of a medical IRRS) or research findings.

4.4.2.5 Attention Mechanisms

Attention mechanisms, first pioneered in the field of *natural language processing (NLP)*, have become a crucial tool in enhancing the interpretability of complex models across various domains, including IRRSs. These mechanisms work by dynamically focusing on specific parts of the input data that are most relevant to the task at hand, whether it is generating a recommendation or retrieving a document. In the context of RSs, attention mechanisms can be employed to identify which aspects of user data (such as past purchase history, browsing behavior, or ratings) are most influential when making a recommendation [84, 150, 346, 375, 442]. For example, Chen et al. [80] leverage attention mechanisms to identify the most relevant parts of user reviews in a recommendation scenario, which are then incorporated into textual explanations offered to the user in addition to the respective recommendation result. Liu et al. [236] generate multi-modal explanations for RSs that account for dynamic user preferences. The presented approach is based on a so-called *attentive recurrent neural network (Ante-RNN)*, which extracts image representations by aligning image regions with corresponding text segments. Users' long-term preferences are modeled through a topical attention mechanism, while recent interactions and short-term interests are captured via a dynamic contextual attention mechanism. Combining visual-semantic alignments with attention weights, the model enhances recommendation performance and facilitates its transparency through both textual and visual interpretations.

In IR, attention mechanisms play a crucial role in enhancing the relevance of search results. They do this by focusing on particular aspects within the query and the documents. For instance, if a query includes specific keywords, the attention model can highlight text passages within documents that contain these keywords or related terms. That is exemplified by Yu et al. in [427], who suggest an approach called *listwise explanation generator (LiEGe)*. LiEGe enhances the interpretability of search result lists by providing explanations for each document derived from attention mechanisms. Specifically, aspect-oriented explanations are generated, whereas aspects correspond to, e.g., topics, concepts, and entities extracted from the user's search query. The system then highlights these explanations to communicate to the user why each retrieved document is relevant to the query.

In general, a key advantage of attention mechanisms is their ability to be visualized. Visualizations can depict where the model's attention is directed during the recommendation or retrieval process. This visualization can take the form of heat maps overlaid on text (i.e., in the case of documents) or graphical representations associated with different user features or item attributes. Such visualizations make it easier for users to understand and interpret the model's decision-making process on a granular level.

4.4.3 Interactive User Interfaces

One important aspect in enhancing the transparency of IRRSs is to offer interactive user interfaces and visualizations. Interactive visualizations allow users to see and manipulate the factors influencing recommendations and retrieval results, providing a deeper understanding of the system's decision-making process and how different user behaviors affect IRRSs' outcomes [361]. Shneiderman, in his book on human-centric AI, calls such an approach "*transparency through exploration*" [360] and advocates for a transition from viewing transparency as a retrospective affair, i.e., explaining the functioning of a trained IRRSs and its outputs, toward providing interactive user interfaces and visualizations that allow for an exploration of how the system, its parametrization, and the user's behavior shape the outcomes. Shneiderman describes such exploratory interfaces as a support tool to help users gradually achieve their objectives while giving them more control over the process and enhancing transparency [361].

For example, Zheng and Toribio [444] suggest tailored user interfaces to enhance transparency in multi-stakeholder recommender systems for such a purpose and then the concept of *explaining* retrieval or recommendation results to users [174].

Collectively, these strategies—from devising interpretable models to enhancing the explainability of IRRSs leveraging XAI techniques to developing interactive user interfaces—represent a multifaceted approach to enhancing the transparency of IRRSs. Each strategy addresses different aspects of the user experience and can contribute to a more trustworthy relationship between users and the systems they interact with.

Many studies within the IRRSs focus on generating explanations for retrieval or recommendation results. Hence, the next section is devoted to the topic of *explanations*. Key research questions in this area include effectively leveraging relevant information sources while ensuring that the explanations produced are accessible and understandable to the respective stakeholders.

4.5 Explanations

Most approaches to enhance the transparency of IRRSs are centered around providing explanations. Explanations are information shown to users that describes the rationale behind the recommendation or retrieval of a specific item or document. In this way, explanations can offer users valuable insights into the system's decision-making process, fostering trust and confidence [146] due to a deeper understanding of *why* particular suggestions are made [363, 383], thereby achieving specific goals, such as increasing the transparency or persuasiveness of systems [136]. In the context of RSs, e.g., Herlocker et al. [174] have found evidence that explanations can lead to increased user acceptance of CF-based RSs. According to Bilac and Raymond [53], explanations can help users choose a particular recommendation and make better decisions.

Tintarev and Masthoff [383] define explanations as an effort "*to make clear by giving a detailed description*" while [438] characterizing them as "*an explainable recommendation aims to answer the question of why.*" Thus, explanations can be viewed as complementary information to a retrieval or recommendation result. They bridge the gap between the algorithmic decision-making process and user understanding, offering insights into why specific recommendations are made and how they align with user preferences and the objectives of the system. The nature and content of explanations can be widely different, ranging from insights into how a user's past behavior influenced an IRRS to explanations based on similarities with other documents or items or users or complex insights derived from the underlying algorithm's processing. Consider the following example.

Example: Explanations of a Job Recommender System
A recent computer science graduate, Alice, has been actively using a job RS to find her first professional role. She is particularly interested in a software developer position at a well-regarded AI company. Despite her qualifications and portfolio, which she believes align well with the company's needs, Alice noticed that she did not receive an invitation to interview for the position.

Fortunately, the job RS provides Alice with a detailed justification in the form of an explanation to help her understand the possible reasons behind this outcome. The system explains that while her academic background and some of her skills are relevant, the job posting received an exceptionally high volume of applications, many of which were from candidates with more extensive portfolios and experience. The explanation helps bridge the gap between the job recommender's decision-making processes and Alice's understanding of why she was not selected for an interview. In this way, Alice can better understand the factors influencing the selection process, i.e., a lack of experience.

4.5.1 Scope of Explanations

Explanations in IRRSs can have either a local or global scope, providing insight into individual results or the overall system behavior. Both are explained in more detail below.

4.5.1.1 Local Explanations

Local explanations in IRRSs focus on individual retrieval results or recommendations produced by the system. They aim to clarify why a specific document or item was retrieved or recommended to a particular user at a certain time. For instance, a local explanation in a movie RS might state, "This film was recommended because you rated similar genres highly in the past." Local explanations are crucial for building user trust and satisfaction, as they provide immediate, understandable insights into specific outcomes [59]. They help users make sense of the system's suggestions on a case-by-case basis, which can be particularly useful for new or unexpected recommendations. For example, a local explanation for our earlier job RS might highlight the most important entries in the CV that influenced the decision to approve or reject Alice's job application.

Several studies in the IRRS domain have proposed approaches to generate local explanations for retrieval and recommendation results. For example, Singh and Anand [414] explore ways to develop a model that can explain the rankings produced by a given base ranker. The explanation model is used to generate document rankings, which are then compared to the rankings generated by the base model. Verman and Ganguly [394] compare various sampling methods for generating explanations of a document's score based on a query by an IR model and propose two evaluation metrics, i.e., *explanation consistency* and *explanation correctness*, to measure the consistency and accuracy of the generated explanations across the different sampling methods.

The results show that the sampling methods utilizing term position information produced less effective explanations in terms of both suggested metrics than those generated by sampling words from documents uniformly or based on a term frequency-inverse document frequency (TF-IDF) approach.

4.5.1.2 Global Explanations

Global explanations provide insights into the overall behavior and functioning of an IRRS. They describe the overall logic and algorithms that drive the system's behavior across all users and scenarios. For example, a global explanation in a movie RS could be: *Our algorithm recommends movies based on a combination of your past viewing history, ratings, and similar preferences of other users with comparable tastes.* Global explanations are essential for users who are interested in understanding the mechanism behind the system, not just the rationale behind individual recommendations. Such explanations can help users identify patterns or biases that may be present in the model (please refer to Sect. 3.3.2 for a discussion of where biases can occur at different stages of the IRRSs' development and usage), offering a broader perspective on how the system operates. For example, a global explanation of our job RS could describe its methodology, data sources, and algorithms used to match job seekers with suitable job listings.

4.5.2 Data Sources for Explanations

Below, we explore the common data sources employed in generating explanations and discuss how they contribute to the user experience.

- **User interactions and user characteristics:** This encompasses a broad spectrum of data, including users' likes, dislikes, browsing history, demographic details, or psychological traits. For instance, in a music RS, an explanation could be this: *This song is recommended based on your preference for jazz music and the fact that other users in your age group also like that genre.* It highlights how the user's interactions (listening history) and characteristics (age group) can be used to explain a recommendation in a music context.
- **Document or item characteristics:** Features of the documents or items being recommended or analyzed can serve as a basis for explanations. For example, an e-commerce RS might highlight attributes like price, quality, or item color that align with the user's interests, e.g., *This jacket is recommended for its waterproof feature and similarity to items you've looked at.* Such an explanation unveils the basis of the recommendation through item attributes. Furthermore, items that are trending or have high ratings might be recommended more often. A corresponding explanation could be this: *This video is trending in your region.*
- **Social data:** Data derived from the aggregated preferences and behaviors of many users or friends (e.g., inferred from connections on social media platforms) can deliver explanations. For instance, a RS might suggest a product because it is popular among or frequently bought by a user's social connections. An explanation here could be this: *Many of your friendship connections also liked this movie.*
- **Context features:** The current context, such as time, location, or weather in which an IRRS is utilized, can be used to explain why a particular item is relevant. The current time and the user's location can influence IRRS results. For example, breakfast recipes might be suggested in the morning, or retrieval and recommendation results might vary based on the device being used, with mobile-optimized content being prioritized for smartphone users.

For example, in Fig. 4.1, we see three example users, Alice, Bob, and Liz, who have purchased various items and provided both reviews and ratings. Inspecting our users, we can observe that all three users prefer products related to music consumption. From Bob's and Liz's reviews, we also can infer that both assess the quality and visual appearance of their purchased items, in this case, the record player and the speakers, respectively. Here, both user preferences and item characteristics are key elements that can be harnessed to generate meaningful explanations for the provided recommendations.

Imagine Liz browsing the online store for a new piece of equipment to enhance her home entertainment system. She has been looking for record players recently and generally prefers high-quality, visually appealing equipment that matches her style. The online store uses a RS that analyzes her browsing habits and purchase history. It recommends a vintage-style record player with a wood finish rated highly by other users. Explanations for this recommendation can now take various forms and styles. We discuss, in the following, the most frequently adopted ones.

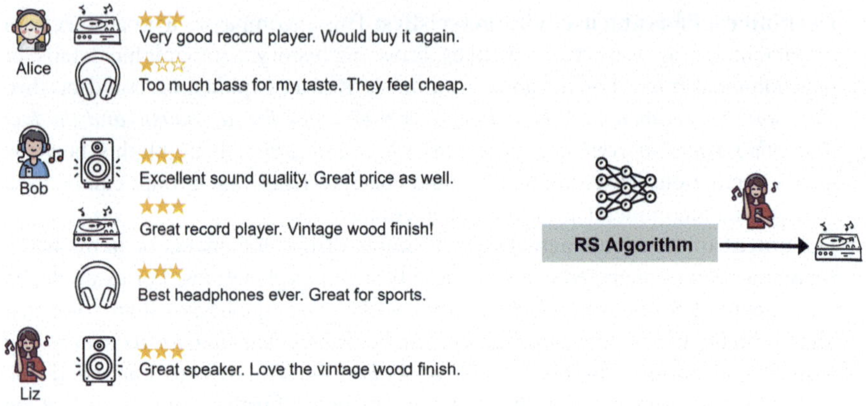

Fig. 4.1: Example data sources that can be exploited to generate explanations

4.5.3 Explanation Styles

The generation of explanations for IRRSs can take various forms, depending on the use case and target audience. The most common styles include explanations based on relevant users, documents, or items closely related to a user's search query or user profile [382]. For example, an IRRS could highlight similar users whose preferences have influenced the recommendations or documents with similar characteristics that influence the retrieval results.

Feature-based explanations offer insights by identifying specific characteristics or attributes that played a significant role in the decision-making process. *Sentence-level explanations* are presented in textual form to explain the reasons behind IRRSs' decisions in natural language. Additionally, *visual explanations* leverage graphical representations, such as heat maps or overlay markings on images, to show which aspects of visual data were most influential. This approach is particularly effective in fields like medical imaging or object recognition, where visual cues are paramount. *Social explanations*, on the other hand, incorporate feedback or input from other users, reflecting a collective or communal reasoning process. This type can be particularly useful in collaborative environments or platforms where user engagement contributes to the system's decision-making. *Counterfactual explanations* provide information on how changes in the input, e.g., user preferences, behavior, or search queries, would affect the outcomes of an IRRS. Such explanations are particularly helpful in cases when users aim to understand how they could potentially achieve more relevant results.

In the following, we briefly discuss these approaches in more detail.

4.5.3.1 Feature-Based Explanations

Feature-based explanations highlight the importance of specific features in the decision-making process. There has been a growing emphasis on the role of metadata in enhancing the transparency of IRRSs, as incorporating detailed metadata about items and user preferences can lead to more precise explanations of why particular recommendations are made. Returning to our earlier example of the job recommender system Alice used:

Example: Job Recommender System
Let us assume that the system recommended against Alice's application for the position due to her lack of experience in a particular programming language. The model's decision could be traced to that specific skillset that was missing in Alice's CV. Hence, Alice could be provided with a detailed explanation of how important expertise in that particular programming language was for the position and that her CV did not list the language.

4.5.3.2 Sentence-Level Explanations

Sentence-level explanations are written in textual form so that humans can understand the reasons behind IRRSs' decisions. Such explanations typically take a simple, intuitive form. For example, an explanation in an e-commerce platform could be written like this: *Users who have bought this item also have bought that item.* The advantage of such explanations lies in their simplicity and that they do not require in-depth technical expertise to understand the rationale behind an IRRS's result. However, the effectiveness of such explanations depends on the language used and the user's familiarity with the domain-specific terminology.

For example, in user-based CF [317], recommendations are generated by identifying a group of users similar to the person seeking a recommendation. The reasoning behind suggesting a particular item is that it has been positively reviewed by similar users, who are considered the person's neighbors in terms of preferences.

With respect to sentence-level explanations, we can distinguish between *template-based* and *generation-based* approaches [223]. Template-based explanations utilize predefined templates filled in with dynamic content based on the specific context of the recommendation or retrieval result. This method relies on a structured format where certain placeholders are replaced with relevant data points.

Example: Template-based Explanations for Music Recommendation
Let's consider a scenario of a jazz aficionado who is a big Miles Davis fan.To make the recommendation process transparent, the system can employ a pre-defined template for explanations that helps explain the relationship between the user's listening behavior and the IRRS outputs. For example, the system might use a template that says: *You're seeing this song because you frequently listen to [genre] and [artist].* When applied, this might transform into a specific explanation like this: *You're seeing this song because you frequently listen to jazz and Miles Davis.*

This method is highly beneficial in settings where explanations need to be direct and easy to understand. It allows users to see a straightforward reason for the recommendations, linking them directly to their previous interactions on the platform, such as songs played, liked, or added to playlists. By filling in the placeholders in the template with details specific to each user's behavior, the system ensures that each explanation is personalized. It ensures a uniform structure across explanations, making them easier for users to understand and predict and is relatively easy to implement and maintain since the templates are predefined and only the dynamic content changes. They are effective for simple IRRS scenarios where the rationale is straightforward, such as genre-based book recommendations. They are particularly useful in scenarios where explanations need to adhere to specific regulatory or transparency requirements.

Another more advanced variant of sentence-level explanations are generation-based explanations. Such explanations leverage *natural language generation (NLG)* technologies to create more dynamic, context-aware explanations [224]. This method uses algorithms and models to generate explanations that can adapt to the user's context and the specific details of the recommendation. Such approaches, while relatively new, have the potential to achieve a higher degree of personalization by incorporating more complex user data and item attributes into the explanations since they can handle vast amounts of scenarios without the need for predefined templates [438]. They are particularly helpful in scenarios when IRRSs engage with the user in a conversational form. Here, the user experience can be enhanced when the explanation feels more like a dialogue with a friend who understands the user's explicit preferences and subtle shifts in taste and interest.

Example: Explaining Diverse Recommendations
Imagine a user who has a diverse music taste, spanning various genres and artists. A generation-based explanation system could analyze their listening patterns, favorite tracks, and frequency of plays to craft an explanation that is both contextually rich and highly personalized. For instance, if a user has been exploring a lot of folk music recently but traditionally listens to rock, the system might recommend a folk-rock artist and explain this choice with a statement like this: *You might enjoy this artist because you've been exploring more folk music lately, and they blend it with your long-time favorite, rock.*

In practice, frequently, hybrid approaches are employed, combining the structure and consistency of template-based methods with the dynamic and personalization of generation-based explanations.

4.5.3.3 Visual Explanations

Visual explanations in IRRSs can significantly enhance user experience and engagement by providing a more intuitive understanding of the rationale behind retrieved documents or recommended items. These explanations leverage graphical representations such as charts, heat maps, or decision trees to illustrate similarities or patterns among documents or items that led to a particular recommendation or retrieval result. How explanations are presented influences the user experience, as shown by Herlocker et al. [174]. They evaluated how various methods of presenting explanations affect the user experience in user-based nearest-neighbor CF (`UserKNN`). Specifically, they investigated whether showing a summary histogram of how similar users rated an item or providing a detailed breakdown of these users' individual ratings led to a higher user acceptance. Their findings suggest that the choice of visualization can influence how users perceive and interact with the recommendations. A summary histogram might offer a broader understanding of general perceptions, while a detailed breakdown helps users explore in more depth who rated the item and how. For an overview of suitable visualization techniques, please refer to Chatti et al. [77].

When designing visual explanations, adopting inclusive design principles is essential to ensure that visualizations are accessible and understandable to a broad spectrum of users. This includes considerations for colorblindness (using high contrast colors and patterns), visual impairments (providing alternative text descriptions and transcripts for audio), cognitive differences (using clear and concise language, avoiding visual clutter), and cultural sensitivities (choosing neutral symbols or images) [290].

4.5.3.4 Social Explanations

Social explanations leverage social graphs and interactions to provide context for recommendations. They might include statements like *Your friend also watched this movie and rated it highly* or *People in your network are currently discussing this article.* [349]. By highlighting the connections between a user's social interactions and potential interests, these explanations not only help clarify why certain recommendations are made but also enhance the relevance of these suggestions. For instance, in a music-streaming service, a social explanation could be this: *Your friends added this song to their workout playlist.* [348].

4.5.3.5 Counterfactual Explanations

Counterfactual explanations explore alternative scenarios to explain why a different recommendation was not made or a different result was not retrieved [191]. The basic idea is to explain how differences in the input data to an IRRS could result in different retrieval or recommendation results [164]. For example, in the context of a music RS, a counterfactual explanation might explain what recommendations a user might receive if they select, for example, the genre heavy metal instead of death metal as their main preference. Hence, counterfactual explanations can shed light on what factors trigger a particular IRRS's result. Since finding suitable counterfactuals (i.e., factors to be changed to obtain different results) can be difficult, several techniques have been suggested to facilitate their detection, including, for example, optimization-based methods [398] or search strategy heuristics [191].

4.6 Evaluation of Transparency

The evaluation of transparency in IRRSs involves assessing how effectively a system communicates its decision-making process to its human users. This involves not only the clarity and understandability of the information provided but also how this information impacts user trust, satisfaction, and decision-making. To quantify the effectiveness of transparency interventions and understand their relationship with user trust and satisfaction, evaluation procedures, benchmarks, and metrics are needed. However, to date, no commonly agreed upon evaluation protocol to assess the impact of transparency-enhancing techniques on IRRSs exists, partly due to a lack of benchmark datasets, different needs and requirements of the involved stakeholders, and also due to the highly subjective nature of such evaluations [22].

One frequently adopted strategy is to conduct *user studies*, where study participants interact with an IRRS that provides different levels of transparency (e.g., various types of explanations for recommendations) [363]. Users are then asked to share their perception of transparency along multiple dimensions, such as understanding how the results were generated and how well they align with the users' preferences. Other strategies involve comprehension tests where users are presented with explanations from the system and then asked questions to assess their understanding of how the recommendations or search results were generated. Furthermore, analyzing user behavior after receiving explanations can offer insights such as if users click on recommendations with explanations more often compared to those with no explanation.

Another evaluation approach is to leverage *fidelity measures* to determine if explanations are consistent across different variations of the input data, when a surrogate model is used, or when an adversarial example is used. To that end, a second prediction is made using such variations to data or models, which is then compared to the actual model outputs. Fidelity is high when both predictions closely resemble each other [22].

A key challenge in evaluating IRRSs concerning transparency is the need for ground truth for explanations. When ground truth explanations are available, they are benchmarks against which generated explanations can be compared. In scenarios where ground truth is unavailable, some approaches utilize an interpretable model as a reference. This allows for evaluating the accuracy of explanation methods by comparing the explanations from the reference model with those produced by the explanation method [22].

The efficiency of a transparency-enhancing approach can also be evaluated through the lens of two distinct perspectives, (1) promotion and (2) satisfaction, as suggested by Bilgic et al. [53]. In the case of *promotion*, the most effective explanation corresponds to the one that best convinces a user to select a particular item. From the *satisfaction* perspective, the most effective explanation is one that gives the user the best insight into the item quality (e.g., how was it rated).

Tackling the topic of transparency from a slightly different perspective, Schelentz et al. [341] introduce a tool called *Transparency-Check* to enhance the transparency of AI-based systems that provide personalization. The tool aims to address user concerns, improve user trust, and comply with legal requirements, such as the GDPR and DSA (see Sect. 4.2.1), and features a checklist that evaluates transparency across four areas of a system: input, processing, output, and user control. The authors evaluate the efficacy of *Transparency-Check* in a user study, which revealed that many real-world systems that offer personalization exhibit a low level of transparency and lack explanations of data processing, decision-making processes, and user control mechanisms.

4.7 Enhancing Transparency via Documentation

Enhancing transparency via documentation is concerned with the necessity to document the system's development process, operational capabilities, and potential limitations. Such documentation facilitates a clear understanding among stakeholders, including developers, users, and regulators. This concept is underpinned by the work of Mitchell et al. [265] on model cards and the OECD's guidelines [287] on transparent and accountable AI system governance, which advocate for comprehensive and accessible documentation as a cornerstone of trustworthy AI development.

The *model cards* approach includes standardized templates and tools to facilitate the creation of comprehensive documentation. These tools guide developers of AI-based systems through the necessary steps to ensure all critical aspects of the AI system are fully documented, from initial design decisions to deployment impacts and beyond. Also various industry stakeholders have adopted the model cards approach to communicate details about the IRRS techniques they employ. For example, Meta [262] employs an approach they call *system cards* that serve as the method for explaining how their AI-based ranking and personalization systems within their products operate. Such system cards provide details on the corresponding algorithms and configurations and consist of descriptions of various models. As the company stresses, the cards should be of help to both experts and non-experts.

In a less standardized form, several studies suggest publishing *articles or blog posts* about the inner workings of the system to enhance transparency and make information accessible to users interested in understanding the system better [51]. This approach not only sheds light on complex functionalities but also encourages a broader engagement from the user community, which is essential in cultivating an informed user base.

4.8 Algorithmic Auditing

In recent years, algorithmic auditing has received widespread attention as a means of ensuring accountability and transparency in algorithms. Algorithmic auditing corresponds to a systematic evaluation of algorithms to assess their performance, impact, and compliance with ethical and legal standards [92]. Algorithmic audits, also known as AI audits, are essential for filling the accountability gap in AI-based systems by providing a framework for comprehensive auditing throughout the development life cycle of these systems [307]. Such audits are essential to scrutinize the functioning and consequences of sociotechnical systems, particularly in ensuring fairness and non-discrimination in algorithmic decision-making processes [393]. Algorithmic auditing is closely related to the broader concept of *algorithmic accountability*, which focuses on assessing the impact and consistency of algorithms with ethical principles and norms [264]. By conducting audits, organizations can identify and address issues such as discrimination, bias (see Sect. 3.3 for a categorization of biases that can occur in IRRSs at various stages), and privacy concerns in algorithmic systems (see Sect. 5.1 for an overview of privacy concerns in IRRSs), thereby enhancing transparency and trust in these systems [185]. The importance of auditing algorithms is further emphasized through works by Raji et al. [308], Bokanyi et al. [55], Merrer et al. [260], and Sandvig et al. [331], which propose various methodologies and frameworks for evaluating and ensuring algorithmic fairness and transparency.

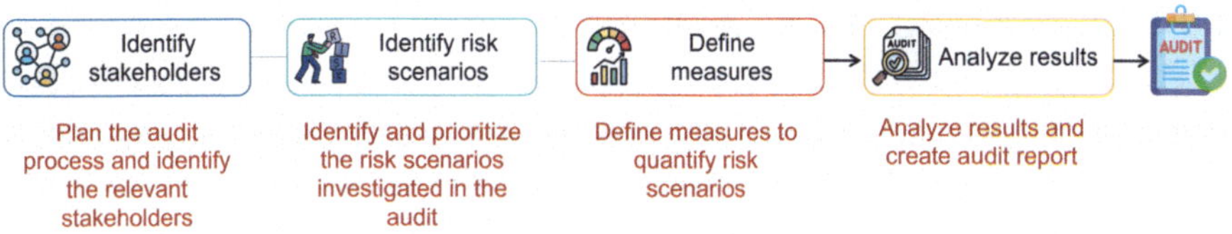

Fig. 4.2: Steps of an auditing process for IRRSs. Visualization based on Meßmer and Degeling [261]

Algorithmic auditing in the context of IRRSs corresponds to a systematic investigation of IRRSs to ensure they produce their results in a transparent, fair, and unbiased fashion [195]. This procedure involves comparing the IRRS's outcomes against a set of predefined criteria [118]. In the context of transparency, such an algorithmic audit could involve assessing the system's level of interpretability or transparency regarding data usage within the system. Furthermore, the implementation of *audit trails* within IRRSs is another strategy to this end. These trails provide a historical record of the system's activities and the decision-making paths taken, which can be crucial for stakeholders who aim to understand past interactions and their outcomes in the frame of an algorithmic audit.

Figure 4.2 depicts steps of an exemplary auditing process that has been proposed by Meßmer and Degeling [261], who suggest a specific process to audit IRRSs following a risk-based approach. That process should serve as a guideline to enable audits according to the DSA (see Sect. 2.1.3). In this process, first, the environment in which the IRRS is deployed is investigated with the aim of defining who should take part in the audit (e.g., providers, independent researchers, legal experts, and representatives from underserved groups). Then, concrete hypotheses need to be defined that serve as a basis for the audit, e.g., such that an IRRS could perpetuate gender bias (please refer to Sect. 3.3 for a list of biases that have already been tested in the context of IRRSs). Then, the methods are defined and applied to assess the hypotheses (e.g., qualitative, quantitative, or mixed methods). Afterward, the collected data is analyzed, and key findings of the audit are summarized in the resulting audit report.

Studies have shown that algorithmic audits play a significant role in evaluating the sociopolitical consequences of search engine behavior, for example, in the context of political communication [205]. These audits help understand and mitigate biases, ensuring that search results and recommendations are not influenced by political agendas or misinformation [106]. Furthermore, algorithmic audits of search engines have been conducted to assess the personalization and composition of politically related search results, highlighting the importance of auditing to maintain neutrality and fairness in information dissemination [324].

For a more detailed discussion of algorithmic auditing approaches, we refer the reader to Bandy [45], who compiled an overview article about algorithmic auditing.

4.9 Summary and Open Challenges

In this chapter, we have discussed the concept of transparency and its importance in IRRSs. We have highlighted critical challenges and barriers to transparency and outlined recent regulatory efforts related to transparency, which are currently either in effect or in preparation in Europe, the USA, and China. Furthermore, we have discussed various approaches and methodologies to enhance the transparency of IRRSs via the adoption of interpretable models, post hoc interpretability, and explanations. Despite the significant efforts made to make IRRSs more transparent and, in turn, better scrutinizable regarding fairness, bias, and privacy violations, achieving full transparency in IRRSs remains a complex and ongoing challenge. We identify several open challenges for the research community to tackle. The following describes a selection of these open challenges:

- **Complexity of DL-based IRRSs:** Contemporary IRRSs typically use complex DL-based algorithms that integrate multiple approaches to produce recommendations or search results. The complex nature of these systems creates a dichotomy between transparency and performance, as fully disclosing the workings of these algorithms might not be feasible without compromising system effectiveness. This tension underscores a critical need in the field: developing advanced methods to achieve high performance and transparency without significant trade-offs. Future research in this area should focus on developing new frameworks or models that can simplify the interpretability of DL-based IRRSs while maintaining or even enhancing their effectiveness.
- **Proprietary algorithms:** Many IRRSs are developed and maintained by corporations that view their algorithms as confidential business assets. This perspective leads to a reluctance to share detailed information about how these systems operate, thus limiting the ability of researchers and the public to evaluate and understand them. Consequently, this lack of transparency can limit advancements in the field and prevent the implementation of effective regulatory and ethical standards. Future work in this area should focus on developing frameworks and incentives that encourage greater openness while respecting the proprietary interests of companies. This could involve creating industry standards for transparency that are not in conflict with business secrets but allow enough insight to ensure the systems are fair, ethical, and accountable. Additionally, partnerships between academic institutions, industry, and regulatory bodies could be formed to foster a culture of shared responsibility and knowledge. These collaborations could lead to the development of new methodologies for independent testing and validation of IRRSs that do not require companies to fully disclose their proprietary algorithms.
- **Privacy considerations:** Transparency efforts in IRRSs, especially those offering personalized services, must carefully manage the balance between openness and the protection of user data. Ensuring transparency without revealing sensitive user information or preferences requires thoughtful consideration and strategies to anonymize data while maintaining the value of transparency. Future work in this

area should tackle several aspects to enhance the transparency of IRRSs without compromising user privacy. Firstly, research and development should focus on advancing and refining techniques for data anonymization and pseudonymization that allow data utility to be retained for analytical purposes while safeguarding individual privacy. This involves creating more sophisticated methods that make re-identification extremely difficult without losing the granularity of data that makes analyses meaningful.

- **Dynamic user data and preferences:** The dynamic nature of user preferences, influenced by changing interests, trends, and situations, adds to the complexity of maintaining transparency. As user preferences evolve, so must the explanations provided by IRRSs, requiring ongoing adjustments to both the models and their explanations to stay relevant and accurate. Such dynamics present a significant challenge as they demand that IRRSs not only adapt to changes in user behavior but also constantly update their explanations to remain meaningful to users. Future work in this area should focus on developing adaptive systems that can dynamically adjust their explanations in real time as user preferences and contexts change.
- **Personalization of explanations:** Different users or stakeholders may require different levels of detail or types of information to understand why they have received a particular recommendation or retrieval result. For instance, some users might value explanations that highlight social proof, such as the following: *This item is popular among users similar to you.* Others might appreciate more technical details about the underlying algorithms: *This result was generated using a CF-variant.* Future work in this area should be concerned with implementing adaptive explanation frameworks that dynamically adjust the explanations to user characteristics (e.g., level of expertise), preferences, and current context.

Summing up, the complex balance between enhancing IRRSs' performance through advanced algorithms and maintaining transparency, given the challenges above, requires innovative solutions. As technology evolves, so must the strategies to ensure IRRSs are effective and transparent to the various stakeholders engaging with IRRSs. We advocate for increased collaboration between academic research, industry, and regulatory bodies to collectively enhance the transparency of IRRSs. Collaboration is essential for fostering an ecosystem where transparency in IRRSs is not merely a compliance requirement but a cornerstone of ethical and user-centric system design. Future IRRS developments shall prioritize user trust, ethical responsibility, and legal compliance, thereby ensuring the responsible evolution of IRRSs in the digital landscape.

4.10 Further Reading

Since this chapter can only provide a brief overview of the extensive research on the transparency and explainability of IRRSs, we would like to point the reader to the resources listed below for more detailed information.

Starting with reproducibility, Bellogín and Said emphasize its importance in IR-RSs. In their view, the reproducibility of experiments in RSs helps increase the transparency of results and evaluation processes, leading to improved accountability [49].

Addressing the topic of explainability specifically in RSs, Zhang and Chen comprehensively summarize the state of the art in explainable recommendation research, giving insights into methodologies and approaches [438]. Similarly, Marconi et al. [247] present a short review of the latest advancements in explainable RSs. Additionally, Afchar et al. [14] discuss explainability specifically in the context of music RSs. Felfernig et al. [135] present strategies to design explanations for group RSs.

Turning to conceptual groundings of explainability, Friedrich and Zanker present a taxonomy of explanation methods to facilitate the generation of explanations in RSs [146], whereas they categorize methods according to specific design principles. The taxonomy exhibits three dimensions, i.e., (1) whether the explanation is a white-box (i.e., the explanation contains information about the underlying model) or a black-box explanation (i.e., the explanation does not contain information about the model), (2) information about the recommendation paradigm, and (3) what information is exploited in the explanation.

Similarly, Nunes and Jannach [284] present a systematic review of explanation approaches and also generate a taxonomy of explanations that includes aspects such as the objective of the explanation (e.g., user acceptance), display style, or the level of detail.

A critical aspect of explainability is user perception, explored in depth by Lu et al. [243]. They present a detailed study that sheds light on user perceptions of explanations of recommendation results, finding that human-generated explanations, such as peer-explanation, are more effective at increasing user intentions, and helping users construct preferences, and ultimately improving user satisfaction.

Lastly, the topic of explainable IR has attracted increasing attention, as evidenced by Anand et al.'s tutorial [23] at the ACM SIGIR conference 2023. The tutorial is based on their survey on explainable IR [22]. Bernard and Balog [51] further contribute to this dialog with a systematic review focused on transparency in IR.

In summary, this chapter highlights the ongoing research efforts dedicated to advancing the transparency and explainability of IRRSs. The field is highly dynamic, with a growing focus on user-centered approaches, highlighting its importance within the IRRS community.

Chapter 5
Privacy and Security

IRRSs have become an essential part of our daily lives. They shape our experiences and access to information, offering suggestions ranging from movies to healthcare. Yet, with this convenience comes a critical question: *How is our privacy protected, and how secure is the data we entrust to these systems?*

This chapter outlines potential privacy and security risks inherent in IRRSs. We explore how personal data and models can be protected and discuss relevant regulations and corresponding technical solutions.

5.1 Introduction to Privacy and Security Risks

In today's technology-driven world, privacy has become a major issue, especially when it comes to systems operating on massive amounts of user-generated data. This concern has grown significantly after events like the Cambridge Analytica scandal in 2018, where user data was misused for political purposes, showing how urgently we need to protect privacy.

Sensitive user data encompasses many types of information, including identity records, biometric identifiers, health information, facial recognition data, smartphone usage patterns, Wi-Fi connectivity logs, transportation, and vehicle usage data, as well as comprehensive video surveillance archives. Such data is collected by companies, organizations, and governments. They use it for deep analysis and as input for various kinds of ML-powered systems. Even seemingly harmless systems like IRRSs, which find and suggest content users might like, rely on sensitive data collection.

This creates a conflict between advancing technology and protecting individual privacy. Better results, e.g., improved accuracy of recommendations or retrieval results in Web search, often result from having more varied and up-to-date data about users. However, collecting this data raises concerns about privacy. The quality

M. Schedl et al., *Technical and Regulatory Perspectives on Information Retrieval and Recommender Systems*, The Information Retrieval Series 50,
https://doi.org/10.1007/978-3-031-69978-8_5

of search and recommendation is inherently linked to the quantity, diversity, and recency of data. Privacy violations could happen when data is collected or when statistics about the data are shared. Because of this, we need to move toward safer ways of conducting statistical analysis and applying ML technologies. Thus, a rigorous analysis of system vulnerabilities is necessary, paving the way for the formulation and implementation of robust privacy frameworks.

At the same time, users also think about this in contradiction. While they are often worried about sharing too much personal information with IRRSs, they also aim to obtain accurate predictions. This creates a tension between the goals of personalizing services and minimizing the disclosure of sensitive data needed for personalized search and recommendations (protecting privacy), especially in IRRSs [273].

A promising approach in this context is *privacy*-preserving ML, which aims to strengthen ML processes to protect user privacy and data integrity. This is distinct from secure ML, which is also analyzed in this chapter and focuses on safeguarding system integrity against intentional attacks. In privacy-preserving efforts, the primary objective is to safeguard the confidentiality of users' sensitive information. The spectrum of these attacks encompasses various adversaries and target points across the life cycle of a ML system, including data collection, model training, and prediction stages.

While centralizing user data simplifies learning, it introduces the risk of abuse and unsolicited data collection by online services, alongside the hazards of data sharing and unauthorized access. Considerable data repositories become susceptible to malicious exploitation as data crosses paths with malevolent servers, possibly giving rise to inference attacks that extract demographic details. These challenges are particularly salient in IRRSs, where a centralized entity manages personal user data to tailor services, exposing this sensitive data to inherent risks. Even when data collection is conducted responsibly or in a trustworthy manner, security violations are still possible. External entities and malicious actors pose threats at various stages of data use. Some notable attacks include *model extraction attacks* that seek to duplicate or approximate ML models, potentially compromising model parameters and training data. Other well-known attacks include *feature estimation attacks*, *reconstruction attacks*, and *membership inference attacks*, with attackers trying to find whether specific samples have been used when training models. The risks emanating from malicious servers, external intrusions, and colluding users pose the need for new research into safeguarding privacy.

Over the span of the last three decades, attacks on IRRSs have not been limited to privacy. The *security* of such systems has been thoroughly examined through two distinct broad categories of attacks: first, *hand-crafted shilling attacks*, which are particularly relevant for RSs, and, second, *adversarial attacks*, which impact both retrieval and RSs. A third and relatively novel area focuses on *ML-based shilling attacks*. These approaches share similarities with adversarial attacks in their use of ML techniques to subtly manipulate recommendation performance while minimizing alterations to the data.

Shilling attacks exploit similarity patterns within users' rating profiles by injecting carefully crafted fake ratings. These fabricated ratings mimic existing ones to achieve specific goals. Among these goals, one goal, the *push attack*, aims to promote certain items into users' recommendation lists. Another, the *nuke attack*, suggests irrelevant items to undermine the system's effectiveness. Conversely, attacks based on *adversarial machine learning (AML)* take a different approach. They focus on understanding how small, deliberate changes to the data can disrupt its expected patterns. These disruptions can manipulate outcomes, often resulting in engineered and potentially harmful effects.

Given these complexities, it is crucial to adopt statistical analyses and ML methodologies to address privacy and security concerns. Protecting privacy and security while improving the accuracy of IRRSs is essential. This requires a deep commitment to privacy-centric models and strategic defenses. Before we discuss such technical details, we review the most important and recent regulations regarding privacy and security, focusing on the European Union, the USA, and China.

5.2 Regulatory Aspects

The digital age has brought undeniable benefits, but it has also raised concerns about how our personal data is collected, used, shared, and protected. To address these concerns, various regions and countries have implemented data privacy and security laws that empower individuals and regulate how organizations handle their information. This section explores the key data privacy and security regulations in three major jurisdictions: the European Union, the USA, and China.

5.2.1 Privacy Regulations

5.2.1.1 Data Protection in Europe: General Data Protection Regulation

The European Union's *General Data Protection Regulation (GDPR)* [309][1] is a comprehensive data privacy law that came into effect in May 2018. It applies to all organizations processing the personal data of individuals residing within the European Economic Area (EEA), regardless of the organization's location. The GDPR empowers individuals with a robust set of rights, including the right to access, rectify, erase, and restrict the processing of their personal data. It also gives individuals the right to object to automated decision-making based on their data. Organizations must have a legal basis for processing data, such as consent, contract fulfillment, or legitimate interests. Additionally, the GDPR mandates data breach notifications, the appointment of data protection officers (DPOs) in certain cases, and restrictions on transferring personal data outside the EEA. By addressing issues like

[1] https://eur-lex.europa.eu/eli/reg/2016/679/oj

unauthorized data collection, lack of transparency, and limited individual control, the GDPR has established a strong framework for data privacy in Europe.

5.2.1.2 Data Protection in the USA: A Patchwork of Regulations

The USA, unlike the EU, does not have a single federal law governing data privacy. Instead, data privacy regulations are a complex patchwork of federal and state laws. Some key federal laws include the *Children's Online Privacy Protection Act (COPPA)*,[2] the *Gramm-Leach-Bliley Act (GLBA)*,[3] and the *Health Insurance Portability and Accountability Act (HIPAA)*.[4]

While the US data privacy landscape is a complex patchwork, the **Children's Online Privacy Protection Act (COPPA)** stands out as a crucial piece of legislation specifically designed to safeguard the privacy of children under 13. Unlike the broader financial and healthcare privacy regulations like GLBA and HIPAA, COPPA directly addresses the unique vulnerabilities of children in the digital age. The exponential growth of online content has opened doors to immense opportunities for learning and entertainment for children. However, this digital playground also presents significant risks to their privacy. Children are often less discerning about sharing personal information online, making them prime targets for data collection practices that can have lasting consequences. COPPA recognizes this power imbalance and empowers parents to act as gatekeepers of their children's online data. By requiring Web sites and online services to obtain verifiable parental consent before collecting, using, or disclosing a child's personal information, COPPA establishes a crucial first line of defense. This parental oversight allows for informed decision-making and helps shield children from the potential harms of unregulated data collection.

The **Gramm-Leach-Bliley Act (GLBA)**, also known as the Financial Modernization Act of 1999, protects consumers' financial information through a combination of requirements. Financial institutions must provide customers with a clear explanation of what data they collect, how it is shared, and the right to opt out of information sharing with non-affiliated companies for marketing purposes. Additionally, GLBA compels institutions to implement data security programs to safeguard customer information and discourages them from collecting more data than necessary. While not explicitly mandated by the Act, some federal regulations require certain institutions to allow consumers access to their information upon request. The *Federal Trade Commission (FTC)*, along with other federal agencies, enforces GLBA. In essence, GLBA empowers consumers with some control over their financial data and ensures its protection through data security measures and limitations on data collection.

---

[2] https://uscode.house.gov/view.xhtml?path=/prelim@title15/chapter91&edition=prelim (15 U.S.C. §6501 et seq.).

[3] https://www.ftc.gov/business-guidance/privacy-security/gramm-leach-bliley-act (15 U.S.C. §§6801–6809).

[4] https://www.cdc.gov/phlp/publications/topic/hipaa.html (Health Insurance Portability and Accountability Act of 1996, Pub. L. No. 104–191, §117, 110 Stat. 1936–1996).

The **Health Insurance Portability and Accountability Act (HIPAA)** is a federal law safeguarding patients' health information. It accomplishes this in two ways: by setting privacy standards and by ensuring data security. Here, data security is mentioned along with privacy, which is different from the security of the IRRSs model that is later discussed. HIPAA requires healthcare providers and insurers to clearly explain how they use patients' medical information and obtain their consent before sharing it. Patients have the right to access and control their health data. Additionally, HIPAA mandates that covered entities, like hospitals and insurers, have robust security measures in place to protect patients' sensitive health information from unauthorized access or disclosure.

Several states, particularly California, have enacted more comprehensive data privacy laws. The **California Consumer Privacy Act (CCPA)**[5] grants Californians rights similar to the GDPR, such as access, deletion, and opting out of data sales. The recently enacted **California Privacy Rights Act (CPRA)**[6] further expands these rights and creates a dedicated enforcement agency. While US laws address similar concerns as the GDPR, focusing on specific data types like children's data, financial information, and health data, the patchwork approach creates challenges for businesses operating across multiple states. The debate around a potential federal data privacy law in the USA is still ongoing.

5.2.1.3 Data Protection in China: Personal Information Protection Law

China's **Personal Information Protection Law (PIPL)**[7,8,9] effective since November 2021, is the country's first comprehensive data privacy framework. Similar to the GDPR, PIPL grants individuals rights to access, rectify, erase, and restrict the processing of their personal data. It emphasizes informed consent and restricts the transfer of personal information outside China. Organizations processing data must conduct data security assessments (data security is mentioned along with privacy, while the security of IRRSs models is later discussed). Before 2024, a security assessment was required if personal information of over 1 million individuals (regardless of data type) was processed or over 100,000 individuals if the data included sensitive personal information. After 2024, the focus has shifted to a cumulative assessment based on two factors: (1) the type of data (potentially impacting national security) or sensitive personal information and (2) the total amount transferred (the

[5] https://oag.ca.gov/privacy/ccpa

[6] https://cppa.ca.gov/regulations

[7] http://www.npc.gov.cn/npc/c2/c30834/202108/t20210820_313088.html

[8] This Web site offers a breakdown of the PIPL by chapter, including an unofficial English translation of the text: https://personalinformationprotectionlaw.com

[9] This Web site provides a full, unofficial English translation of the PIPL: https://www.china-briefing.com/news/the-personal-information-protection-law-in-china-a-legal-analysis

combined volume of personal information exported throughout the year is considered). However, no further details are provided in the law, and they will be defined in future regulations. While PIPL is a significant step toward data privacy in China, its enforcement details are still evolving.

5.2.2 Security Regulations

5.2.2.1 Security in Europe

Europe takes a multipronged approach to addressing AI-powered attacks (i.e., attacks leveraging AI techniques) or attacks on AI systems through various regulations. Enacted in 2018, the **General Data Protection Regulation (GDPR)**[10] [155] prioritizes user privacy and data security. It can be used to hold organizations accountable for vulnerabilities in their ML models. For instance, if an ML attack manipulates a RS to leak sensitive user data, the GDPR might be applicable. Organizations must implement appropriate technical and organizational measures to safeguard personal data and ensure its integrity (Article 32).

The **Product Liability Directive (PLD)**[11] [301] applies to products placed on the EU market and could be used to hold manufacturers liable for damages caused by faulty AI systems vulnerable to ML attacks. If an attack exploits a vulnerability in an AI-powered product, causing harm (e.g., a medical device malfunction), the PLD could be invoked to hold the manufacturer responsible (Article 1).

The European Commission has recently developed a comprehensive AI regulation, known as the **Artificial Intelligence Act (AI Act)**,[12] addressing issues like fairness, transparency, and accountability in AI systems. This regulation includes provisions related to the robustness of AI models. The EU AI Act does not directly regulate the security of individual ML models. However, by focusing on the security of the entire AI system and risk management for high-risk applications, it indirectly promotes the secure development and deployment of ML models. Security requirements apply to the entire AI system, encompassing its design, development, and deployment. This implicitly includes the security of the ML model within the system. Furthermore, the AI Act mandates security risk assessments for high-risk AI systems. These assessments also consider the design of the system, including the security of the machine learning model used. Previously, in 2020, the *Joint Research Centre* paved the way by publishing a report to provide a

> Policy-oriented description of the current perspectives of AI and its implications in society, an objective view on the current landscape of AI, focusing on the aspects of robustness and explainability. This also includes a technical discussion of the current risks associated with AI in terms of security, safety, and data protection, and a presentation of the scientific

[10] https://eur-lex.europa.eu/eli/reg/2016/679/oj

[11] https://eur-lex.europa.eu/legal-content/EN/TXT/?uri=celex%3A31985L0374

[12] https://digital-strategy.ec.europa.eu/en/policies/regulatory-framework-ai

solutions that are currently under active development in the AI community to mitigate these risks.[13]

5.2.2.2 Security in the USA

The US approach to ML security regulations is more fragmented, relying on existing laws and agency guidelines. The **Federal Trade Commission (FTC) Act**[14] [134] in §45 prohibits unfair and deceptive trade practices. The FTC could potentially use this act against companies whose AI systems are vulnerable to ML attacks that cause harm to consumers. For instance, if an attack manipulates an AI-powered credit scoring system to deny loans unfairly, the FTC might take action under the provisions of the FTC Act's deceptive practices.

Furthermore, the *National Highway Traffic Safety Administration (NHTSA)* and the *National Transportation Safety Board (NTSB)* have issued non-binding guidelines[15,16] for the development and deployment of automated vehicles. These guidelines emphasize the importance of safety and security, which could encompass considerations for potential attacks on self-driving car systems. Even though the regulation is not directly related to IRRSs, the reader may find it a useful example of how US administrations regulate security for critical AI applications.

Certain industries in the USA, like finance and healthcare, have their own regulations that focus on software systems requirements. Nonetheless, the same regulations apply to ML systems and ML attacks. For example, the **Gramm-Leach-Bliley Act (GLBA)** (15 U.S.C. §6801 et seq.)[17] [162] in finance requires institutions to protect customer data, which could extend to securing AI models used for financial decisions from manipulation. The regulation also involves AI tools to support human decisions, thus including IRRSs.

5.2.2.3 Security in China

China's regulatory landscape regarding attacks on ML systems is still evolving, and China does not have any specific regulations on ML attacks as of today. However, this does not mean the issue is ignored. China is actively involved in standardization efforts related to AI security, which could pave the way for future regulations. The national standards body, *Standardization Administration of China (SAC)*, has published guidelines for building novel AI systems,[18] which includes considerations

---

[13] https://ai-watch.ec.europa.eu/publications/robustness-and-explainability-artificial-intelligence_en

[14] https://www.law.cornell.edu/wex/ftc

[15] https://www.nhtsa.gov/vehicle-safety/automated-vehicles-safety

[16] https://www.ntsb.gov/Advocacy/safety-topics/Pages/automated-vehicles-investigations.aspx

[17] https://www.ftc.gov/business-guidance/privacy-security/gramm-leach-bliley-act

[18] https://www.gov.cn/zhengce/zhengceku/2020-08/09/content_5533454.htm

for security and resilience of AI models. These guidelines, although not legally binding, could influence future regulatory developments. While these guidelines are broad in scope, covering AI systems in general, they have important implications for IRRSs as well. Some key points from these guidelines that are particularly relevant to IRRSs include (1) data security, emphasizing the importance of data protection and privacy, which is crucial for IRRSs that often handle large amounts of user data; (2) model robustness, ensuring AI models are robust against various types of attacks, including adversarial attacks (directly relates to our discussion on securing IRRSs against manipulation); (3) transparency and explainability, stressing the need for AI systems to be transparent and explainable, which is an ongoing challenge in complex IRRSs; and (4) ethical considerations, emphasizing the ethical use of AI, including fairness in recommendations and avoiding bias, which is particularly relevant for RSs. Overall, while there are no comprehensive ML security regulations yet, existing legal frameworks and evolving approaches in China demonstrate a growing awareness of ML security and the potential risks posed by ML attacks.

5.3 Fundamentals and Theoretical Background of Privacy and Data Protection

This section explores the relationship between user privacy and data utilization in the context of ML and IRRSs. We begin by introducing a privacy-by-design learning paradigm, i.e., *federated learning*, *homomorphic encryption*, and *secure multiparty computation*, and then we outline the potential threats to user privacy that arise throughout the data life cycle, encompassing its collection, storage, and subsequent use. To address these concerns, we present several data security and privacy-preserving techniques, including *differential privacy*, *k-anonymity*, *ℓ-diversity*, *t-closeness*, and *δ-presence*. We examine how these techniques can be employed to mitigate privacy risks associated with data-intensive tasks. This section also acknowledges the inherent trade-off between ensuring robust privacy protection and maintaining IRRSs' competitive performance.

5.3.1 Federated Learning

The traditional ML paradigm is usually referred to as *centralized learning* (see Fig. 5.1a) and involves aggregating all data to a central server where the model is trained. This approach simplifies implementation and allows comprehensive data analysis and model optimization since the entire dataset is accessible in one location. However, it raises significant concerns about data privacy and security, and it creates potential single points of failure. *Decentralized learning* (see Fig. 5.1b) eliminates the central server entirely, with nodes—users' end devices in IRRSs—communicating and collaborating directly to train a model in a peer-to-peer fashion.

This enhances robustness and fault tolerance but poses challenges in coordination and communication management. *Distributed learning* (see Fig. 5.1c), applicable in both centralized and decentralized setups, involves splitting the training process across multiple machines to handle large datasets and complex models more efficiently. In a centralized distributed setup, data is divided among nodes that return computations to a central server, while a decentralized distributed setup involves nodes independently processing and exchanging results. This approach leverages parallel processing for faster training but demands careful management of data partitioning and synchronization.

In 2016, Google introduced the concept of *federated learning (FL)* [252], representing a collaborative learning framework that offers an effective structure for partitioning the holistic ML workflow into discrete components. FL addresses the limitations of the other paradigms by keeping data on local devices, which train models individually and only share model updates with a central server. This method enhances privacy and reduces data transfer costs but requires sophisticated aggregation methods to ensure model accuracy and convergence. Figure 5.1 visually illustrates the differences between the learning paradigms. In the FL paradigm (see Fig. 5.1d), numerous clients (such as an extensive array of mobile or Internet of Things devices) collectively train an ML model overseen by a central server. The rationale of FL is decentralizing the model training on users' devices to keep personal data private and protected. Concisely, each participant within the federation acquires the current shared global model from the central server and subsequently enhances it by learning from the sensitive data localized on their respective devices, thereby incorporating these refinements via a targeted update. The central server then combines these updates provided by users into an updated shared global model.

From the privacy perspective, the FL paradigm builds upon the common principle of *data minimization*, where data is protected by respecting the simple assumption that sensitive data will never leave the user device. This materializes through the selective scope of collected updates, confined to the minimal essential information necessary for the learning task at hand, thereby exemplifying *focused collection*. Further, the aggregation process is executed at the earliest juncture feasible (termed *early aggregation*), while both accumulated and processed data are promptly discarded, aligning with the principle of *minimal retention*. By performing computations on the device containing sensitive data, FL also respects the principle of *data locality*, ensuring users' rights to *data ownership*, encompassing the possession and governance over their data.

FL, following all these guiding principles, and further combined with privacy-preserving technologies to ensure *data anonymization* (described in the following sections), is an important tool to preserve user privacy and data confidentiality. Moreover, when the training of the ML model involves privacy-sensitive user data (e.g., medical data whose ownership only belongs to the patients), the adoption of FL becomes essential.

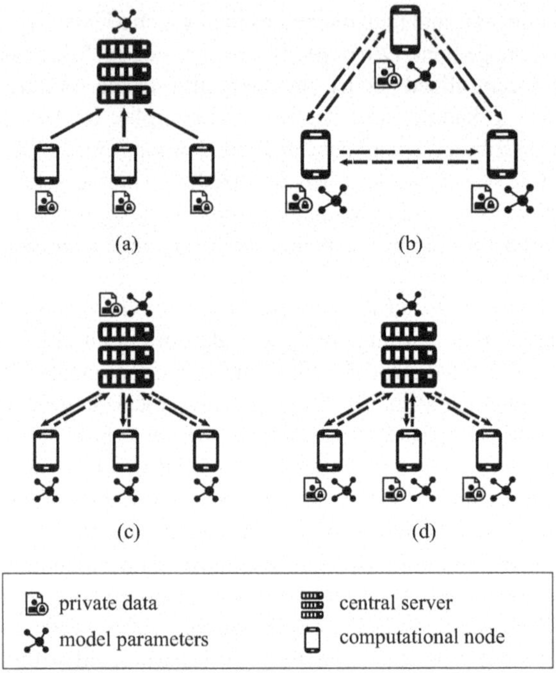

Fig. 5.1: Information flow over the network in four IRRS architectures. Solid lines represent training data flow, dashed lines represent model parameters flow. (**a**) Centralized learning. (**b**) Decentralized learning. (**c**) Distributed learning. (**d**) Federated learning

Several recent studies have explored the application of FL to RSs, with a focus on user privacy. Yang et al. in 2020 provided a foundational analysis, defining the problem and potential solutions [426]. Building on this, Ali et al. discuss the general suitability of FL for privacy-preserving RSs [20]. FL is also leveraged to address specific challenges in recommendations, such as the cold start problem [399]. The overall effectiveness of federated RSs is explored by Tan et al. [376] and Jalalirad et al. [186]. Additionally, Anelli et al., in various works from 2019 to 2022, propose methods like FedRank and user-controlled federated MF that empower users to participate in model training while keeping their data confidential [27, 28, 30]). Their research builds upon the core principles of FL, differentiating it from traditional distributed learning approaches. This line of work contributes to a growing body of research on privacy-preserving RSs, as evidenced in the recent survey by Chronis et al. [90]. Additional works investigate theoretical aspects [29] and methods for incorporating user feedback [405].

5.3.2 *Homomorphic Encryption: Secure Computations on Encrypted Data*

The concept of *homomorphic encryption (HE)* was first envisioned in 1978 by Ronald Rivest, Leonard Adleman, and Michael Dertouzos [322]. However, the first practical construction of a fully homomorphic encryption scheme came much later in 2009 by Craig Gentry. With HE, it is possible to perform complex calculations on confidential data without ever revealing it. Unlike traditional encryption, where data becomes unusable until decrypted, HE allows computations directly on encrypted data (this possibility is detailed in the following section about secure multiparty computation).

HE schemes come in two primary categories. *Partially homomorphic encryption (PHE)* supports either addition or multiplication on encrypted data. This enables specific computations like finding minimum or maximum values without decryption. *Fully homomorphic encryption (FHE)*, on the other hand, allows for both addition and multiplication, opening doors to a wider range of computations.

HE utilizes complex mathematical structures to create a virtual world where calculations on encrypted data mirror operations in the real world. Imagine data as numbers hidden within layers of mathematical operations. HE allows adding or multiplying these layers without ever accessing the core data itself.

Benefits and Challenges: HE offers significant advantages. It allows for privacy-preserving analysis, enabling secure analysis of sensitive data on cloud platforms without compromising confidentiality. Additionally, computations remain encrypted with HE, reducing the attack surface for data breaches and enhancing overall security.

However, HE also faces challenges. Current HE schemes are computationally expensive, impacting processing speed and efficiency. While FHE offers greater flexibility, it is still under development, with limitations on supported operations and data sizes.

Despite these challenges, HE is a revolutionary technology with high potential. As research progresses, HE holds promise for unlocking new avenues in secure data analysis and collaboration across various fields.

Several research efforts have explored using HE [322] to achieve privacy-preserving RSs. Kim et al. [197] propose a method for efficient MF using FHE. This approach allows the RS to process encrypted user data while still generating accurate recommendations. Building on this concept, Erkin et al. [128] present a method for generating private recommendations using a combination of HE and data packing techniques, aiming to further improve efficiency. Additionally, Sobitha Ahila and Shunmuganathan [17] investigate the role of HE in RSs for e-commerce applications, highlighting its potential for user privacy preservation. While these works focus on item recommendations, Badsha et al. [39] explore a privacy-preserving user-based CF technique based on HE, similar to Mukherjee et al. [271].

5.3.3 Secure Multiparty Computation

Secure *multiparty computation (MPC)* is a cryptographic technique that allows multiple parties to jointly compute a function on their private inputs without revealing those inputs to each other. With secure MPC, competitors can analyze market trends together without revealing their individual sales figures, or researchers can collaborate on sensitive medical data while keeping patient information strictly confidential.

Traditionally, collaborating on data analysis often requires sharing it. This raises privacy concerns, as parties might be hesitant to share sensitive information for fear of exposing their secrets. Secure MPC offers a solution by enabling a secure collaboration environment. Thereby, MPC protocols rely on complex cryptographic techniques. Here is a simplified breakdown of the process:

- **Secret sharing**: Each party transforms their private input (like sales figures) into several encrypted shares using cryptographic tools. These shares are then distributed to all other participants. Imagine splitting a secret recipe into several encrypted pieces and giving each collaborator a part.
- **Shared computation**: Each party performs calculations on their own encrypted shares, following a carefully designed protocol. These calculations involve complex mathematical operations that ensure no party can glean any information about the original data from their individual share. Think of each collaborator manipulating their encrypted recipe fragment without understanding the whole recipe.
- **Result reconstruction**: Finally, the parties combine their processed shares in a specific way. This cryptographic magic allows them to reconstruct the final result of the function (like market trends) without ever revealing their original inputs. Imagine putting together the encrypted recipe fragments to unveil the final dish without anyone knowing the exact ingredients.

There are two main security models in MPC: semi-honest security and malicious security. In the *semi-honest security* scenario, parties follow the protocol honestly but might try to learn additional information from the exchanged messages. Secure MPC protocols ensure that no party learns more than their designated output, even if they try to peek at what others are doing. In the *malicious security* scenario, it is assumed a more adversarial setting where some parties might deviate from the protocol or try to disrupt the computation entirely. In this case, secure MPC protocols guarantee correctness and privacy. Indeed, the final result is computed accurately, and no party learns anything beyond its designated output, even if it cheats.

Benefits and Challenges: MPC allows parties to work together on sensitive data analysis while safeguarding individual privacy (privacy-preserving collaboration). Distributing the computation among multiple parties makes it harder for a single point of failure or attack. MPC can be adapted to handle multiple participants and complex computations. However, MPC also faces some challenges, including computational overhead. The complex cryptographic operations involved can be computationally expensive, impacting efficiency. Moreover, designing secure and efficient MPC protocols for specific functions can be complex. Finally, while research is ongoing, not all computations can be performed efficiently using MPC yet.

Secure MPC represents a powerful tool for unlocking collaboration on sensitive data without compromising privacy. While it faces computational limitations and functional boundaries, ongoing research is making it more efficient and versatile. As technology advances, MPC has the potential to revolutionize data analysis and collaboration across diverse fields, fostering secure and innovative solutions for the future.

Several studies have explored secure MPC for privacy-preserving CF in healthcare RSs. Kaur et al. [194] propose an efficient multiparty scheme specifically designed for healthcare data, addressing the challenge of scattered data across different institutions. Their method leverages secure MPC techniques to allow collaboration without revealing individual patient information. Also, Shmueli and Tassa contributed two significant works in this area. In 2017, they presented secure multiparty protocols for item-based CF [358]. They refined their approach in 2020, proposing mediated secure multiparty protocols for CF [359], which can be particularly useful when a trusted third party is involved.

5.3.4 *k-anonymity*

One concept particularly stands out when it comes to data anonymity for privacy protection in IRRSs: *k-anonymity*. This term, coined by Pierangela Samarati and Latanya Sweeney, has become pivotal in safeguarding individuals' privacy within anonymized datasets. While its origins trace back to the pioneering work of Tore Dalenius in 1986, its relevance is still significant today [102]. As a starting point, the interested reader may also find helpful Sweeney's work on k-anonymity [373].

k-anonymity ensures personal information is shielded from prying eyes while remaining helpful in enhancing user experiences. At its core, k-anonymity addresses the challenge of releasing sensitive, person-specific data without jeopardizing individuals' identities. It achieves this through data generalization, masking, and pseudonymization, rendering individuals indistinguishable within a dataset. In short, k-anonymity protects user identities by ensuring a minimum number of users that share similar data points.

To give some examples of the use of k-anonymity in IRRSs, Zhang et al. [434] propose a method for privacy-aware CF that utilizes k-anonymity. This approach aims to achieve a balance between user privacy and the accuracy of recommendations. Salas' work [330] complements this area by introducing a measure to quantify the privacy offered by anonymization techniques like k-anonymity in RSs. Prior research by Casino et al. [71] also explored achieving k-anonymity in CF through microaggregation, a process that groups similar data points together. Understanding user perspectives on the privacy-accuracy trade-off is equally important. Valdez and Ziefle [391] examine user attitudes toward privacy in health RSs, highlighting the potential for users to accept some privacy risks in exchange for more valuable recommendations.

5.3.4.1 Definition

We start by defining the data holder's private dataset, where each user represents a distinct entity. The dataset corresponds to the set of personal data collected for an IRRS. For simplicity, the examples will refer to a limited set of sensitive attributes. Nevertheless, without loss of generality, the studied techniques could apply to any IRRS. An important concept in this context is quasi-identifiers (QIs), which are defined as combinations of attributes that could be used to disclose user identity (e.g., the combination of birthplace and birth date). These QIs must be protected to ensure anonymity. Specifically, each release of data should ensure that every combination of QI values can be linked to at least k individuals indistinguishably.

More formally: *A dataset satisfies* k*-anonymity if, for each quasi-identifier, every sequence of values in the dataset appears at least* k *times.*

5.3.4.2 Generalization

In the data release, these QIs must be protected. Specifically, each release of data should ensure that every combination of QI values can be linked to at least k individuals indistinguishably. To adhere to this anonymity requirement, it is essential to determine how many individuals the released information corresponds to, which may involve linking the released data with externally available information—a task impractical for the data holder. However, we can assume the data holder knows which attributes may appear in external datasets, thereby identifying the QIs. Nonetheless, the specific values of external data cannot be assumed. Therefore, for k-anonymity, we assume that the anonymized dataset is released, and we assess whether a malicious agent has enough information to find user identities. To achieve this, we rely on the definition given in Sect. 5.3.4.1.

Our initial approach to achieving k-anonymity involves defining and utilizing generalization relationships between domains and the values that attributes can take. In a conventional relational database system, *domains* describe the set of values that attributes can have. For instance, there may be domains for ZIP codes, numbers, and strings. We extend this concept to facilitate the generalization of attribute values. In the original dataset, where values are as specific as possible, each attribute is within the *ground domain* (i.e., a domain that is publicly known). For instance, a ZIP code like 02139 belongs to the ground ZIP code domain. To achieve k-anonymity, we generalize the ZIP code to be less informative. This involves introducing a more *general domain*, thus mapping the *private domain* (i.e., a domain containing fine-grained information about individuals) into the generalized one (i.e., a domain containing only coarse-grained information). This mapping is defined through a generalization relationship, representing a partial order on the set of domains.

This generalization concept implies the existence of a domain generalization hierarchy for each domain, ensuring compatibility among all domains within a hierarchy. Additionally, a value generalization relationship, represented by a partial order, associates each value in a domain with a unique value in a directly generalized domain, forming a value generalization hierarchy.

More concisely: ***Generalization*** *facilitates the transformation of specific attribute values into broader categories, reducing the risk of re-identification. It involves introducing a more general domain, represented by a partial order, and mapping the private domain into the generalized one. This ensures compatibility among all domains within a hierarchy.*

Example: Generalization in k-anonymity
Imagine a healthcare IRRS deployed in a clinic. The system retrieves and recommends information based on patient data, which can be highly sensitive. In this example, we focus on a fragment of personal information, but it could be easily extended to any personal or sensitive information of an IRRS, including personal preferences. This data might include a patient's ZIP code, which can be used to infer details about their socioeconomic status and potentially even their home address. Initially, specific ZIP codes like 02139 are part of the ground domain. To ensure the anonymity of the patients, we generalize ZIP codes by replacing the last digit with 0, thus mapping the private domain into a more generalized one (e.g., 02139 $\rightarrow$ 02130). This mapping is guided by a generalization relationship, representing a partial order on the set of domains.

5.3.4.3 Suppression

We previously explored how a generalized dataset can be derived from a private dataset, offering a more generalized representation of the data while adhering to a k-anonymity constraint. Generalization presents the advantage of releasing all individual users from the dataset, albeit in a more generalized format. A complementary approach to achieving k-anonymity is *suppression*.

Suppression involves removing specific data from the dataset to prevent their release. This technique, familiar in disclosure control, operates at the user level, meaning an entire user can be suppressed if necessary. Suppression acts as a moderating force during the generalization process, particularly when dealing with outliers, i.e., users with occurrences less than the specified k value. To illustrate, consider the scenario where k-anonymity with $k = 2$ is desired. Suppose the attribute "Date of Birth" undergoes several generalizations, ranging from specific dates to broader intervals. The presence of outliers in the dataset may necessitate extensive generalization steps across various attributes to meet the k-anonymity requirement. In practice, this often results in the generalization of nearly all attributes. However, if the outliers are suppressed, the need for extensive generalization decreases. Essentially, suppression allows for a reduction in the degree of generalization required. It is crucial to note that the definition of suppression differs from that of generalization. Suppression permits users from the private dataset to have no corresponding generalized users in the disclosed dataset. These users, without a counterpart in the disclosed data, are the ones that have been suppressed.

More concisely: ***Suppression*** *involves the removal of specific data from the dataset, ensuring they are not released. This moderates the generalization process, particularly when dealing with outliers – users with occurrences less than the specified k value. By suppressing outliers, the need for extensive generalization decreases.*

Example: Suppression in k-anonymity

Suppression entails the removal of specific data from the user information to prevent its release. This technique operates at the user level, so entire users can be suppressed. Suppression serves as a complementary strategy to generalization, particularly in scenarios where outliers exist in users with occurrences less than the specified k value. In Table 5.1, an example of a dataset containing patient information is provided (Table 5.1).

Patient ID	Age	Health Condition
1	25	Diabetes
2	45	Heart Disease
3	90	Cancer

Table 5.1: Example of a common dataset of patients

For instance, we aim for k-anonymity with $k = 2$. If the attribute "Age" undergoes extensive generalization to achieve anonymity (e.g., suppose substituting the age for patients 1 and 2 with a "20–50" label), the presence of outliers (i.e., patient 3 with age 90) may necessitate further generalization across multiple attributes (i.e., creating a new label "20–90" to comprise the three patients). However, by suppressing outliers (i.e., removing patient 3), the extent of generalization required can be reduced (i.e., patients 1 and 2 will keep a more reasonable label: "20–50").

5.3.5 ℓ-diversity

ℓ-diversity [245] is a privacy-preserving data anonymization technique that extends the k-anonymity model. It addresses limitations in k-anonymity by ensuring diversity within anonymized groups, particularly for sensitive attributes. k-anonymity anonymizes data by ensuring each record belongs to a group of at least k indistinguishable records based on QI attributes. While k-anonymity provides a basic level of privacy, it suffers from key weaknesses, i.e., its proneness to two types of attacks:

- **Homogeneity Attack**: If all records within a k-anonymous group share the same sensitive value, an attacker with some background knowledge can easily re-identify individuals.
- **Background Knowledge Attack**: Even with diverse sensitive values within a group, if an attacker possesses additional knowledge about a specific individual (e.g., age or ZIP code), they can potentially link the individual to a particular record.

ℓ-diversity addresses these shortcomings by ensuring diversity within anonymized groups for the sensitive attribute (e.g., a disease). Formally, a dataset is considered ℓ-diverse for a sensitive attribute S if, for every group of k indistinguishable records based on QIs (QI group), there exist at least ℓ well-represented distinct diseases within the group.

ℓ-diversity is typically achieved through careful data manipulation techniques that preserve privacy while maintaining data utility. The goal is not to falsify individual records but rather to transform the dataset as a whole. Some common approaches include generalization, suppression, data swapping (i.e., exchanging sensitive attributes between records within the same QI group, maintaining overall statistics while increasing diversity), adding noise (to increase diversity without significantly altering overall data characteristics), and microaggregation (i.e., grouping similar records and replacing individual values with group averages or representatives)

It is important to note that these techniques are applied to the entire dataset, not just to individual records that might compromise privacy. The goal is to transform the data in a way that makes it ℓ-diverse while preserving as much utility as possible.

Example: ℓ-diversity in Health-Related Search and Retrieval

Consider a dataset with age and ZIP code as QI attributes and disease (cancer, diabetes, flu) as the sensitive attribute. Suppose $k = 3$ (minimum group size). Let us show ℓ-diversity through two examples (Tables 5.2 and 5.3):

Age	ZIP Code	Disease
30	10001	Cancer
30	10001	Cancer
30	10001	Cancer

Table 5.2: Example of not ℓ-diverse (low diversity) dataset

Tables 5.2 violates ℓ-diversity because only one disease (cancer) is present, even though the group size is 3 (meeting k-anonymity). An attacker can easily identify someone with cancer given the unique age and ZIP code.

Age	ZIP Code	Disease
30	10001	Cancer
30	10001	Diabetes
30	10001	Flu

Table 5.3: Example of ℓ-diverse (high diversity) dataset

Tables 5.3 satisfies ℓ-diversity because there are 3 distinct and well-represented diseases (at least $\frac{1}{3}$ of the group has each disease). An attacker cannot easily find who has which disease.

The introduction of ℓ introduces a trade-off between privacy and data utility. Higher ℓ values enhance privacy by requiring more diversity within groups, but this might lead to increased data suppression (hiding values) or generalization (replacing values with broader categories), potentially reducing the usability of the anonymized data. Indeed, generalization and suppression help create bigger groups that contain more diverse attributes. Here, the attributes considered for generalization and suppression are different from the ones considered for ℓ-diversity.

Several extensions of ℓ-diversity have been proposed, including:

- **Discernibility-based ℓ-diversity:** This variant focuses on the probability of correctly identifying an individual based on the QI and sensitive attribute values.
- **Inconsistent ℓ-diversity:** This model allows for some groups to fall below the ℓ threshold as long as the overall probability of re-identification remains low.

ℓ-diversity offers some important advantages over k-anonymity. Notably, ℓ-diversity ensures diversity within anonymized groups for sensitive attributes. Furthermore, ℓ-diversity mitigates the impact of homogeneity attacks and background knowledge attacks. Overall, ℓ-diversity provides a more robust approach to data anonymization compared to k-anonymity by addressing its limitations. However, it introduces a trade-off between privacy and data utility. The choice of appropriate ℓ values and specific variants of ℓ-diversity depends on the specific data context and the desired privacy-utility balance.

5.3.6 t-closeness

t-closeness [225] is a data anonymization technique that refines ℓ-diversity, offering a more rigorous approach to privacy preservation. While ℓ-diversity ensures a minimum number of well-represented values for the sensitive attribute within anonymized groups, t-closeness focuses on the distribution of these values.

Example: Motivations and Limitations of ℓ-diversity in a Health-Related Scenario
Imagine a medical dataset with QI attributes (age and ZIP code) and disease (cancer, diabetes, flu) as the sensitive attribute. ℓ-diversity ensures each QI group of, say, $k = 3$ patients has at least ℓ distinct diseases. However, it has limitations:

- **Threshold issues:** Choosing ℓ can be subjective. A high ℓ might not be achievable, and a low ℓ might not offer enough protection.
- **Distribution insensitivity:** ℓ-diversity only guarantees a minimum number of distinct values, not necessarily a distribution that reflects the overall data. For example, a group might cover two diseases out of three (cancer, diabetes, flu), thereby satisfying ℓ-diversity with $\ell = 2$), but with an uneven distribution (2 cancer, 1 diabetes, 0 flu) compared to the entire dataset (e.g., 20 cancer, 60 diabetes, 300 flu).

t-closeness addresses these limitations by introducing a distance metric to compare the distribution of the sensitive attribute within an anonymized group to the overall data distribution. Formally, a dataset is considered t-close for a sensitive attribute S if, for every QI group, the distance between the distribution of S within the group (denoted by P_g) and the overall distribution of S (denoted by P_U) is less than or equal to a predefined threshold t. Therefore, t-closeness is further defined by the following key aspects:

- **Distance metric:** Various metrics quantify how similar two distributions are. A common choice is the earth mover's distance (EMD), which measures the minimum effort (work) needed to transform one distribution into another. Imagine piles of dirt representing the distribution of disease (P_g). EMD then calculates the minimum amount of dirt you need to move between piles to obtain the overall distribution P_U.
- **Threshold t:** This parameter defines the maximum allowable difference between the group's sensitive attribute distribution and the overall distribution. A lower t denotes stricter privacy requirements.

Example: High and Low t-closeness
Consider a dataset with blood type (A, B, AB, 0) as the sensitive attribute. Suppose $k = 3$ (minimum group size) and $t = 0.5$ as maximum allowable EMD. Please note that EMD is computed between frequency distributions. In this example, we have a discrete distribution with a given fixed order of the

blood types (A, B, AB, 0) only for explanatory purposes. Consider the following dataset:

Age	ZIP Code	Blood Type
25	12345	A
25	12345	A
25	12345	B

Table 5.4: Not t-close group (high EMD)

This group has a **high EMD** (0.69) because all As are concentrated in one record (i.e., for A/B/AB/0, the distribution is 0.66/0.33/0/0), while the overall data has a more balanced distribution in our example (0.35/0.35/0.2/0.1).

Let us now take a look at the following dataset:

Age	ZIP Code	Blood Type
25	12345	A
25	12345	B
25	12345	AB

Table 5.5: t-close group (low EMD)

Here, the distribution within the group (i.e., for A/B/AB/0 the distribution is 0.33/0.33/0.33/0) is closer to the overall data distribution compared to the previous example, resulting in a **low EMD** of 0.44. Therefore, the first example (Table 5.4) represents a dataset in which the blood type group is not t-close, whereas the second one (Table 5.5) represents a t-close dataset with respect to the blood type group.

t-closeness builds upon ℓ-diversity by introducing a distribution-aware approach to privacy preservation. While it requires careful selection of the distance metric and threshold t, it offers a more robust privacy guarantee compared to ℓ-diversity. The choice between these techniques depends on the specific data context, desired privacy level, and acceptable level of data utility.

5.3.7 δ-presence

δ-presence is a privacy metric that goes beyond simply counting how anonymous a dataset is (like k in k-anonymity). It focuses on the information leakage about an individual's presence in a dataset after anonymization, thereby unveiling privacy risks in anonymized data. In simpler terms, it tells us how much the uncertainty about an individual being in the data changes after anonymization. For computing

δ-presence, we will now assume that the population information is known and a malicious agent wants to find if a specific, known user is in the anonymized dataset.

Example: Motivation for δ-presence in a Health-Related Scenario
Imagine a hospital dataset with patient IDs and diseases. Anonymization techniques like k-anonymity group patient records based on age and ZIP code, hiding the original identifiers (IDs). However, traditional metrics like the number of records in a group (k) do not tell us how much safer a patient's information is after anonymization. δ-presence helps bridge this gap.

δ-presence quantifies the privacy risk associated with an individual's record being present in a dataset. Formally, this is shown in Eq. 5.1, where $\delta(QI_{group}, D)$ represents the δ-presence of an individual in the original dataset D belonging to a specific QI group, $n(QI_{group} \in D)$ is the number of patients of the same QI group in the dataset D, and $\mathcal{N}(QI_{group})$ is the number of individuals in the entire population who share the same QIs.

$$\delta(QI_{group}, D) = \frac{n(QI_{group} \in D)}{\mathcal{N}(QI_{group})} \tag{5.1}$$

Analogously, $\delta(QI_{group}, D')$ can be computed, where D' is the anonymized dataset (e.g., with generalized or suppressed identifiers).

Let us suppose that two patients are 34 years old and have ZIP code 12345. Unfortunately, they are the only users in the entire population with these identifiers. It is straightforward to observe that, for each of them, their δ-presence is 1. Therefore, a δ-presence value of 1 indicates no change in privacy and, thus, a high risk of re-identification of single individuals. The attacker can still be certain (or uncertain) about each of these patients being in the dataset, regardless of anonymization (that has not been implemented in this small example). A value closer to 0 signifies stronger privacy (e.g., suppose there are 1,500 individuals sharing the same identifiers in the population). The lower the chance of guessing a patient's presence after anonymization, the better.

Example: High and Low δ-presence

High δ-presence (Low Privacy): Consider a small clinic with only 10 patients, given in Table 5.6. Anonymization groups patients by age. Let us assume there are two patients who are 30 years old. Imagine a malicious agent knowing the presence of a specific patient with age 30 and wanting to know her disease. Let us assume that, in this example, the population is composed of the clinic patients. The attacker can be certain (δ-presence equal to 1) about that patient's disease, because she must be one of the two in the 30-year-old group who both suffer from stomach ulcer.

Age	Patient ID	Disease
20	1	Heart disease
20	2	Flu
25	3	Diabetes
25	4	Cancer
30	5	Stomach ulcer
30	6	Stomach ulcer
35	7	Blood pressure
35	8	Allergies
40	9	Migraine
40	10	Stomach ulcer

Table 5.6: Original dataset D

Low δ-presence (High Privacy): Now, let us consider a large hospital dataset, given in Table 5.7, which is potentially anonymized with other techniques, such as ℓ-diversity, to ensure diverse diseases within age groups. Even if an attacker knows a patient's age (e.g., 30) and ZIP code (e.g., 12345), but these are common, and there are many different diseases in the group (5 in our example), it becomes much harder to find the exact record, thus, the disease. Supposing that the overall population belonging to the QI group is composed of 500 individuals, this scenario results in a lower δ-presence value, being $\delta\left(QI_{(30,12345)}, D'\right) = \frac{5}{500} = 0.01$.

Age	ZIP code	Disease
30	12345	Cancer
30	12345	Diabetes
30	12345	Flu
30	12345	Blood pressure
30	12345	Stomach ulcer

Table 5.7: Anonymized dataset D'

Here, even though the attacker knows the age and ZIP code, there are five common diseases within that group. We could suppose that anonymization by ℓ-diversity would have ensured this diversity. Without any additional information, it is difficult to find the specific patient's disease. This scenario would lead to a lower δ-presence value (0.01).

Some important considerations and limitations should be mentioned:

- δ-presence assumes the attacker has some background knowledge about the target individual.
- It does not account for complex attacks that combine information from multiple sources.
- Calculating δ-presence can be difficult for very large datasets.

δ-presence provides a valuable tool for understanding how anonymization protects individual privacy. It complements existing metrics by focusing on the change in uncertainty about an individual's presence in the data. However, its limitations should be considered, and it is often used alongside other techniques for a comprehensive privacy analysis.

5.3.8 Differential Privacy

Differential privacy (DP) has become a cornerstone of modern data analysis, particularly when dealing with sensitive datasets. It offers a mathematically grounded framework for ensuring strong privacy guarantees for individuals contributing data while simultaneously enabling researchers to extract valuable insights from the collective information [122].

The core principle of DP revolves around the introduction of *controlled randomness*, often referred to as noise, into the data or statistics released for analysis. This strategic noise addition acts as a cloak, obfuscating the identification of any specific individual within the dataset. Usually, this noise could be applied to the data feeding the IRRS or to the model parameters.

However, achieving this obfuscation presents a non-trivial balancing act. The noise needs to be calibrated to effectively mask individual-level details. Yet, it should not be so substantial that it renders the aggregated data unusable for broader analysis purposes or making personalized recommendations.

DP leverages the concept of *privacy loss*, quantified by the parameter ε (epsilon). A mechanism is considered ε-differentially private if the outcome of any function f on datasets differing by at most one record remains indistinguishable. Formally, for any two neighboring datasets D and D' (i.e., datasets differing by a single element), and for any subset of outputs S, Eq. 5.2 holds.

$$\mathcal{P}(f(D) \in S) \leq e^{\varepsilon} \cdot \mathcal{P}(f(D') \in S) \tag{5.2}$$

Here, $\mathcal{P}$ denotes probability. This formulation guarantees that the probability of observing a particular outcome S from the function f applied to dataset D is at most e^{ε} times greater than the probability of observing the same outcome from f applied to the neighboring dataset D' that must be protected. A smaller ε signifies stronger privacy guarantees, implying that the inclusion or exclusion of a single data point has a minimal impact on the analysis output. This control over ε allows for tailoring privacy guarantees to specific risk tolerances and data sensitivity levels.

Several mechanisms can be employed to achieve DP, each with its own advantages and trade-offs. Here are some prominent examples:

- **Laplace mechanism**: This mechanism adds Laplace noise, drawn from a Laplace distribution to the information extraction result (e.g., the age of a patient or a user preference). The scale parameter of the Laplace distribution controls the amount of noise added, directly impacting the privacy-utility trade-off.
- **Gaussian mechanism**: Similar to the Laplace mechanism, Gaussian noise is added to the information extraction result. However, Gaussian noise might be less efficient for certain types of information compared to Laplace noise.
- **Kernel smoothing**: This technique smoothens the distribution of the data by applying a kernel function, effectively blurring individual data points and achieving DP.

The selection of an appropriate mechanism depends on the specific information that should be extracted from the data and the desired balance between privacy and utility. Indeed, if detailed data (e.g., exact movie ratings, or a detailed list of all the enjoyed items) is required to obtain accurate recommendations or search results, protecting privacy could be substantially detrimental to the overall performance.

Example: Differential Privacy Applications in Healthcare

The healthcare domain presents a compelling use case for differential privacy. Often, valuable insights for medical research and public health initiatives reside in sensitive patient data. For example, suppose an IR system to search for the best therapies for a patient. Despite the potential benefits, empowering such systems with AI or ML could jeopardize user privacy. DP empowers researchers to leverage this data for analysis while upholding strong patient privacy. Here are some detailed examples of how DP could protect privacy in various IR scenarios:

- **Analyzing disease prevalence**: Researchers can utilize DP to release statistics on the prevalence of specific diseases within a population. By adding controlled noise to the counts of individuals diagnosed with a particular disease, DP ensures that an individual's decision to participate in the study has a negligible effect on the reported statistics. This allows for robust analysis of disease patterns without compromising patient privacy.
- **Identifying risk factors**: DP can be employed to study the association between various factors and specific health outcomes. For instance, researchers might investigate the link between lifestyle choices and the risk of developing a chronic disease. By applying DP to the analysis, they can identify potential risk factors without revealing individual patient information.
- **Pharmaceutical research**: Clinical trials often involve collecting sensitive data from participants. DP can be used to release aggregate statistics on the effectiveness and safety of new drugs without compromising individual patient data. This facilitates transparent and efficient drug development processes while safeguarding patient privacy.

Example: Differential Privacy in Healthcare/Disease Prevalence Analysis
Suppose we have a healthcare dataset containing information about patients' diagnoses (Table 5.8). We want to release statistics on the prevalence of a specific disease while preserving DP.

Patient ID	Disease diagnosis
1	Disease A
2	Disease B
3	Disease A
4	Disease C
5	Disease A

Table 5.8: Original private dataset

Let us say we want to release the number of patients diagnosed with Disease A. We add Laplace noise to the count to achieve DP (Table 5.9).

Count	Noisy count
3	3.5

Table 5.9: Disease A count with differential privacy

In this example, the Laplace noise added to the count of patients diagnosed with Disease A preserves DP while providing information about disease prevalence.

Example: Differential Privacy in Healthcare/Risk Factor Analysis
Consider a scenario where researchers want to study the association between smoking and the risk of developing a specific health condition (Table 5.10).

Patient ID	Smoking status
1	Non-smoker
2	Smoker
3	Non-smoker
4	Smoker
5	Smoker

Table 5.10: Original dataset

We want to release aggregated statistics on the risk of health conditions for smokers and non-smokers without revealing individual smoking statuses. The following table summarizes the patients with the studied health condition (Table 5.11).

Smoking status	Noisy risk factor	Real risk factor
Non-Smoker	0.3	0.4
Smoker	0.7	0.6

Table 5.11: Risk factor analysis with differential privacy

By adding an appropriate amount of noise (e.g., Laplace noise that averages to 0.1 for smokers and −0.1 for non-smokers), we ensure that DP is preserved while still providing valuable insights into the association between smoking and the risk of developing the health condition without revealing if the smokers in a datasets composed of five individuals are three or four.

DP has emerged as a promising framework for building privacy-preserving RSs [272]. Friedman et al. [143] were among the first to explore applying DP to MF, a common technique in RSs. Their approach adds mathematical noise to the data in a way that guarantees user privacy while still allowing for accurate recommendations. McSherry and Mironov [253] solidify this foundation, demonstrating how DP could be incorporated into existing RS algorithms. Building on this work, Berlioz et al. [50] apply DP to MF and analyze its impact on recommendation accuracy. Shin et al. [357] propose a method that utilizes local DP, a variant that offers additional privacy guarantees. While DP offers strong theoretical foundations, Liu et al. [237] explore combining it with randomized perturbation techniques for a hybrid approach. More recent work by Liu et al. [233] investigates condensed local DP for RSs, while Shen and Jin [354] propose an instance-based approach using DP, where data is obfuscated on user devices, thus providing a user-based DP protection.

5.4 Security in Retrieval and Recommender Systems

As IRRSs become increasingly prevalent and influential in our digital lives, ensuring their security and robustness has emerged as a critical research challenge. This section explores the various security threats faced by IRRSs and the strategies developed to defend against them.

We begin by examining the background and key concepts in IRRS security, including the two primary attack types: *shilling attacks* and *adversarial ML attacks*. However, traditional security approaches for ML classification and regression models do not exactly fit IRRSs. Therefore, specialized security approaches have been proposed. In detail, ML classification models and IR systems share enough similarities to describe together the security approaches applying to both. In fact, the body of literature on security (attacks and defenses) of classification and regression systems is also used for IR systems with slight modifications. In contrast, RSs strongly differ in terms of architecture and security requirements. Even though approaches to security in RSs are inspired from previous ones in the ML literature, they evolved with field-specific adaptions.

Therefore, this section delves into the unique characteristics of IRRSs that differentiate them from traditional classification systems, highlighting why specialized security approaches are necessary. The section continues with (adversarial) empirical risk minimization to give the reader a better understanding and provide them with the fundamental concepts to address adversarial attacks along with a classification of the attacks based on timing, knowledge, and goals. The discussion then progresses to a detailed exploration of adversarial attacks for ML classification and retrieval systems, providing formal definitions and examples of prominent attack strategies. This is followed by an examination of defense mechanisms designed to counteract these threats, including techniques for increasing model robustness and detecting adversarial examples. Finally, the chapter focuses specifically on adversarial attacks and defenses in the context of RSs, showcasing how general security principles are adapted to address the unique challenges posed by CF and user-item interactions.

5.4.1 Background and Preliminaries

The security of IRRSs has been a growing concern for researchers in recent decades. Two primary attack types have emerged: *shilling attacks* and *adversarial machine learning (AML) attacks*.

- **Shilling attacks:** This area focuses on manipulating RSs—this kind of attack is more popular for recommendation systems—through the injection of fabricated user profiles and ratings. Early research explored techniques like *profile injection attacks* where attackers create fake accounts with ratings designed to influence recommendations. These attacks can be categorized as *push attacks* (promoting specific items) or *nuke attacks* (degrading system trust by recommending irrelevant items).
- **Adversarial machine learning attacks:** This more recent area explores manipulating IRRSs using ML techniques. Pioneering works [160, 374] investigate *adversarial perturbations*, i.e., minimal data modifications designed to disrupt the system's underlying statistical assumptions, and steer search results and recommendations toward malicious goals. These attacks often leverage the *data stationary assumption*, i.e., the expectation that the data distribution remains consistent, and aims to disrupt it for manipulation.

A nascent third area combines these approaches: *machine-learned shilling attacks*, using ML to generate more sophisticated and believable fake profiles for shilling attacks. This convergence highlights the evolving nature of recommendation security threats.

Understanding these attack methodologies is crucial for developing robust IRRSs. Shilling attacks exploit user and item similarity patterns, while AML attacks target the system's ML models. By recognizing these vulnerabilities, researchers can design mitigation strategies and build more secure IRRSs that are resistant to manipulation.

While ML for classification, retrieval, and recommendation share similarities, adversarial attacks on IRRSs present unique challenges:

- **Poisoning vs. direct attacks:** Unlike classification and retrieval systems, where attacks often directly manipulate individual data points, RS research has historically focused on shilling attacks, i.e., injecting fabricated user profiles with ratings. In a dataset with N users, a shilling attack injects a fraction of malicious users (denoted by $\alpha \cdot N$, where α is a small value) with ratings for a limited number of items. The goal is to manipulate recommendations toward a specific outcome, like promoting certain items to achieve a competitive market advantage. Shilling attacks have a long history in RS research, with two main development phases. A first research direction focused on hand-crafted fake profiles, following various rating strategies such as random, popular, and bandwagon approaches. Random strategies involve assigning arbitrary ratings to appear more natural and evade detection systems. Popular strategies consistently give high ratings to well-liked items to blend in with genuine users. Bandwagon strategies follow trending opinions or ratings to mimic authentic user behavior. A second direction studies machine-learned shilling attacks, first introduced by Li et al. [221]. This work employed adversarial learning to generate malicious user profiles for poisoning recommendation models. Due to their effectiveness against modern RS models, AML attacks have recently garnered significant research attention.
- **Focus on collaborative filtering:** Classification and retrieval attacks typically aim to manipulate the prediction of a single data point. However, RS attacks leverage CF principles: (1) identifying user similarities based on ratings and (2) generating recommendations. This user-item interdependence results in several unique characteristics. Firstly, it provides *improved robustness*. Predictions rely on user groups rather than individual users, making them less susceptible to single-point manipulation. Secondly, it can lead to *cascade effects*, where attacks on a single user might negatively impact recommendations for similar users. Lastly, RS attacks deal with *discrete data* and face challenges related to *imperceptibility*. Unlike adversarial examples in image classification that leverage the continuous nature of pixel values, RSs deal with discrete data such as user IDs, item IDs, and integer ratings. Perturbing these values can lead to nonsensical data. For example, adding a value to a user ID might create a new, non-existent user, or adding a value to a rating could result in an out-of-range rating. As a result, existing adversarial attacks from general ML cannot be directly applied to RSs. Furthermore, unlike computer vision attacks where perturbations need to be visually inconspicuous, the concept of imperceptibility in the context of RS attacks remains an open challenge.

These unique characteristics highlight the need for specialized adversarial attack methods tailored to the specificities of IRRSs. Therefore, in the following, we first highlight the most important classification and retrieval attacks (Sect. 5.4.2) and defenses (Sect. 5.4.3). Subsequently, we elaborate on common adaptations made in the RS field (respectively, in Sects. 5.4.4 and 5.4.5). Before that, we introduce some fundamental concepts and examples of adversarial attacks in ML.

5.4.1.1 Adversarial Examples

Before discussing security challenges faced by IRRSs, it is crucial to understand the origins and fundamental concepts of adversarial attacks in ML. A pivotal moment in the study of ML security came in 2013 with the work of Szegedy et al. [374]. Their research on adversarial examples opened up a new field of study and highlighted a significant vulnerability in deep neural networks (DNNs) that had previously gone unnoticed. This work laid the foundation for much of the subsequent research in AML, including the attacks and defenses we discuss later in the context of IRRSs

Adversarial examples challenge the robustness of DNNs. Szegedy et al. [374] in 2013 demonstrated that adding carefully chosen, human-imperceptible perturbations to an image can trick a well-trained DNN into misclassifying it with high confidence. Szegedy et al.'s findings can be summarized as follows: First, adding imperceptible noise to an image (e.g., of a panda) can cause a DNN to classify it as something entirely different (e.g., a gibbon). This finding was surprising because DNNs are expected to generalize well on unseen data and resist minor modifications. Furthermore, Szegedy et al. [374] introduced the term "adversarial examples" and proposed an optimization method to generate such perturbations. They initially hypothesized that the culprit was the non-linearity of DNNs.

In 2014, Goodfellow et al. [160] suggested a "counterintuitive hypothesis": the linearity of DNNs, not their non-linearity, might be the key factor in adversarial vulnerability. This "linearity hypothesis" is supported by the fact that DNN training often encourages linear behavior, especially with activation functions like ReLU and MaxOut. Although these functions make models theoretically non-linear, architectural design and training steer them toward the linear region to avoid vanishing gradients. Common strategies to train DNNs include (1) using non-saturating activation functions, (2) adopting weight initializations that enable DNNs to work in not saturating (quasi-linear) regions of the activations functions, or (3) early stopping to stop the training before the model activations begin working in their highly non-linear ranges. To support their hypothesis, Goodfellow et al. demonstrated that linear models [160] can effectively fool DNNs.[19] These findings highlight the vulnerability of DNNs to adversarial examples and the need for further research on robustness in DL.

Several research papers have investigated adversarial attacks and detection in RSs. Cao et al. [68] explore attacks on reinforcement learning-based RSs. Christakopoulou and Banerjee [88] focus on adversarial attacks from an ML perspective. Lin et al. [229] examine methods for attacking RSs with augmented user profiles. Wu et

[19] The interested reader may find more details on this method later in Sect. 5.4.2.2.

al. [416] propose adversarial poisoning training to improve RS robustness. Tang et al. [378] investigate the robustness of multimedia RSs. Additionally, Wu et al. [415] explore triple adversarial learning for mitigating poisoning attacks. Anelli et al. [259] propose a denoising method to strengthen visual RSs against adversaries. Formal analyses studied the recommendation quality of adversarially trained models [32]. Frameworks like ELLIOT [25, 26] facilitate reproducible evaluation. Studies examined adversarial training effects on bias [36]. Adversarial personalized ranking optimization [31] and semantic-aware shilling attacks exploiting knowledge graphs [34] were also proposed.

Recent work has also highlighted the vulnerability of IR systems to adversarial attacks. Prinz et al. [300] present the first work on end-to-end white-box adversarial attacks in MIR systems, specifically targeting instrument classification. Their approach can significantly reduce the accuracy of classifiers by introducing imperceptible modifications to the audio data. This area of research intersects with broader IR concerns. Park and Chang [293] propose adversarial sampling techniques to improve the robustness of IR models. Several studies focus on adversarial attacks against specific retrieval tasks. Parry et al. [294] analyze the impact of adversarial examples on sequence-to-sequence relevance models, while Liu et al. [240] explore topic-oriented attacks against black-box neural ranking models. Recent work by Wu et al. [418] introduces PRADA, a practical black-box attack method for neural ranking models, highlighting the potential real-world implications of these attacks.

5.4.1.2 Empirical Risk Minimization and Adversarial Empirical Risk Minimization

We now focus on a fundamental concept in ML that plays a crucial role in understanding and addressing adversarial attacks: *empirical risk minimization (ERM)* and its adversarial counterpart.

ERM forms the backbone of many supervised learning algorithms, including those used in retrieval and recommendation tasks. However, as we explore in this section, the traditional ERM framework falls short when confronted with adversarial examples, i.e., carefully crafted inputs designed to mislead ML models. To bridge this gap and enhance the robustness of ML systems, researchers have developed *adversarial empirical risk minimization (AERM)*. This approach extends the classical ERM paradigm to account for potential adversarial manipulations of the input data.

In the following, we discuss the mathematical foundations of ERM and AERM, examining how these frameworks are formulated, their objectives, and their key differences. This understanding is crucial as we also explore specific adversarial attacks and defense mechanisms in the context of IRRSs.

In the supervised learning paradigm, we are presented with a training dataset $D = (x_i, y_i)_{i=1}^n$, where each x_i represents a feature vector in the input space and y_i denotes the corresponding label in the output space.

The primary objective of ERM is to minimize the expected risk, also known as the generalization error, of a predictive model. This is achieved by identifying an optimal candidate function $f(x;\theta)$ that minimizes the empirical risk, defined as the average loss incurred on the training dataset.

Despite its effectiveness in optimizing classifiers, ERM does not inherently ensure robustness against adversarial samples. Adversarial examples, crafted with malicious intent, can exploit vulnerabilities in trained models, leading to erroneous predictions.

Contrary to ERM's goal of optimizing model performance across the entire dataset, adversarial attacks focus on manipulating individual data points to induce misclassification. Specifically, these attacks aim to perturb input samples minimally so that the model produces an incorrect output.

Let $f(x;\theta)$ represent a classifier parameterized by θ and (x, y) denote a data point with its true label. An adversary seeks to generate an adversarial example $x_{\text{adv}} = x + \delta$ by introducing a perturbation δ to the original sample x, such that $f(x_{\text{adv}};\theta) \neq f(x;\theta)$. The perturbation δ is constrained to adhere to certain bounds, often quantified by a norm, to limit its magnitude and preserve perceptual similarity.

The classical ERM formulation is insufficient for training models robust against adversarial examples. To achieve robustness, a reformulation of the ERM paradigm is necessary. In adversarial supervised learning, we consider an adversary capable of modifying the training data distribution in a specific way, such as manipulating input features to induce prediction errors.

Equation 5.3 defines the *adversarial empirical risk minimization (AERM)* problem, where $\mathcal{B}$ represents the set of allowed perturbations and $\mathcal{L}$ is the loss function.

$$\min_{\theta} \sup_{\delta \in \mathcal{B}} \mathcal{L}(f(\mathbf{x} + \delta;\theta), y), \tag{5.3}$$

The AERM problem can be viewed as a composite problem: First, the *inner maximization attack* seeks a perturbation δ that maximizes the prediction loss of the model $\mathcal{L}$. As a counterpart, the *outer minimization defense*, representing the defensive strategy, aims to find model parameters θ that minimize the adversarial loss produced by the inner maximization attack.

5.4.1.3 Timing, Knowledge, and Goals of Adversarial Attacks

ML algorithms are susceptible to various attacks, ranging from simple hand-crafted attacks to ML-enhanced attacks, which aim to trick the ML system into making wrong decisions. This section explains how we categorize these attacks based on three key aspects: *timing* (when the attack occurs), *knowledge* (how much information the attacker has about the system), and *goal* (what the attacker wants to achieve).

Timing of the attack: The timing of an attack determines when it disrupts the learning process of the ML system. There are two main categories: evasive attacks and poisoning attacks. *Evasive attacks* target the decisions made by the already trained model. Imagine a spam filter. An evasive attacker might try to modify an email to bypass the filter's detection (like adding typos or changing keywords). In contrast, *poisoning attacks* happen before the model is trained. The attacker adds misleading data (called "poison") to the training data. This can cause the trained model to make biased or incorrect predictions. Imagine training a classifier to recognize cats in images. A poisoning attack might involve adding many pictures of dogs to the training data, confusing the model.

Attacker's knowledge: The attacker's knowledge level of the ML system influences the attack strategy. On one end of the spectrum sits the *perfect-knowledge attacker*, also known as *white-box attacker*, which has complete knowledge of the system, including the learning algorithm and the data used for training. This is the most powerful attack scenario but also the least realistic. The *limited-knowledge attacker*, also known as *gray-box attacker*, might have some insights, such as the type of ML model used or the format of the training data, but not the full picture. To exploit the target model's weaknesses, they may attempt to build a similar system to learn by analogy. Finally, the *zero-knowledge attacker*, also known as *black-box attacker*, has no prior information about the system. This attacker has to interact with the system itself to learn and develop an attack strategy.

Attacker's goals: The attacker's ultimate goal shapes the type of adversarial attack they launch. In a *targeted attack*, the adversary aims to steer the system toward making a specific misclassification, i.e., wrong decision. For example, an attacker might try to manipulate a RS to suggest a particular product to users. In contrast, *untargeted attacks* seek to disrupt the system's overall performance by causing any kind of misclassification, thereby making the system unreliable. Imagine an attacker trying to disrupt a spam filter by modifying emails in unpredictable ways. By understanding these different objectives (i.e., the classification and the attacker's objectives), we can develop more robust defenses to safeguard ML systems from manipulation and ensure they continue to deliver reliable results.

5.4.2 Adversarial Attacks to Classification and Retrieval Systems

This section formally introduces and defines prominent attack and defense strategies used in ML systems, commonly employed in classification and retrieval tasks—image classification is one of the first research fields that scrutinized these attacks [160]—and then adapted for RSs (see Sect. 5.4.4).

Classification, IR, and RSs are all related fields within ML, but they have distinct characteristics that affect how adversarial attacks and defenses apply to them. Classification and IR are often treated together in adversarial attacks because they share some common characteristics: both typically deal with a single input (query or data point) at a time; the adversarial goal is often to manipulate a single prediction or ranking; and finally, continuous input spaces (e.g., text embeddings, image pixels) allow for small, imperceptible perturbations. RSs, however, are treated differently because they rely heavily on the interdependence between users and items. In particular, in CF, attacks can have cascading effects, and the discrete nature of user-item interactions makes traditional perturbation-based attacks less applicable.

Understanding these attacks and developing effective defenses is crucial for ensuring the reliability and security of ML systems. This section outlines adversarial attacks and defenses, focusing on the concept of *adversarial robustness*. We discuss how optimization techniques can be used to train models that are less susceptible to manipulation.

Adversarial attacks target the decision-making process of an ML model. Attackers create slightly modified versions of real data points, called adversarial examples(see Sect. 5.4.1.1 to have a first introduction to adversarial examples). These modifications are often imperceptible to humans but can significantly alter the model's output. Here, we examine three common attack models.

5.4.2.1 Limited-Memory Broyden-Fletcher-Goldfarb-Shanno Attack

The *limited-memory Broyden–Fletcher–Goldfarb–Shanno (L-BFGS) attack* [374] seeks minimally distorted adversarial examples. It formulates an optimization problem, formally given in Eq. 5.4, that minimizes the distortion while maximizing the model's prediction error. L-BFGS leverages the ℓ_2 norm to constrain the magnitude of the modifications, ensuring the adversarial example remains similar to the original data point.

$$\min_{\delta} \quad c \cdot f(x+\delta) - \mathcal{L}(x, y) + \lambda \cdot ||\delta||_2^2 \tag{5.4}$$

This equation represents the optimization problem for generating adversarial examples using L-BFGS. Here, x represents the original input, δ is the perturbation added to x, $f(x+\delta)$ is the prediction made by the model on the adversarial example, $\mathcal{L}(x, y)$ is the (classification or regression) loss function measuring the discrepancy between the predicted output and the true label y, $||\delta||_2^2$ represents the ℓ_2 norm of the perturbation, and c and λ are hyperparameters.

5.4.2.2 Fast Gradient Sign Method

The *fast gradient sign method (FGSM) attack* [160] exploits the linearity of DNNs in high-dimensional space. It utilizes the gradient of the loss function, which indicates how the model's output changes with respect to the input. By taking the sign of the gradient (see Eq. 5.5), FGSM creates an adversarial example in the direction that maximizes the loss function, essentially pushing the input away from the decision boundary. Variants of FGSM include *fast gradient value (FGV)* [326] that uses the actual gradient value, the *basic iterative method (BIM)* [208] (also known as *iterative FGSM*), and the *projected gradient descent (PGD)* [246] approaches that iteratively apply FGSM with small steps for more refined attacks.

$$x_{adv\text{FGSM}} = x + \epsilon \cdot \text{sign}(\nabla_x \mathcal{L}(x, y)) \tag{5.5}$$

This equation represents the FGSM attack, where x is the original input, $x_{adv\text{FGSM}}$ is the adversarial example, ϵ is the perturbation magnitude, $\nabla_x \mathcal{L}(x, y)$ is the gradient of the loss function with respect to the input, and sign(·) denotes taking the sign of each element.

5.4.2.3 Carlini and Wagner (CW-ℓ_0, CW-ℓ_2, CW-ℓ_∞)

The powerful *Carlini and Wagner attack* model [69] finds adversarial perturbations under various distance metrics, like ℓ_0 (number of non-zero elements), ℓ_2 (Euclidean distance), and ℓ_∞ (maximum absolute difference). Similar to L-BFGS, it transforms the constrained problem into an unconstrained one, according to Eq. 5.6, where $f(\cdot)$ is the prediction function.

$$\min_{\delta} \quad ||\delta||_p^p + c \cdot f(x + \delta) \tag{5.6}$$

The most common formulation is CW-ℓ_2 for targeted attacks to misclassify an input into a specific category, given in Eq. 5.7 (here reported for the sake of completeness):

$$\min_{\delta} \quad ||\delta||_2^2 + c \cdot f(x + \delta) \tag{5.7}$$

This equation represents the optimization problem for generating adversarial examples using the CW-ℓ_2 attack. Here, x represents the original input, δ is the perturbation added to x, $||\delta||_2^2$ represents the squared ℓ_2 norm of the perturbation, $f(x + \delta)$ is the prediction made by the model on the adversarial example, and c is a hyperparameter controlling the trade-off between perturbation size and model misclassification.

These attack models showcase adversaries' ingenuity in generating malicious examples. Understanding their techniques is essential for developing robust defenses.

5.4.3 Adversarial Defenses for Classification and Retrieval Systems

There are two main approaches to defending against adversarial attacks to ML systems. First, *increasing model robustness* aims to train models that can correctly classify both clean and adversarial samples. The goal is to make the model less sensitive to irrelevant data variations that attackers might exploit. On the other hand, one can aim at *detecting and rejecting adversarial examples* before they influence the model's output [19, 68, 188]. This approach treats the problem as anomaly detection, identifying data points that deviate significantly from normal patterns.

In retrieval and classification tasks, there are two common techniques for increasing model robustness, through robust optimization and distillation.

Robust optimization is a theoretically grounded framework integrating robustness directly into the learning process. It formulates adversarial robustness as a robust optimization problem, formally given by Eq. 5.8, that seeks to find a model that performs well even under the worst-case scenario of adversarial perturbations:

$$\min_{\theta} \max_{\delta} \mathcal{L}(f(x + \delta; \theta), y) \tag{5.8}$$

where f is the learning model characterized by the parameter θ, δ is the allowed perturbation, and $\mathcal{L}$ is the loss function of the model. For a deeper dive into this topic, consider pioneering research works, such as Szegedy et al.'s [374], and adversarial training by Goodfellow et al. [160], a common approach within this framework. It is a data augmentation technique where the model is exposed to adversarial examples during training. This process can be viewed as solving the inner maximization problem in the robust optimization formulation (see Eq. 5.8). During training, the model not only learns from clean data but also from adversarial examples that it has generated itself. A worst-case loss function is used as a regularization term to achieve a trade-off between robustness on adversarial samples and accuracy on clean data.

Distillation is a heuristic approach aiming to make gradient-based attacks harder. It involves training a smaller, more robust model (student) by learning from the predictions of a larger, more complex model (teacher). By rescaling the output function of the student model, distillation can make gradients unstable, hindering the effectiveness of gradient-based attacks.

5.4.4 Adversarial Attacks in Recommender Systems

In computer vision, adversarial attacks often manipulate loss functions used for image classification tasks, like cross-entropy loss in neural networks. Similarly, attacks on RSs adapt these strategies, exploiting specific loss functions employed in RS tasks. For instance, several studies have scrutinized the robustness of embedding parameters in MF models trained with Bayesian personalized ranking (BPR), a leading ranking-based approach for recommendation. These investigations typically involve introducing perturbations to user embeddings, item embeddings, or both.

One of the pioneering adversarial attacks against RS embedding parameters was proposed by He et al. [169]. They explored the robustness of BPR to perturbations on user and item representations in the latent space. Their approach, inspired by FGSM [160] (see Sect. 5.4.2.2), linearizes the loss function $\mathcal{L}$ around an initial zero-perturbation and applies a max-norm constraint. The adversarial perturbation Δ^{adv} is defined in Eq. 5.9, where $\Pi = \frac{\partial \mathcal{L}(\Theta+\Delta)}{\partial \Delta}$, where Δ is the perturbation, Θ is the current set of model parameters, ϵ controls the magnitude of adversarial perturbations, and $||\cdot||$ denotes the ℓ_2-norm.

$$\Delta^{adv} = \epsilon \cdot \frac{\Pi}{||\Pi||} \tag{5.9}$$

He et al. applied this perturbation to the current model parameters ($\Theta^{adv} = \Theta + \Delta^{adv}$) and observed that small perturbations obtained from FGSM (e.g., $\epsilon = 0.5$) significantly degraded recommendation accuracy.

Building upon this work, subsequent studies have investigated similar perturbations against various recommendation approaches, including visual-based recommenders [378], tensor factorization machines [81], and DL-based models [428, 429]. Analogous to advancements in computer vision, the single-step FGSM attack has been extended to an iterative strategy in the RS domain [208]. This iterative approach refines the perturbation using gradient information, resulting in more effective attacks compared to the single-step FGSM. The effectiveness of multi-step attacks has been demonstrated in weakening state-of-the-art model-based recommenders [208], potentially deteriorating their performance to a level worse than random recommendations.

The Carlini and Wagner attack has also been adapted to RSs by Du et al. [120]. They illustrated its utilization in manipulating the model's performance during the testing phase. Similarly to previous strategies, they tailored Carlini and Wagner's approach to a specific recommender model, i.e., neural collaborative filtering (NCF) in their experiments [170]. The Carlini and Wagner optimization problem (see Eq. 5.6) aims to find an adversarial perturbation with minimal magnitude that significantly alters the model's prediction for a user-item pair. Their findings demonstrated a high success rate in manipulating the predicted relevance of user-item interactions.

These studies underscore the susceptibility of model-based recommenders to even minor adversarial perturbations applied to model parameters. An attacker with access to the model could potentially manipulate recommendations by subtly altering the latent factors. Moreover, these findings raise concerns regarding the stability of model training under real-world conditions. Even slight deviations from intended user behavior during training could lead to significant performance degradation.

5.4.5 Adversarial Defenses in Recommender Systems

Two primary defense mechanisms have been proposed to mitigate adversarial attacks in RSs: adversarial personalized ranking (APR) and stage-wise hints training.

5.4.5.1 Adversarial Personalized Ranking

He et al. [169] introduced *adversarial personalized ranking (APR)*, the first method to modify the classical loss function of a BPR model by incorporating adversarial training. Analogous to adversarial training in computer vision, APR integrates an adversarial regularization term into the loss function, encouraging the model to become more robust to parameter perturbations. This training procedure has been shown to enhance model robustness against FGSM attacks and has been applied to various recommender models, e.g., visual BPR (VBPR [377]), collaborative denoising autoencoder and adversarial collaborative autoencoder (CDAE and ACAE [428, 429]), pairwise interaction tensor factorization (PITF [316]), and adversarial tensor factorization (ATF [81]). Furthermore, adversarial training can improve the model's generalization ability, potentially leading to better recommendation accuracy metrics (e.g., NDCG and HR). Variations of adversarial training, such as flexible ϵ-bounded perturbations [386] and directional adversarial training [424], have been proposed. However, these methods may not be effective against iterative adversarial attacks [24].

5.4.5.2 Stage-Wise Hints Training

Du et al. [120] proposed *stage-wise hints training* as a defensive distillation approach to bolster the robustness of deep recommender models against Carlini and Wagner attacks. Defensive distillation entails training a smaller *student model* to mimic the predictions of a larger, more complex *teacher model*. In this context, the student model learns from the teacher's latent vectors (user and item embeddings) transferred in a stage-wise manner. Additionally, the student model incorporates a noisy layer to further fortify the robustness of its parameters against perturbations. This defense strategy has proven effective in reducing the success rate of Carlini and Wagner [69] attacks compared to an undefended recommendation model.

5.5 Summary and Open Challenges

This chapter explored the relationship between IRRSs and privacy and security, emphasizing their challenges and potential solutions. The critical role of user data in powering these models necessitates finding a balance between optimizing IRRSs' accuracy and protecting user privacy. The chapter highlighted the pressing need for privacy-preserving ML techniques to mitigate the risks associated with data collection and utilization within IRRSs. We emphasized the distinction between privacy-preserving and secure ML, where the former studies how to release collective datasets without putting individual privacy at risk and how to create ML models avoiding malicious agents stealing personal information, while the latter focuses on safeguarding systems against targeted and untargeted attacks. A significant portion of the chapter explored the spectrum of privacy threats plaguing ML and IRRSs. Centralized data repositories introduce vulnerabilities, potentially exposing user data to breaches and unauthorized access. Malicious actors can exploit these vulnerabilities to launch inference attacks, potentially deciphering sensitive user details. We further investigated shilling attacks, a prevalent threat specifically for RSs. These attacks manipulate recommendation algorithms by injecting fabricated rating patterns, aiming to sway recommendations toward specific items or erode user trust in the system. The chapter contrasted hand-crafted shilling attacks with more recent ML-based shilling attacks against IRRSs.

This chapter also laid bare the complexities inherent in trustworthy IRRSs. Some of the open challenges that persist in this domain include the following:

- **How should we balance privacy and accuracy?** A fundamental challenge lies in striking a balance between the personalization achieved through user data and the protection of user privacy [274]. Excessively stringent privacy measures can hamper the accuracy of search results and recommendations, while lax data collection and storage practices raise privacy concerns. Future research should explore methods to optimize recommendation accuracy while minimizing the data required and maximizing user control over their data.
- **Are the numerous privacy-preserving techniques enough?** The landscape of privacy threats constantly evolves, demanding IRRSs to adapt. New data collection techniques (e.g., wearables, brain-computer interfaces, eye-tracking) and user behaviors (i.e., how the user interacts with the system, e.g., scrolling, swiping, touching the screen, talking with an assistant) necessitate the continuous development and refinement of privacy-preserving algorithms and robust defenses against novel attack strategies.
- **How could we put the user in control of the system?** Enhancing user trust in IRRSs necessitates transparency regarding data collection practices and how user data is utilized. Furthermore, empowering users with granular control over their data is paramount. This includes allowing users to opt out of data collection or specific data uses, as well as providing mechanisms for users to access and rectify their data.
- **Can we establish effective regulations shared across countries?** Creating and establishing clear lines of accountability for privacy breaches and data misuse is crucial. Regulatory frameworks need to keep pace with technological advancements, ensuring that IRRSs operate within a responsible and ethical paradigm.
- **How to create more efficient privacy-preserving ML techniques?** As IRRSs become increasingly sophisticated, the need for privacy-preserving ML techniques intensifies. However, cryptography techniques, such as homomorphic encryption [322], are significantly computationally expensive. Further research should explore novel algorithms that can deliver accurate outcomes while minimizing privacy risks and overhead computation.
- **Could we have robust and yet personalized results?** The robustification of ML models against adversarial attacks has been shown to produce accurate but less personalized search and recommendation results. This empirical observation raises the need for new defense strategies that are able to protect the underlying model while preserving a high degree of personalization.

In conclusion, trustworthy IRRSs necessitate a multifaceted approach that prioritizes user privacy and security without compromising the core functionality of these systems. By addressing the open challenges outlined above, researchers and developers can cultivate a future where IRRSs provide users with valuable suggestions while preserving their privacy and the system's security.

5.6 Further Reading

This chapter provided a high-level overview of privacy and security challenges in IRRSs. Due to the vast amount of ongoing research, it obviously could not cover every aspect of the field. Therefore, the following resources offer a deeper dive into specific topics for readers who wish to explore further.

If the reader is interested in the technical details of privacy-preserving algorithms, we summarize an essential list of valuable resources. The reader may also find them in the corresponding sections, but they have also been collected here to ease this task. For federated learning, the foundational paper is [252] by McMahan et al. Diving deeper into specific privacy techniques, Sweeney's work on k-anonymity is a key starting point [373]. Additional concepts to explore include differential privacy [122], ℓ-diversity [245] as an extension of k-anonymity, and t-closeness [225], which builds on those ideas. Finally, while not explicitly mentioned, understanding privacy risks in anonymized data is essential. Addressing this topic, Giomi et al.'s work [157] provides a helpful framework.

For the specific field of RSs, a recent survey has been published by Ogunseyi et al. in [289]. The interested reader may also find an introduction to privacy facets in RSs in the chapter *Privacy Aspects of Recommender Systems* [144] of the 2nd edition of the *Recommender Systems Handbook* [319].

As for security of IRRSs, work on AML offers valuable insights into potential vulnerabilities, many of which apply also to IRRSs. Understanding how attackers might exploit weaknesses in IRRSs allows developers to implement robust defenses. Farooq offers a general survey of adversarial attacks in IR [132], while the interested reader is also invited to explore the recent survey by Deldjoo et al. [33] for RSs. Finally, a detailed overview of attacks and defenses in the context of RSs can be found in chapter *Adversarial Recommender Systems: Attach, Defense, and Advances* [33] of the 3rd edition of the *Recommender Systems Handbook* [320].

Chapter 6
Conclusions and Open Challenges

As we conclude our exploration of bias, fairness, transparency, and privacy aspects of IRRSs, we find ourselves at a crossroads marked by rapid technological advances and the urgent need for ethical guidance. This concluding chapter synthesizes the key themes discussed throughout this work and outlines a roadmap for future research directions in this critical field.

6.1 Summary

In this book, we have explored three vital dimensions of trustworthiness in IRRSs: (1) bias, fairness, and non-discrimination, (2) transparency, and (3) privacy and security. We summarized key regulatory efforts in the EU, the USA, and China for all three dimensions (Chap. 2). While this book has comprehensively covered these three directions, it is essential to note that they represent only a part of the broader framework that comprises seven critical dimensions of trustworthiness in IRRSs.

With respect to *bias, fairness, and non-discrimination* (Chap. 3), we outlined how biases in data and algorithms can lead to unfair outcomes and explored strategies for mitigating these biases to create more unbiased and fair systems. That included discussions on categories of biases and fairness criteria, origins of bias, the role of different stakeholders, and how to identify, measure, and mitigate harmful biases.

Concerning *transparency* (Chap. 4), we outlined the fundamentals and background of transparency and the benefits and challenges. We discussed approaches to enhance transparency and evaluate it in IRRSs. Since transparency in IRRSs is strongly linked to the topic of explanations, we discuss how to create explanations, data sources for explanations, and explanation styles. We concluded the chapter with a discussion on algorithmic auditing as a compliance tool. That involves regular reviews and checks of algorithms to ensure they adhere to ethical standards and regulations, providing a systematic approach to maintain transparency and accountability in IRRSs.

M. Schedl et al., *Technical and Regulatory Perspectives on Information Retrieval and Recommender Systems*, The Information Retrieval Series 50,
https://doi.org/10.1007/978-3-031-69978-8_6

In our discussion of *privacy and security* (Chap. 5), we reflected on privacy risks present in IRRSs. We outlined critical theoretical privacy backgrounds, including federated learning, homomorphic encryption, secure multiparty computation, and differential privacy. We then highlighted security concerns in IRRSs and attack strategies before outlining potential mitigation/defense strategies.

6.2 Open Challenges and Future Research Avenues

Continuing from our exploration of bias, fairness, transparency, and privacy, we recognize that our work is just the beginning of what needs to be a rigorous and ongoing examination of the trustworthiness of IRRSs. In the following, we describe several open challenges and key areas where future research could significantly enhance the current state of the art in IRRSs.

6.2.1 Discrepancy Between Metrics, Human Perception, and Regulations

One of the significant challenges in advancing IRRS technology is the evident discrepancy between measurable metrics of bias, fairness, and diversity and how humans perceive these metrics. While IRRS algorithms can be tuned to optimize such metrics, the subjective assessment of humans might lead to different bias perceptions. For example, users can think they are treated fairly by a IRRS, while the system may still disadvantage certain user groups. That could be particularly true if less visible individuals or groups or less commonly recognized factors, such as regional differences, are not accounted for in the algorithmic design. Also, if mainstream users feel that an IRRS meets their needs, they might not realize that the algorithm does not address the minority group well. Since bias mitigation strategies frequently lead to a trade-off between algorithmic performance and fairness, the majority group could even perceive their experience as compromised when fairness is increased for minority groups. That can make it challenging for system designers to aim to create IRRSs that cater equally to all users. Here, transparency in how results are retrieved or recommendations are generated is critical, and explanations of trade-offs could help communicate the reasoning behind such mitigation efforts.

Another issue is that metrics need to align with regulations and ethical standards. Ensuring that metrics capture both the algorithmic performance and fairness of IRRSs while adhering to ethical and regulatory guidelines is, to date, still an evolving field, on the one hand, since regulatory frameworks often struggle to keep pace with the rapid evolution of AI technologies and, on the other hand, because what is considered fair or unbiased might vary between cultural contexts and legal systems.

6.2.2 Assessing Whether Users Actually Prefer Trustworthy Results

One the one hand, researchers—especially those working on trustworthy IRRSs—aim at making their algorithms and systems as unbiased and transparent as possible. However, the majority of users may care little about these things or even prefer biased results that conform to existing stereotypes, as evidenced, for instance, by Wang et al. [401] in a career recommendation scenario. This may often be the result of deeply rooted societal and cultural norms or beliefs, which are hard to break down. However, it may also be owed to the fact that many users care much more about the relevance and accuracy of results than about bias and fairness. In turn, companies providing IR and RS services are unwilling to increase fairness when this comes at the expense of lower user satisfaction. Also, some users may not want to be distracted by explanations as long as the system provides relevant results to a query or appropriate recommendations. For developers, this means that integrating explanations into their IRRSs should be carefully realized and should perhaps also be adjustable to the preferences and needs of the individual users, i.e., to their preferred level of bias and transparency.

6.2.3 Understanding the Capabilities and Limitations of Existing Solutions

Existing solutions for enhancing fairness, diversity, transparency, and privacy in IRRSs have demonstrated promising results, but they still need improvement. The effectiveness of these solutions can be constrained by the data they are trained on, the specificity of algorithms, and the contexts in which they are applied. Understanding these boundaries is essential for further development and setting realistic stakeholder expectations. This awareness also guides caution in applying these technologies, particularly in high-stakes domains such as employment, finance, and law enforcement.

6.2.4 Taking a Multistakeholder Perspective

Developing solutions that genuinely address the concerns of fairness, diversity, and transparency requires the involvement of multiple stakeholders. That includes the technologists who design and implement IR and RS technology and the end users, policymakers, ethicists, and representatives from affected communities. Each group brings unique perspectives and values, highlighting different aspects of the problem and potential solutions. A collaborative approach ensures that the systems developed are technologically robust, socially responsible, and ethically sound.

6.2.5 Taking an Interdisciplinary Perspective

Effective communication between different stakeholders and bridging the gaps between relevant research communities—computer science, law, ethics, economics, sociology, and psychology—is crucial for fostering interdisciplinarity. These disciplines contribute different methods, theories, and insights, enriching the understanding of and approaches to IR and RS technologies. Enhancing dialog and collaboration across these fields makes it possible to develop comprehensive solutions that are informed by a broader range of knowledge and are more likely to be accepted and effective in diverse social contexts.

In summary, we hope that this book serves as a foundation for those interested in the trustworthiness considerations of IRRSs. We strongly believe that the path forward involves a collaborative, interdisciplinary approach that should engage academics, industry stakeholders, end users, policymakers, and other relevant stakeholders in an interdisciplinary dialog and result in exciting joint efforts to ensure that IRRSs advance in a manner that is both innovative and aligned with broader societal values.

References

[1] B. Abdollahi, O. Nasraoui, Using explainability for constrained matrix factorization, in *Proceedings of the eleventh ACM Conference on Recommender Systems* (2017), pp. 79–83

[2] H. Abdollahpouri, G. Adomavicius, R. Burke, I. Guy, D. Jannach, T. Kamishima, J. Krasnodebski, L.A. Pizzato, Multistakeholder recommendation: Survey and research directions. User Model. User Adapt. Interact. **30**(1), 127–158 (2020)

[3] H. Abdollahpouri, R. Burke, Multi-stakeholder recommendation and its connection to multi-sided fairness, in *Proceedings of the Workshop on Recommendation in Multi-stakeholder Environments co-located with the 13th ACM Conference on Recommender Systems (RecSys 2019), Copenhagen, Denmark, September 20, 2019*, volume 2440 of *CEUR Workshop Proceedings*, ed. by R. Burke, H. Abdollahpouri, E.C. Malthouse, K.P. Thai, Y. Zhang (CEUR-WS.org, 2019)

[4] H. Abdollahpouri, R. Burke, B. Mobasher, Controlling popularity bias in learning-to-rank recommendation, in *Proceedings of the Eleventh ACM Conference on Recommender Systems* (2017), pp. 42–46

[5] H. Abdollahpouri, R. Burke, B. Mobasher, Managing popularity bias in recommender systems with personalized re-ranking (2019), pp. 413–418

[6] H. Abdollahpouri, M. Mansoury, R. Burke, B. Mobasher, The unfairness of popularity bias in recommendation, in *Workshop on Recommendation in Multi-stakeholder Environments (RMSE'19), in conjunction with the 13th ACM Conference on Recommender Systems, RecSys'19* (2019)

[7] H. Abdollahpouri, M. Mansoury, R. Burke, B. Mobasher, The unfairness of popularity bias in recommendation, in *Proceedings of the Workshop on Recommendation in Multi-stakeholder Environments co-located with the 13th ACM Conference on Recommender Systems (RecSys 2019), Copenhagen, Denmark, September 20, 2019*, volume 2440 of *CEUR Workshop Proceedings*, ed. by R. Burke, H. Abdollahpouri, E.C. Malthouse, K.P. Thai, Y. Zhang (CEUR-WS.org, 2019)

M. Schedl et al., *Technical and Regulatory Perspectives on Information Retrieval and Recommender Systems*, The Information Retrieval Series 50,
https://doi.org/10.1007/978-3-031-69978-8

[8] H. Abdollahpouri, M. Mansoury, R. Burke, B. Mobasher, The connection between popularity bias, calibration, and fairness in recommendation, in *Fourteenth ACM Conference on Recommender Systems* (2020), pp. 726–731

[9] H. Abdollahpouri, M. Mansoury, R. Burke, B. Mobasher, E. Malthouse, User-centered evaluation of popularity bias in recommender systems, in *Proceedings of the 29th ACM Conference on User Modeling, Adaptation and Personalization* (2021), pp. 119–129

[10] A. Abolghasemi, S. Verberne, A. Askari, L. Azzopardi, Retrievability bias estimation using synthetically generated queries, in *Proceedings of the 32nd ACM International Conference on Information and Knowledge Management, CIKM 2023, Birmingham, United Kingdom, October 21–25, 2023*, ed. by I. Frommholz, F. Hopfgartner, M. Lee, M. Oakes, M. Lalmas, M. Zhang, R.L.T. Santos (ACM, New York, 2023), pp. 3712–3716

[11] A. Acharya, B. Singh, N. Onoe, LLM based generation of item-description for recommendation system, in *Proceedings of the 17th ACM Conference on Recommender Systems, RecSys 2023, Singapore, Singapore, September 18–22, 2023*, ed. by J. Zhang, L. Chen, S. Berkovsky, M. Zhang, T.D. Noia, J. Basilico, L. Pizzato, Y. Song (ACM, New York, 2023), pp. 1204–1207

[12] Ada health. https://ada.com. Accessed 13 Feb 2024

[13] G. Adomavicius, J. Bockstedt, S. Curley, J. Zhang, Recommender systems, consumer preferences, and anchoring effects, in *RecSys 2011 Workshop on Human Decision Making in Recommender Systems* (2011), pp. 35–42

[14] D. Afchar, A.B. Melchiorre, M. Schedl, R. Hennequin, E.V. Epure, M. Moussallam, Explainability in music recommender systems (2022). arXiv preprint arXiv:2201.10528

[15] A.H. Afridi, Transparency for beyond-accuracy experiences: a novel user interface for recommender systems. Proc. Comput. Sci. **151**, 335–344 (2019)

[16] C.C. Aggarwal, *Recommender Systems—The Textbook* (Springer, Berlin, 2016)

[17] S.S. Ahila, K.L. Shunmuganathan, Role of agent technology in web usage mining: homomorphic encryption based recommendation for e-commerce applications. Wirel. Pers. Commun. **87**(2), 499–512 (2016)

[18] M.S. Aksoy, A review of rules family of algorithms. Math. Comput. Appl. **13**(1), 51–60 (2008)

[19] A. Aldahdooh, W. Hamidouche, S.A. Fezza, O. Déforges, Adversarial example detection for DNN models: a review and experimental comparison. Artif. Intell. Rev. **55**(6), 4403–4462 (2022)

[20] W. Ali, R. Kumar, Z. Deng, Y. Wang, J. Shao, A federated learning approach for privacy protection in context-aware recommender systems. Comput. J. **64**(7), 1016–1027 (2021)

[21] E. Amigó, Y. Deldjoo, S. Mizzaro, A. Bellogín, A unifying and general account of fairness measurement in recommender systems. Inf. Process. Manag. **60**(1), 103115 (2023)

[22] A. Anand, L. Lyu, M. Idahl, Y. Wang, J. Wallat, Z. Zhang, Explainable information retrieval: a survey (2022). arXiv preprint arXiv:2211.02405

[23] A. Anand, P. Sen, S. Saha, M. Verma, M. Mitra, Explainable information retrieval, in *Proceedings of the 46th International ACM SIGIR Conference on Research and Development in Information Retrieval* (2023), pp. 3448–3451

[24] V.W. Anelli, A. Bellogín, Y. Deldjoo, T.D. Noia, F.A. Merra, MSAP: multi-step adversarial perturbations on recommender systems embeddings, in *Proceedings of the Thirty-Fourth International Florida Artificial Intelligence Research Society Conference, North Miami Beach, Florida, USA, May 17–19, 2021*, ed. by E. Bell, F. Keshtkar (2021)

[25] V.W. Anelli, A. Bellogín, A. Ferrara, D. Malitesta, F.A. Merra, C. Pomo, F.M. Donini, T.D. Noia, Elliot: a comprehensive and rigorous framework for reproducible recommender systems evaluation, in *SIGIR '21: The 44th International ACM SIGIR Conference on Research and Development in Information Retrieval, Virtual Event, Canada, July 11–15, 2021*, ed. by F. Diaz, C. Shah, T. Suel, P. Castells, R. Jones, T. Sakai (ACM, New York, 2021), pp. 2405–2414

[26] V.W. Anelli, A. Bellogín, A. Ferrara, D. Malitesta, F.A. Merra, C. Pomo, F.M. Donini, T.D. Noia, V-elliot: design, evaluate and tune visual recommender systems, in *RecSys '21: Fifteenth ACM Conference on Recommender Systems, Amsterdam, The Netherlands, 27 September 2021–1 October 2021*, ed. by H. J. C. Pampín, M. A. Larson, M. C. Willemsen, J. A. Konstan, J. J. McAuley, J. Garcia-Gathright, B. Huurnink, and E. Oldridge (ACM, New York, 2021), pp. 768–771

[27] V.W. Anelli, Y. Deldjoo, T.D. Noia, A. Ferrara, Towards effective device-aware federated learning, in *AI*IA 2019—Advances in Artificial Intelligence—XVIIIth International Conference of the Italian Association for Artificial Intelligence, Rende, Italy, November 19–22, 2019, Proceedings*, volume 11946 of Lecture Notes in Computer Science, ed. by M. Alviano, G. Greco, F. Scarcello (Springer, Berlin, 2019), pp. 477–491

[28] V.W. Anelli, Y. Deldjoo, T.D. Noia, A. Ferrara, Prioritized multi-criteria federated learning. Intelligenza Artificiale **14**(2), 183–200 (2020)

[29] V.W. Anelli, Y. Deldjoo, T.D. Noia, A. Ferrara, F. Narducci, FedeRank: user controlled feedback with federated recommender systems, in *Advances in Information Retrieval—43rd European Conference on IR Research, ECIR 2021, Virtual Event, March 28–April 1, 2021, Proceedings, Part I*, volume 12656 of Lecture Notes in Computer Science, ed. by D. Hiemstra, M. Moens, J. Mothe, R. Perego, M. Potthast, F. Sebastiani (Springer, Berlin, 2021), pp. 32–47

[30] V.W. Anelli, Y. Deldjoo, T.D. Noia, A. Ferrara, F. Narducci, User-controlled federated matrix factorization for recommender systems. J. Intell. Inf. Syst. **58**(2), 287–309 (2022)

[31] V.W. Anelli, Y. Deldjoo, T.D. Noia, D. Malitesta, F.A. Merra, A study of defensive methods to protect visual recommendation against adversarial manipulation of images, in *SIGIR '21: The 44th International ACM SIGIR Conference on Research and Development in Information Retrieval, Virtual Event,*

Canada, July 11–15, 2021, ed. by F. Diaz, C. Shah, T. Suel, P. Castells, R. Jones, T. Sakai (ACM, 2021), pp. 1094–1103

[32] V.W. Anelli, Y. Deldjoo, T.D. Noia, F.A. Merra, A formal analysis of recommendation quality of adversarially-trained recommenders, in *CIKM '21: The 30th ACM International Conference on Information and Knowledge Management, Virtual Event, Queensland, Australia, November 1–5, 2021*, ed. by G. Demartini, G. Zuccon, J. S. Culpepper, Z. Huang, and H. Tong (ACM, New York, 2021), pp. 2852–2856

[33] V.W. Anelli, Y. Deldjoo, T.D. Noia, F.A. Merra, Adversarial recommender systems: Attack, defense, and advances, in *Recommender Systems Handbook*, ed. by F. Ricci, L. Rokach, B. Shapira (Springer, New York, 2022)

[34] V.W. Anelli, Y. Deldjoo, T.D. Noia, E.D. Sciascio, F.A. Merra, Sasha: semantic-aware shilling attacks on recommender systems exploiting knowledge graphs, in *The Semantic Web—17th International Conference, ESWC 2020, Heraklion, Crete, Greece, May 31–June 4, 2020, Proceedings* (2020), pp. 307–323

[35] V.W. Anelli, S. Kalloori, B. Ferwerda, L. Belli, A. Tejani, F. Portman, A. Lung-Yut-Fong, B. Chamberlain, Y. Xie, J. Hunt, M.M. Bronstein, W. Shi, Recsys 2021 challenge workshop: Fairness-aware engagement prediction at scale on twitter's home timeline, in *RecSys '21: Fifteenth ACM Conference on Recommender Systems, Amsterdam, The Netherlands, 27 September 2021–1 October 2021*, ed. by H.J.C. Pampín, M.A. Larson, M.C. Willemsen, J.A. Konstan, J.J. McAuley, J. Garcia-Gathright, B. Huurnink, E. Oldridge (ACM, New York, 2021), pp. 819–824

[36] V.W. Anelli, T.D. Noia, F.A. Merra, The idiosyncratic effects of adversarial training on bias in personalized recommendation learning, in *RecSys '21: Fifteenth ACM Conference on Recommender Systems, Amsterdam, The Netherlands, 27 September 2021–1 October 2021*, ed. by H.J.C. Pampín, M.A. Larson, M.C. Willemsen, J.A. Konstan, J.J. McAuley, J. Garcia-Gathright, B. Huurnink, E. Oldridge (ACM, New York, 2021), pp. 730–735

[37] J. Anthis, K. Lum, M. Ekstrand, A. Feller, A. D'Amour, C. Tan, The impossibility of fair LLMs, 2024

[38] L. Azzopardi, Cognitive biases in search: a review and reflection of cognitive biases in information retrieval, in *CHIIR '21: ACM SIGIR Conference on Human Information Interaction and Retrieval, Canberra, ACT, Australia, March 14–19, 2021*, ed. by F. Scholer, P. Thomas, D. Elsweiler, H. Joho, N. Kando, C. Smith (ACM, 2021), pp. 27–37

[39] S. Badsha, X. Yi, I. Khalil, E. Bertino, Privacy preserving user-based recommender system, in *37th IEEE International Conference on Distributed Computing Systems, ICDCS 2017, Atlanta, GA, USA, June 5–8, 2017*, ed. by K. Lee, L. Liu (IEEE Computer Society, 2017), pp. 1074–1083

[40] R. Baeza-Yates, Bias on the web. Commun. ACM **61**(6), 54–61 (2018)

[41] R. Baeza-Yates, B. A. Ribeiro-Neto, *Modern Information Retrieval—The Concepts and Technology Behind Search*, 2nd edn. (Pearson Education, Harlow, 2011)

[42] N. Balasubramaniam, M. Kauppinen, A. Rannisto, K. Hiekkanen, S. Kujala, Transparency and explainability of ai systems: from ethical guidelines to requirements. Inform. Softw. Technol. **159**, 107197 (2023)
[43] G. Balloccu, L. Boratto, G. Fenu, F.M. Malloci, M. Marras, Explainable recommender systems with knowledge graphs and language models, in *European Conference on Information Retrieval* (Springer, Berlin, 2024), pp. 352–357
[44] K. Balog, F. Radlinski, S. Arakelyan, Transparent, scrutable and explainable user models for personalized recommendation, in *Proceedings of the 42nd International ACM SIGIR Conference on Research and Development in Information Retrieval* (2019), pp. 265–274
[45] J. Bandy, Problematic machine behavior: a systematic literature review of algorithm audits (2021)
[46] J. Barria-Pineda, Exploring the need for transparency in educational recommender systems, in *Proceedings of the 28th ACM Conference on User Modeling, Adaptation and Personalization* (2020)
[47] C. Bauer, M. Schedl, Global and country-specific mainstreaminess measures: definitions, analysis, and usage for improving personalized music recommendation systems. PloS One **14**(6), e0217389 (2019)
[48] V. Bellini, A. Schiavone, T. Di Noia, A. Ragone, E. Di Sciascio, Knowledge-aware autoencoders for explainable recommender systems, in *Proceedings of the 3rd Workshop on Deep Learning for Recommender Systems* (2018), pp. 24–31
[49] A. Bellogín, A. Said, Improving accountability in recommender systems research through reproducibility. User Model. User-Adapt. Interact. **31**(5), 941–977 (2021)
[50] A. Berlioz, A. Friedman, M.A. Kâafar, R. Boreli, S. Berkovsky, Applying differential privacy to matrix factorization, in *Proceedings of the 9th ACM Conference on Recommender Systems, RecSys 2015, Vienna, Austria, September 16–20, 2015*, ed. by H. Werthner, M. Zanker, J. Golbeck, G. Semeraro (ACM, New York, 2015), pp. 107–114
[51] N. Bernard, K. Balog, A systematic review of fairness, accountability, transparency and ethics in information retrieval. ACM Comput. Surv. (2023)
[52] H. Bharadhwaj, Layer-wise relevance propagation for explainable recommendations (2018). arXiv preprint arXiv:1807.06160
[53] M. Bilgic, R.J. Mooney, Explaining recommendations: satisfaction vs. promotion, in *Beyond Personalization Workshop, IUI*, vol. 5 (2005), p. 153
[54] J. Black, P. Esch, Ai-enabled recruiting: what is it and how should a manager use it? Bus. Horizons **63**, 215–226 (2020)
[55] E. Bokányi, A. Hannák, Understanding inequalities in ride-hailing services through simulations. Sci. Rep. **10**(1), 1–11 (2020)
[56] E. Bonilla-Silva, *Racism Without Racists: Color-Blind Racism and the Persistence of Racial Inequality in the United States* (Rowman & Littlefield Publishers, 2006)
[57] G. Bonnin, D. Jannach, Automated generation of music playlists: survey and experiments. ACM Comput. Surv. **47**(2), 26:1–26:35 (2014)

[58] L. Boratto, G. Fenu, M. Marras, Connecting user and item perspectives in popularity debiasing for collaborative recommendation. Inf. Process. Manag. **58**(1), 102387 (2021)

[59] C. Bove, J. Aigrain, M.-J. Lesot, C. Tijus, M. Detyniecki, Contextualization and exploration of local feature importance explanations to improve understanding and satisfaction of non-expert users, in *Proceedings of the 27th international conference on intelligent user interfaces* (2022), pp. 807–819

[60] J.K. Bower, S. Patel, J.E. Rudy, A.S. Felix, Addressing bias in electronic health record-based surveillance of cardiovascular disease risk: finding the signal through the noise. Curr. Epidemiol. Rep. **4**, 346–352 (2017)

[61] I. Burke, R. Burke, G. Kuljanin, Fair candidate ranking with spatial partitioning: lessons from the SIOP ML competition, in *Proceedings of the First Workshop on Recommender Systems for Human Resources (RecSys in HR 2021) Co-located with the 15th ACM Conference on Recommender Systems (RecSys 2021)*, vol. 2967 (CEUR-WS, 2021)

[62] R. Burke, H. Abdollahpouri, E.C. Malthouse, K.P. Thai, Y. Zhang, Recommendation in multistakeholder environments, in *Proceedings of the 13th ACM Conference on Recommender Systems, RecSys 2019, Copenhagen, Denmark, September 16–20, 2019*, ed. by T. Bogers, A. Said, P. Brusilovsky, D. Tikk (ACM, New York, 2019), pp. 566–567

[63] J. Burrell, How the machine 'thinks': understanding opacity in machine learning algorithms. Big Data Soc. **3**(1), 2053951715622512 (2016)

[64] D. Cai, Y. Wang, L. Liu, S. Shi, Recent advances in retrieval-augmented text generation, in *SIGIR '22: The 45th International ACM SIGIR Conference on Research and Development in Information Retrieval, Madrid, Spain, July 11–15, 2022*, ed.. by E. Amigó, P. Castells, J. Gonzalo, B. Carterette, J. S. Culpepper, G. Kazai (ACM, New York, 2022), pp. 3417–3419

[65] I. Calzada, Citizens' data privacy in China: the state of the art of the personal information protection law (PIPL). Smart Cities **5**(3), 1129–1150 (2022)

[66] California consumer privacy act (CCPA). https://cloud.google.com/security/compliance/ccpa. Accessed 13 Feb 2024

[67] California privacy protection agency. https://cppa.ca.gov/. Accessed 13 Feb 2024

[68] Y. Cao, X. Chen, L. Yao, X. Wang, W.E. Zhang, Adversarial attacks and detection on reinforcement learning-based interactive recommender systems, in *Proceedings of the 43rd International ACM SIGIR conference on research and development in Information Retrieval, SIGIR 2020, Virtual Event, China, July 25–30, 2020*, ed. by J. Huang, Y. Chang, X. Cheng, J. Kamps, V. Murdock, J. Wen, Y. Liu (ACM, New York, 2020), pp. 1669–1672

[69] N. Carlini, D.A. Wagner, Towards evaluating the robustness of neural networks, in *IEEE Symposium on Security and Privacy* (IEEE Computer Society, 2017), pp. 39–57

[70] M. Caro-Martínez, G. Jiménez-Díaz, J. A. Recio-García, Conceptual modeling of explainable recommender systems: an ontological formalization to guide their design and development. J. Artif. Intell. Res. **71**, 557–589 (2021)

[71] F. Casino, J. Domingo-Ferrer, C. Patsakis, D. Puig, A. Solanas, Privacy preserving collaborative filtering with k-anonymity through microaggregation, in *IEEE 10th International Conference on e-Business Engineering, ICEBE 2013, Coventry, United Kingdom, September 11–13, 2013*, (IEEE Computer Society, 2013), pp. 490–497

[72] CCPA transparency chart. https://iapp.org/resources/article/cacpa-what-to-disclose-and-where-to-disclose-it/. Accessed 13 Feb 2024

[73] L.E. Celis, D. Straszak, N.K. Vishnoi, Ranking with fairness constraints, in *45th International Colloquium on Automata, Languages, and Programming, ICALP 2018, July 9–13, 2018, Prague, Czech Republic*, volume 107 of LIPIcs, ed. by I. Chatzigiannakis, C. Kaklamanis, D. Marx, D. Sannella (Schloss Dagstuhl-Leibniz-Zentrum für Informatik, 2018), pp. 28:1–28:15

[74] Ò. Celma, *Music Recommendation and Discovery—The Long Tail, Long Fail, and Long Play in the Digital Music Space* (Springer, Berlin, 2010)

[75] G.B. Chapman, E.J. Johnson, Incorporating the irrelevant: Anchors in judgments of belief and value, in *Heuristics and Biases: The Psychology of Intuitive Judgment* (2002), pp. 120–138

[76] Charter of Fundamental Rights of the European Union. https://eur-lex.europa.eu/legal-content/EN/TXT/PDF/?uri=CELEX:12012P/TXT. Accessed 13 Mar 2024

[77] M.A. Chatti, M. Guesmi, A. Muslim, Visualization for recommendation explainability: a survey and new perspectives. ACM Trans. Interact. Intell. Syst. **14**(3), 1–40 (2024)

[78] H.A. Chaudhari, S. Lin, O. Linda, A general framework for fairness in multistakeholder recommendations (2020). CoRR, abs/2009.02423

[79] Y.-K. Che, J. Hörner, Recommender systems as mechanisms for social learning. Q. J. Econ. **133**(2), 871–925 (2018)

[80] C. Chen, M. Zhang, Y. Liu, S. Ma, Neural attentional rating regression with review-level explanations, in *Proceedings of the 2018 World Wide Web Conference* (2018), pp. 1583–1592

[81] H. Chen, J. Li, Adversarial tensor factorization for context-aware recommendation, in *RecSys* (ACM, New York, 2019), pp. 363–367

[82] J. Chen, H. Dong, X. Wang, F. Feng, M. Wang, X. He, Bias and debias in recommender system: a survey and future directions. ACM Trans. Inf. Syst. **41**(3), 67:1–67:39 (2023)

[83] J. Chen, J. Sun, Understanding the chinese data security law. Int. Cybersecur. Law Rev. **2**(2), 209–221 (2021)

[84] J. Chen, F. Zhuang, X. Hong, X. Ao, X. Xie, Q. He, Attention-driven factor model for explainable personalized recommendation, in *The 41st International ACM SIGIR Conference on Research & Development in Information Retrieval* (2018), pp. 909–912

[85] Q. Chen, T. Zhang, M. Nie, Z. Wang, S. Xu, W. Shi, Z. Cao, Fashion-GPT: integrating LLMs with fashion retrieval system, in *Proceedings of the 1st Workshop on Large Generative Models Meet Multimodal Applications, LGM3A*

2023, Ottawa ON, Canada, 2 November 2023, ed. by Z. Wang, C. Long, S. Xu, B. Gan, W. Shi, Z. Cao, T. Chua (ACM, New York, 2023), pp. 69–78
[86] X. Chen, Z. Qin, Y. Zhang, T. Xu, Learning to rank features for recommendation over multiple categories, in *Proceedings of the 39th International ACM SIGIR Conference on Research and Development in Information Retrieval* (2016), pp. 305–314
[87] X. Cheng, D. Luo, X. Chen, L. Liu, D. Zhao, R. Yan, Lift yourself up: retrieval-augmented text generation with self-memory, in *Advances in Neural Information Processing Systems 36: Annual Conference on Neural Information Processing Systems 2023, NeurIPS 2023, New Orleans, LA, USA, December 10–16, 2023*, ed. by A. Oh, T. Naumann, A. Globerson, K. Saenko, M. Hardt, S. Levine (2023)
[88] K. Christakopoulou, A. Banerjee, Adversarial attacks on an oblivious recommender, in *Proceedings of the 13th ACM Conference on Recommender Systems, RecSys 2019, Copenhagen, Denmark, September 16–20, 2019* (2019), pp. 322–330
[89] F. Christof, Diese sexistischen Antworten liefert der KI-Chatbot des AMS (2024). https://futurezone.at/digital-life/chatbot-ams-chatgpt-berufsinfomat-kritik-sexismus-stereotype-kosten-mangel/402729334.
[90] C. Chronis, I. Varlamis, Y. Himeur, A.N. Sayed, T. M. Al-Hasan, A. Nhlabatsi, F. Bensaali, G. Dimitrakopoulos, A survey on the use of federated learning in privacy-preserving recommender systems. IEEE Open J. Comput. Soc. **5**, 227–247 (2024)
[91] A. Collins, D. Tkaczyk, A. Aizawa, J. Beel, A study of position bias in digital library recommender systems (2018). CoRR, abs/1802.06565
[92] S. Costanza-Chock, I. D. Raji, J. Buolamwini, Who audits the auditors? Recommendations from a field scan of the algorithmic auditing ecosystem, in *2022 ACM Conference on Fairness, Accountability, and Transparency* (2022)
[93] H. Cramer, V. Evers, S. Ramlal, M. Someren, L. Rutledge, N. Stash, L. Aroyo, B. Wielinga, The effects of transparency on trust in and acceptance of a content-based art recommender. User Model. User-Adapt. Interact. **18**, 455–496 (2008)
[94] H. Cramer, V. Evers, S. Ramlal, M. Someren, L. Rutledge, N. Stash, L. Aroyo, B. Wielinga, The effects of transparency on trust in and acceptance of a content-based art recommender. User Model. User-Adapt. Interact. **18**, 455–496 (2008)
[95] H. Cramer, V. Evers, S. Ramlal, M. Van Someren, L. Rutledge, N. Stash, L. Aroyo, B. Wielinga, The effects of transparency on trust in and acceptance of a content-based art recommender. User Model. User-Adapt. Interact. **18**(5), 455 (2008)
[96] N. Craswell, B. Mitra, E. Yilmaz, D. Campos, E.M. Voorhees, Overview of the TREC 2019 deep learning track (2020). CoRR, abs/2003.07820
[97] N. Craswell, O. Zoeter, M. J. Taylor, B. Ramsey, An experimental comparison of click position-bias models, in *Proceedings of the International Conference on Web Search and Web Data Mining, WSDM 2008, Palo Alto, California,*

USA, February 11–12, 2008, ed. by M. Najork, A.Z. Broder, S. Chakrabarti (ACM, New York, 2008), pp. 87–94

[98] K.A. Creel, Transparency in complex computational systems. Philos. Sci. **87**, 568–589 (2020)

[99] R. Creemers, China's emerging data protection framework, J. Cybersecur. **8**(1), tyac011 (2022)

[100] P. Cremonesi, F. Garzotto, R. Pagano, M. Quadrana, Recommending without short head, in *23rd International World Wide Web Conference, WWW '14, Seoul, Republic of Korea, April 7–11, 2014, Companion Volume*, ed. by C. Chung, A.Z. Broder, K. Shim, T. Suel (ACM, New York, 2014), pp. 245–246

[101] R.G. Crowder, *Principles of Learning and Memory: Classic Edition* (Psychology Press, 2014)

[102] T. Dalenius, Finding a needle in a haystack or identifying anonymous census records. J. Official Stat. **2**(3), 329–336 (1986)

[103] K. Daniel, *Thinking, Fast and Slow* (2017)

[104] A. Dash, A. Chakraborty, S. Ghosh, A. Mukherjee, K.P. Gummadi, Fairir: mitigating exposure bias from related item recommendations in two-sided platforms. IEEE Trans. Comput. Soc. Syst. **10**(3), 1301–1313 (2023)

[105] J. Dastin, Amazon scraps secret AI recruiting tool that showed bias against women, in *Ethics of Data and Analytics* (Auerbach Publications, 2018), pp. 296–299

[106] F. Daucê, B. Loveluck, Codes of conduct for algorithmic news recommendation: the yandex.news controversy in Russia. First Monday (2021)

[107] C. de Ruijt, S. Bhulai, Job recommender systems: a review (2021). CoRR, abs/2111.13576

[108] J. Deese, R.A. Kaufman, Serial effects in recall of unorganized and sequentially organized verbal material. J. Exp. Psychol. **54**(3), 180 (1957)

[109] R. Deffayet, T. Thonet, J. Renders, M. de Rijke, Generative slate recommendation with reinforcement learning, in *Proceedings of the Sixteenth ACM International Conference on Web Search and Data Mining, WSDM 2023, Singapore, 27 February 2023–3 March 2023*, ed. by T. Chua, H.W. Lauw, L. Si, E. Terzi, P. Tsaparas (ACM, New York, 2023), pp. 580–588

[110] Y. Deldjoo, D. Jannach, A. Bellogin, A. Difonzo, D. Zanzonelli, Fairness in recommender systems: research landscape and future directions. User Model. User-Adapt. Interact. **34**(1), 59–108 (2024)

[111] S. Delecraz, L. Eltarr, M. Becuwe, H. Bouxin, N. Boutin, O. Oullier, Making recruitment more inclusive: Unfairness monitoring with a job matching machine-learning algorithm, in *Proceedings of the 2nd International Workshop on Equitable Data and Technology*, FairWare '22 (Association for Computing Machinery, New York, 2022), pp. 34–41

[112] P. Delobelle, B. Berendt, Fairdistillation: mitigating stereotyping in language models, in *Machine Learning and Knowledge Discovery in Databases—European Conference, ECML PKDD 2022, Grenoble, France, September 19–23, 2022, Proceedings, Part II*, volume 13714 of Lecture Notes in Com-

puter Science, ed. by M. Amini, S. Canu, A. Fischer, T. Guns, P.K. Novak, G. Tsoumakas (Springer, Berlin, 2022), pp. 638–654

[113] Z.-H. Deng, L. Huang, C.-D. Wang, J.-H. Lai, S. Y. Philip, Deepcf: a unified framework of representation learning and matching function learning in recommender system, in *Proceedings of the AAAI Conference on Artificial Intelligence*, vol. 33 (2019), pp. 61–68

[114] L. Determann, J. Tam, The California privacy rights act of 2020: a broad and complex data processing regulation that applies to businesses worldwide. J. Data Protect. Privacy **4**(1), 7–21 (2020)

[115] J. Devlin, M. Chang, K. Lee, K. Toutanova, BERT: pre-training of deep bidirectional transformers for language understanding, in *Proceedings of the 2019 Conference of the North American Chapter of the Association for Computational Linguistics: Human Language Technologies, NAACL-HLT 2019, Minneapolis, MN, USA, June 2–7, 2019, Volume 1 (Long and Short Papers)*, ed. by J. Burstein, C. Doran, T. Solorio (Association for Computational Linguistics, 2019), pp. 4171–4186

[116] T. Di Noia, N. Tintarev, P. Fatourou, M. Schedl, Recommender systems under European ai regulations. Commun. ACM **65**(4), 69–73 (2022)

[117] D. Di Palma, Retrieval-augmented recommender system: enhancing recommender systems with large language models, in *Proceedings of the 17th ACM Conference on Recommender Systems, RecSys 2023, Singapore, Singapore, September 18–22, 2023*, ed. by J. Zhang, L. Chen, S. Berkovsky, M. Zhang, T.D. Noia, J. Basilico, L. Pizzato, Y. Song (ACM, New York, 2023), pp. 1369–1373

[118] V. Do, S. Corbett-Davies, J. Atif, N. Usunier, Online certification of preference-based fairness for personalized recommender systems. Proc. AAAI Conf. Artif. Intell. **36**, 6532–6540 (2022)

[119] R. Dobelli, *The Art of Thinking Clearly: Better Thinking, Better Decisions* (Hachette UK, 2013)

[120] Y. Du, M. Fang, J. Yi, C. Xu, J. Cheng, D. Tao, Enhancing the robustness of neural collaborative filtering systems under malicious attacks. IEEE Trans. Multimedia **21**(3), 555–565 (2019)

[121] R. Dwivedi, D. Dave, H. Naik, S. Singhal, R. Omer, P. Patel, B. Qian, Z. Wen, T. Shah, G. Morgan, et al., Explainable ai (xai): core ideas, techniques, and solutions. ACM Comput. Surv. **55**(9), 1–33 (2023)

[122] C. Dwork, Differential privacy, in *Automata, Languages and Programming, 33rd International Colloquium, ICALP 2006, Venice, Italy, July 10–14, 2006, Proceedings, Part II*, volume 4052 of Lecture Notes in Computer Science, ed. by M. Bugliesi, B. Preneel, V. Sassone, I. Wegener (Springer, Berlin, 2006), pp. 1–12

[123] J.L. Eberhardt, *Biased: Uncovering the Hidden Prejudice that Shapes What We See, Think, and Do* (Penguin, 2020)

[124] D.M. Eddy, W. Hollingworth, J.J. Caro, J. Tsevat, K.M. McDonald, J. B. Wong, Model transparency and validation: a report of the ISPOR-SMDM

modeling good research practices task force-7. Med. Decis. Making **32**, 733–743 (2012)

[125] S. Eide, D.S. Leslie, A. Frigessi, Dynamic slate recommendation with gated recurrent units and Thompson sampling. Data Min. Knowl. Discov. **36**(5), 1756–1786 (2022)

[126] M.D. Ekstrand, A. Das, R. Burke, F. Diaz, Fairness in information access systems. Found. Trends® Inform. Retrieval **16**(1–2), 1–177 (2022)

[127] A. Epps-Darling, H. Cramer, R. T. Bouyer, Artist gender representation in music streaming, in *Proceedings of the 21th International Society for Music Information Retrieval Conference, ISMIR 2020, Montreal, Canada, October 11–16, 2020*, ed. by J. Cumming, J.H. Lee, B. McFee, M. Schedl, J. Devaney, C. McKay, E. Zangerle, T. de Reuse (2020), pp. 248–254

[128] Z. Erkin, T. Veugen, T. Toft, R.L. Lagendijk, Generating private recommendations efficiently using homomorphic encryption and data packing. IEEE Trans. Inf. Forensics Secur. **7**(3), 1053–1066 (2012)

[129] G. Escobedo, M. Moscati, P. Muellner, S. Kopeinik, D. Kowald, E. Lex, M. Schedl, Making alice appear like bob: a probabilistic preference obfuscation method for implicit feedback recommendation models, in *Machine Learning and Knowledge Discovery in Databases. Research Track*, ed. by A. Bifet, J. Davis, T. Krilavičius, M. Kull, E. Ntoutsi, I. Žliobaitė (Springer, Cham, 2024), pp. 349–365

[130] M. Fabbri, How and to which extent will the provisions of the digital services act of the European union impact on the relationship between users and platforms as information providers? in *Proceedings of the 2023 AAAI/ACM Conference on AI, Ethics, and Society* (2023)

[131] W. Fan, X. Zhao, X. Chen, J. Su, J. Gao, L. Wang, Q. Liu, Y. Wang, H. Xu, L. Chen, Q. Li, A comprehensive survey on trustworthy recommender systems (2022). CoRR, abs/2209.10117

[132] S. Farooq, A survey on adversarial information retrieval on the web (2019). CoRR, abs/1911.11060

[133] Z. Fatemi, C. Xing, W. Liu, C. Xiong, Improving gender fairness of pre-trained language models without catastrophic forgetting, in *Proceedings of the 61st Annual Meeting of the Association for Computational Linguistics (Volume 2: Short Papers), ACL 2023, Toronto, Canada, July 9–14, 2023*, ed. by A. Rogers, J.L. Boyd-Graber, N. Okazaki (Association for Computational Linguistics, 2023), pp. 1249–1262

[134] Federal trade commission (FTC) act (15 u.s.c. art. 45). https://www.law.cornell.edu/wex/ftc. Accessed 26 June 2024

[135] A. Felfernig, N. Tintarev, T. N. T. Tran, M. Stettinger, Designing explanations for group recommender systems (2021). ArXiv, abs/2102.12413

[136] A. Felfernig, N. Tintarev, T. N. Trang Tran, M. Stettinger, Explanations for groups, in *Group Recommender Systems: An Introduction* (Springer, Berlin, 2023), pp. 109–131

[137] M.R. Fernandes, Confirmation bias in social networks. Math. Soc. Sci. **123**, 59–76 (2023)

[138] Z.T. Fernando, J. Singh, A. Anand, A study on the interpretability of neural retrieval models using DeepSHAP, in *Proceedings of the 42nd International ACM SIGIR Conference on Research and Development in Information Retrieval* (2019), pp. 1005–1008

[139] M. Ferrari Dacrema, P. Cremonesi, D. Jannach, Are we really making much progress? A worrying analysis of recent neural recommendation approaches, in *Proceedings of the 13th ACM Conference on Recommender Systems*, RecSys '19 (Association for Computing Machinery, New York, 2019), pp. 101–109

[140] A. Ferraro, X. Serra, C. Bauer, Break the loop: gender imbalance in music recommenders, in *CHIIR '21: ACM SIGIR Conference on Human Information Interaction and Retrieval, Canberra, ACT, Australia, March 14–19, 2021*, ed. by F. Scholer, P. Thomas, D. Elsweiler, H. Joho, N. Kando, C. Smith (ACM, New York, 2021), pp. 249–254

[141] B. Ferwerda, E. Ingesson, M. Berndl, M. Schedl, I don't care how popular you are! investigating popularity bias in music recommendations from a user's perspective, in *Proceedings of the 2023 Conference on Human Information Interaction and Retrieval*, CHIIR '23 (Association for Computing Machinery, New York, 2023), pp. 357–361

[142] E. Franks, B. Lee, H. Xu, Report: China's new ai regulations. Global Privacy Law Rev. 5(1) (2024)

[143] A. Friedman, S. Berkovsky, M.A. Kâafar, A differential privacy framework for matrix factorization recommender systems. User Model. User Adapt. Interact. **26**(5), 425–458 (2016)

[144] A. Friedman, B.P. Knijnenburg, K. Vanhecke, L. Martens, S. Berkovsky, Privacy aspects of recommender systems, in *Recommender Systems Handbook*, ed. by F. Ricci, L. Rokach, B. Shapira (Springer, Berlin, 2015), pp. 649–688

[145] B. Friedman, H. Nissenbaum, Bias in computer systems. ACM Trans. Inf. Syst. **14**(3), 330–347 (1996)

[146] G. Friedrich, M. Zanker, A taxonomy for generating explanations in recommender systems. AI Mag. **32**, 90–98 (2011)

[147] G. Frosio, C. Geiger, Taking fundamental rights seriously in the digital services act's platform liability regime. Eur, Law J. **29**(1–2), 31–77 (2023)

[148] I.O. Gallegos, R.A. Rossi, J. Barrow, M.M. Tanjim, S. Kim, F. Dernoncourt, T. Yu, R. Zhang, N.K. Ahmed, Bias and fairness in large language models: a survey (2023). CoRR, abs/2309.00770

[149] C. Ganhör, D. Penz, N. Rekabsaz, O. Lesota, M. Schedl, Unlearning protected user attributes in recommendations with adversarial training, in *SIGIR '22: The 45th International ACM SIGIR Conference on Research and Development in Information Retrieval, Madrid, Spain, July 11–15, 2022*, ed. by E. Amigó, P. Castells, J. Gonzalo, B. Carterette, J.S. Culpepper, G. Kazai (ACM, Berlin, 2022), pp. 2142–2147

[150] J. Gao, X. Wang, Y. Wang, X. Xie, Explainable recommendation through attentive multi-view learning, in *Proceedings of the AAAI Conference on Artificial Intelligence*, vol. 33 (2019), pp. 3622–3629

[151] R. Gao, C. Shah, Counteracting bias and increasing fairness in search and recommender systems, in *Proceedings of the 14th ACM Conference on Recommender Systems*, RecSys '20 (Association for Computing Machinery, New York, 2020), pp. 745–747
[152] Y. Gao, Y. Xiong, X. Gao, K. Jia, J. Pan, Y. Bi, Y. Dai, J. Sun, Q. Guo, M. Wang, H. Wang, Retrieval-augmented generation for large language models: a survey (2023). CoRR, abs/2312.10997
[153] L. Gates, D. Leake, Evaluating CBR explanation capabilities: survey and next steps, in *ICCBR Workshops* (2021), pp. 40–51
[154] Y. Ge, S. Liu, Z. Fu, J. Tan, Z. Li, S. Xu, Y. Li, Y. Xian, Y. Zhang, A survey on trustworthy recommender systems. ACM Trans. Recomm. Syst. (2024). Just Accepted
[155] General data protection regulation (GDPR) - regulation (eu) 2016/679. https://eur-lex.europa.eu/eli/reg/2016/679/oj. Accessed 23 June 2024
[156] G. Gigerenzer, W. Gaissmaier, Heuristic decision making. Ann. Rev. Psychol. **62**, 451–482 (2011)
[157] M. Giomi, F. Boenisch, C. Wehmeyer, B. Tasnádi, A unified framework for quantifying privacy risk in synthetic data. Proc. Priv. Enhancing Technol. **2023**(2), 312–328 (2023)
[158] L. Goeuriot, G. J. Jones, L. Kelly, H. Müller, J. Zobel, Medical information retrieval: introduction to the special issue. Inform. Retrieval J. **19**, 1–5 (2016)
[159] G. Gomroki, H. Behzadi, R. Fattahi, J.S. Fadardi, Identifying effective cognitive biases in information retrieval. J. Inform. Sci. **49**(2), 348–358 (2023)
[160] I.J. Goodfellow, J. Shlens, C. Szegedy, Explaining and harnessing adversarial examples, in *3rd International Conference on Learning Representations, ICLR 2015, San Diego, CA, USA, May 7–9, 2015, Conference Track Proceedings* (2015)
[161] B. Goodman, S. Flaxman, European union regulations on algorithmic decision-making and a "right to explanation". AI Mag. **38**(3), 50–57 (2017)
[162] Gramm-Leach-Bliley Act (GLBA) (15 u.s.c. art. 6801 et seq.). https://www.ftc.gov/business-guidance/privacy-security/gramm-leach-bliley-act. Accessed 23 June 2024
[163] M. Guesmi, M.A. Chatti, S. Joarder, Q.U. Ain, C. Siepmann, H. Ghanbarzadeh, R. Alatrash, Justification vs. transparency: why and how visual explanations in a scientific literature recommender system. Information **14**(7), 401 (2023)
[164] R. Guidotti, A. Monreale, F. Giannotti, D. Pedreschi, S. Ruggieri, F. Turini, Factual and counterfactual explanations for black box decision making. IEEE Intell. Syst. **34**(6), 14–23 (2019)
[165] R. Guidotti, A. Monreale, S. Ruggieri, F. Turini, F. Giannotti, D. Pedreschi, A survey of methods for explaining black box models. ACM Comput. Surv. **51**(5), 1–42 (2018)
[166] L. Hajibayova, Guardians of the knowledge: relevant, irrelevant, or algorithmic? Inform. Res. **24**(4) (2019)

[167] M. Hardt, E. Price, E. Price, N. Srebro, Equality of opportunity in supervised learning, in *Proceedings of the Advances in Neural Information Processing Systems (NIPS)*, ed. by D. Lee, M. Sugiyama, U. Luxburg, I. Guyon, R. Garnett, vol. 29 Barcelona (Curran Associates, 2016), pp. 3315–3323

[168] F.M. Harper, J.A. Konstan, The MovieLens datasets: history and context. ACM Trans. Interact. Intell. Syst. **5**(4), 19:1–19:19 (2016)

[169] X. He, Z. He, X. Du, T. Chua, Adversarial personalized ranking for recommendation, in *SIGIR* (ACM, New York, 2018), pp. 355–364

[170] X. He, L. Liao, H. Zhang, L. Nie, X. Hu, T. Chua, Neural collaborative filtering, in *Proceedings of the 26th International Conference on World Wide Web, WWW 2017, Perth, Australia, April 3–7, 2017*, ed. by R. Barrett, R. Cummings, E. Agichtein, E. Gabrilovich (ACM, New York, 2017), pp. 173–182

[171] C. Healey, J. Enns, Attention and visual memory in visualization and computer graphics. IEEE Trans. Vis. Comput. Graph. **18**(7), 1170–1188 (2011)

[172] F. Henkel, G. Widmer, Real-time music following in score sheet images via multi-resolution prediction. Front. Comput. Sci. **3**, 718340 (2021)

[173] R. Hepworth-Sawyer, J. Hodgson, L. King, M. Marrington, *Gender in Music Production* (CRC Press, Boca Raton, 2020)

[174] J.L. Herlocker, J.A. Konstan, J. Riedl, Explaining collaborative filtering recommendations, in *Proceedings of the 2000 ACM Conference on Computer Supported Cooperative Work* (2000), pp. 241–250

[175] W. Hersh, W. Hersh, Weston, *Information Retrieval: A Biomedical and Health Perspective* (Springer, Berlin, 2020)

[176] High-Level Expert Group on Artificial Intelligence. Ethics Guidelines for Trustworthy AI. https://ec.europa.eu/newsroom/dae/document.cfm?doc_id=60419. Accessed 15 Mar 2024

[177] High-Level Expert Group on Artificial Intelligence. Ethics guidelines for trustworthy ai (2019)

[178] E. Hine, L. Floridi, Artificial intelligence with American values and Chinese characteristics: a comparative analysis of American and Chinese governmental ai policies. AI Soc. **39**(1), 257–278 (2024)

[179] A.L. Hoffmann, S.T. Roberts, C.T. Wolf, S. Wood, Beyond fairness, accountability, and transparency in the ethics of algorithms: contributions and perspectives from LIS. Proc. Assoc. Inform. Sci. Technol. **55**(1), 694–696 (2018)

[180] G. Hofstede, *Culture's Consequences: Comparing Values, Behaviors, Institutions and Organizations Across Nations* (Sage, New York, 2001)

[181] Y. Hou, J. Li, Z. He, A. Yan, X. Chen, J.J. McAuley, Bridging language and items for retrieval and recommendation (2024). CoRR, abs/2403.03952

[182] Y. Hu, Y. Koren, C. Volinsky, Collaborative filtering for implicit feedback datasets, in *Proceedings of the 8th IEEE International Conference on Data Mining (ICDM 2008), December 15–19, 2008, Pisa, Italy* (IEEE Computer Society, 2008), pp. 263–272

[183] W. Hua, L. Li, S. Xu, L. Chen, Y. Zhang, Tutorial on large language models for recommendation, in *Proceedings of the 17th ACM Conference on Recommender Systems, RecSys 2023, Singapore, Singapore, September 18–22, 2023*,

ed. by J. Zhang, L. Chen, S. Berkovsky, M. Zhang, T.D. Noia, J. Basilico, L. Pizzato, Y. Song. (ACM, Berlin, 2023), pp. 1281–1283

[184] J. Huber, J.W. Payne, C. Puto, Adding asymmetrically dominated alternatives: violations of regularity and the similarity hypothesis. J. Consum. Res. **9**(1), 90–98 (1982)

[185] B. Imana, A. Korolova, J. Heidemann, Auditing for discrimination in algorithms delivering job ads. *Proceedings of the Web Conference 2021* (2021)

[186] A. Jalalirad, M. Scavuzzo, C. Capota, M.R. Sprague, A simple and efficient federated recommender system, in *Proceedings of the 6th IEEE/ACM International Conference on Big Data Computing, Applications and Technologies, BDCAT 2019, Auckland, New Zealand, December 2–5, 2019*, ed. by K. Johnson, J. Spillner, X. Zhao, O. Datskova, B. Varghese (ACM, New York, 2019), pp. 53–58

[187] D. Jannach, L. Lerche, I. Kamehkhosh, M. Jugovac, What recommenders recommend: an analysis of recommendation biases and possible countermeasures. User Model. User-Adapt. Interact. **25**, 427–491 (2015)

[188] W. Jiang, Z. He, J. Zhan, W. Pan, Attack-aware detection and defense to resist adversarial examples. IEEE Trans. Comput. Aided Des. Integr. Circuits Syst. **40**(10), 2194–2198 (2021)

[189] Z. Jiang, F.F. Xu, L. Gao, Z. Sun, Q. Liu, J. Dwivedi-Yu, Y. Yang, J. Callan, G. Neubig, Active retrieval augmented generation, in *Proceedings of the 2023 Conference on Empirical Methods in Natural Language Processing, EMNLP 2023, Singapore, December 6–10, 2023*, ed. by H. Bouamor, J. Pino, K. Bali (Association for Computational Linguistics, 2023), pp. 7969–7992

[190] F. Jourdan, T. T. Kaninku, N. Asher, J.-M. Loubes, L. Risser, How optimal transport can tackle gender biases in multi-class neural network classifiers for job recommendations. Algorithms **16**(3), 174 (2023)

[191] V. Kaffes, D. Sacharidis, G. Giannopoulos, Model-agnostic counterfactual explanations of recommendations, in *Proceedings of the 29th ACM Conference on User Modeling, Adaptation and Personalization* (2021), pp. 280–285

[192] D. Kahneman, *Thinking, Fast and Slow* (Farrar, Straus and Giroux, New York, 2011)

[193] M. Kaminskas, D. Bridge, Diversity, serendipity, novelty, and coverage: a survey and empirical analysis of beyond-accuracy objectives in recommender systems. ACM Trans. Interact. Intell. Syst. **7**(1), 2:1–2:42 (2017)

[194] H. Kaur, N. Kumar, S. Batra, An efficient multi-party scheme for privacy preserving collaborative filtering for healthcare recommender system. Fut. Gener. Comput. Syst. **86**, 297–307 (2018)

[195] E. Kazim, A. Koshiyama, A. Hilliard, R. Polle, Systematizing audit in algorithmic recruitment. J. Intell. **9**, 46 (2021)

[196] P.J. Keenan, Do norms still matter-the corrosive effects of globalization on the vitality of norms. Vand. J. Transnat'l L. **41**, 327 (2008)

[197] J. Kim, D. Koo, Y. Kim, H. Yoon, J. Shin, S. Kim, Efficient privacy-preserving matrix factorization for recommendation via fully homomorphic encryption. ACM Trans. Priv. Secur. **21**(4), 17:1–17:30 (2018)

[198] Ö. Kirnap, F. Diaz, A. Biega, M. D. Ekstrand, B. Carterette, E. Yilmaz, Estimation of fair ranking metrics with incomplete judgments, in *WWW '21:*

The Web Conference 2021, Virtual Event / Ljubljana, Slovenia, April 19–23, 2021, ed. by J. Leskovec, M. Grobelnik, M. Najork, J. Tang, L. Zia (ACM/IW3C2, 2021), pp. 1065–1075

[199] A. Klimashevskaia, M. Elahi, D. Jannach, C. Trattner, L. Skjærven, Mitigating popularity bias in recommendation: potential and limits of calibration approaches, in *Advances in Information Retrieval: Workshop on Algorithmic Bias in Search and Recommendation (BIAS) in conjunction with the 42nd European Conference on IR Research (ECIR)* (Springer, Berlin, 2022), pp. 82–90

[200] A. Klimashevskaia, D. Jannach, M. Elahi, C. Trattner, A survey on popularity bias in recommender systems (2023). CoRR, abs/2308.01118

[201] P. Knees, M. Schedl, M. Goto, Intelligent user interfaces for music discovery. Trans. Int. Soc. Music Inform. Retrieval **3**(1), 165–179 (2020)

[202] B.P. Knijnenburg, M.C. Willemsen, Z. Gantner, H. Soncu, C. Newell, Explaining the user experience of recommender systems. User Model. User Adapt. Interact. **22**(4–5), 441–504 (2012)

[203] D. Kowald, G. Mayr, M. Schedl, E. Lex, A study on accuracy, miscalibration, and popularity bias in recommendations, in *Advances in Bias and Fairness in Information Retrieval—4th International Workshop, BIAS 2023, Dublin, Ireland, April 2, 2023, Revised Selected Papers*, volume 1840 of Communications in Computer and Information Science, ed. by L. Boratto, S. Faralli, M. Marras, G. Stilo (Springer, Berlin, 2023), pp. 1–16

[204] D. Kowald, M. Schedl, E. Lex, The unfairness of popularity bias in music recommendation: a reproducibility study, in *European Conference on Information Retrieval* (Springer, Berlin, 2020), pp. 35–42

[205] D. Kravets, A. Ryzhova, F. Toepfl, A. Beseler, Different platforms, different plots? The kremlin-controlled search engine Yandex as a resource for Russia's informational influence in Belarus during the covid-19 pandemic. Journalism **24**, 2762–2780 (2023)

[206] D. Kumar, T. Grosz, E. Greif, N. Rekabsaz, M. Schedl, Identifying words in job advertisements responsible for gender bias in candidate ranking systems via counterfactual learning, in *Proceedings of the 3rd Workshop on Recommender Systems for Human Resources (RecSys in HR 2023) co-located with the 17th ACM Conference on Recommender Systems (RecSys 2023), Singapore, Singapore, 18th-22nd September 2023*, volume 3490 of CEUR Workshop Proceedings, ed, by M. Kaya, T. Bogers, D. Graus, C. Johnson, J. Decorte (CEUR-WS.org, 2023)

[207] D. Kumar, T. Grosz, N. Rekabsaz, E. Greif, M. Schedl, Fairness of recommender systems in the recruitment domain: an analysis from technical and legal perspectives. Front. Big Data - Recommender Syst. **6**, 1245198 (2023)

[208] A. Kurakin, I.J. Goodfellow, S. Bengio, Adversarial examples in the physical world, in *5th International Conference on Learning Representations, ICLR 2017, Toulon, France, April 24–26, 2017, Workshop Track Proceedings* (2017)

[209] K.-H. Lai, Z.-R. Yang, P.-Y. Lai, C.-D. Wang, M. Guizani, M. Chen, Knowledge-aware explainable reciprocal recommendation, in *Proceedings of the AAAI Conference on Artificial Intelligence*, vol. 38 (2024), pp. 8636–8644

[210] A. Lambrecht, C. Tucker, Algorithmic bias? An empirical study of apparent gender-based discrimination in the display of stem career ads. Manag. Sci. **65**(7), 2966–2981 (2019) © 2019 INFORMS This manuscript has been accepted for publication in Management Science. The version of record can be found at https://doi.org/10.1287/mnsc.2018.3093

[211] J.-B. Lamy, B. Sekar, G. Guezennec, J. Bouaud, B. Séroussi, Explainable artificial intelligence for breast cancer: a visual case-based reasoning approach. Artif. Intell. Med. **94**, 42–53 (2019)

[212] Latham and Watkins. *China's New AI Regulations* (2023). https://www.lw.com/en/admin/upload/SiteAttachments/Chinas-New-AI-Regulations.pdf. Accessed 13 Feb 2024

[213] V. Laurim, S. Arpaci, B. Prommegger, H. Krcmar, Computer, whom should i hire? Acceptance criteria for artificial intelligence in the recruitment process 1–10 (2021)

[214] D.M. Lazer, M.A. Baum, Y. Benkler, A.J. Berinsky, K.M. Greenhill, F. Menczer, M.J. Metzger, B. Nyhan, G. Pennycook, D. Rothschild, et al., The science of fake news. Science **359**(6380), 1094–1096 (2018)

[215] D.B. Leake, CBR in context: the present and future, in *Case-Based Reasoning: Experiences, Lessons, and Future Directions* (1996), pp. 3–30

[216] G. Lederrey, R. West, When sheep shop: measuring herding effects in product ratings with natural experiments, in *Proceedings of the 2018 World Wide Web Conference on World Wide Web, WWW 2018, Lyon, France, April 23–27, 2018*, ed. by P. Champin, F. Gandon, M. Lalmas, P.G. Ipeirotis (ACM, New York, 2018), pp. 793–802

[217] O. Lesota, S. Brandl, M. Wenzel, A.B. Melchiorre, E. Lex, N. Rekabsaz, M. Schedl, Exploring cross-group discrepancies in calibrated popularity for accuracy/fairness trade-off optimization, in *Proceedings of the 2nd Workshop on Multi-Objective Recommender Systems co-located with 16th ACM Conference on Recommender Systems (RecSys 2022), Seattle, WA, USA, 18th-23rd September 2022*, volume 3268 of *CEUR Workshop Proceedings*, ed. by H. Abdollahpouri, S. Sahebi, M. Elahi, M. Mansoury, B. Loni, Z. Nazari, M. Dimakopoulou (CEUR-WS.org, 2022)

[218] O. Lesota, G. Escobedo, Y. Deldjoo, B. Ferwerda, S. Kopeinik, E. Lex, N. Rekabsaz, M. Schedl, Computational versus perceived popularity miscalibration in recommender systems, in *Proceedings of the 46th International ACM SIGIR Conference on Research and Development in Information Retrieval, SIGIR 2023, Taipei, Taiwan, July 23–27, 2023*, ed. by H. Chen, W.E. Duh, H. Huang, M.P. Kato, J. Mothe, B. Poblete (ACM, New York, 2023), pp. 1889–1893

[219] O. Lesota, A.B. Melchiorre, N. Rekabsaz, S. Brandl, D. Kowald, E. Lex, M. Schedl, Analyzing item popularity bias of music recommender systems: are different genders equally affected? in *Proceedings of the 15th ACM Conference on Recommender Systems (Late-Breaking Results)* (Amsterdam, 2021)

[220] E. Lex, D. Kowald, P. Seitlinger, T.N.T. Tran, A. Felfernig, M. Schedl, Psychology-informed recommender systems. Found. Trends Inf. Retr. **15**(2), 134–242 (2021)

[221] B. Li, Y. Wang, A. Singh, Y. Vorobeychik, Data poisoning attacks on factorization-based collaborative filtering, in *Advances in Neural Information Processing Systems 29: Annual Conference on Neural Information Processing Systems 2016, December 5–10, 2016, Barcelona, Spain* (2016), pp. 1885–1893

[222] D. Li, J. Lian, L. Zhang, K. Ren, T. Lu, T. Wu, X. Xie, *Recommender Systems—Frontiers and Practices* (Springer, Berlin, 2024).

[223] L. Li, Y. Zhang, L. Chen, Generate neural template explanations for recommendation, in *Proceedings of the 29th ACM International Conference on Information & Knowledge Management* (2020), pp. 755–764

[224] L. Li, Y. Zhang, L. Chen, Personalized prompt learning for explainable recommendation. ACM Trans. Inf. Syst. **41**(4), 1–26 (2023)

[225] N. Li, T. Li, S. Venkatasubramanian, t-closeness: privacy beyond k-anonymity and l-diversity, in *Proceedings of the 23rd International Conference on Data Engineering, ICDE 2007, The Marmara Hotel, Istanbul, Turkey, April 15–20, 2007*, ed. by R. Chirkova, A. Dogac, M. T. Özsu, T.K. Sellis (IEEE Computer Society, 2007), pp. 106–115

[226] P. Li, X. Zhu, X. Su, Neural_bpr: multi-processing popularity bias mitigating method in recommendation systems. Electron. Commer. Res. Appl. **62**, 101323 (2023)

[227] Y. Li, M. Yamashita, H. Chen, D. Lee, Y. Zhang, Fairness in job recommendation under quantity constraints, in *AAAI-23 Workshop on AI for Web Advertising* (2023)

[228] D. Liang, R.G. Krishnan, M.D. Hoffman, T. Jebara, Variational autoencoders for collaborative filtering, in *Proceedings of the 2018 World Wide Web Conference on World Wide Web, WWW 2018, Lyon, France*, ed. by P. Champin, F.L. Gandon, M. Lalmas, P.G. Ipeirotis (ACM, New York, 2018), pp. 689–698

[229] C. Lin, S. Chen, H. Li, Y. Xiao, L. Li, Q. Yang, Attacking recommender systems with augmented user profiles, in *CIKM '20: The 29th ACM International Conference on Information and Knowledge Management, Virtual Event, Ireland, October 19–23, 2020*, ed. by M. d'Aquin, S. Dietze, C. Hauff, E. Curry, P. Cudré-Mauroux (ACM, New York, 2020), pp. 855–864

[230] H. Lin, H. Wu, A right to an explanation of algorithmic decision-making in China. Hong Kong LJ **52**, 1163 (2022)

[231] R. Ling, Confirmation bias in the era of mobile news consumption: the social and psychological dimensions. Digit. J. **8**(5), 596–604 (2020)

[232] Z.C. Lipton, The mythos of model interpretability. Queue **16**(3), 31–57 (2018)

[233] A. Liu, Y. Yao, X. Cheng, Recommender systems with condensed local differential privacy, in *Machine Learning for Cyber Security—Third International Conference, ML4CS 2020, Guangzhou, China, October 8–10, 2020, Proceedings, Part I*, volume 12486 of Lecture Notes in Computer Science, ed. by X. Chen, H. Yan, Q. Yan, X. Zhang (Springer, 2020), pp. 355–365

[234] H. Liu, A. Gegov, F. Stahl, Categorization and construction of rule based systems, in *Engineering Applications of Neural Networks: 15th International Conference, EANN 2014, Sofia, Bulgaria, September 5–7, 2014. Proceedings 15* (Springer, Berlin, 2014), pp. 183–194

[235] N. Liu, Y. Ge, L. Li, X. Hu, R. Chen, S.-H. Choi. Explainable recommender systems via resolving learning representations, in *Proceedings of the 29th ACM International Conference on Information & Knowledge Management* (2020), pp. 895–904

[236] P. Liu, L. Zhang, J.A. Gulla, Dynamic attention-based explainable recommendation with textual and visual fusion. Inform. Process. Manag. **57**(6), 102099 (2020)

[237] X. Liu, A. Liu, X. Zhang, Z. Li, G. Liu, L. Zhao, X. Zhou, When differential privacy meets randomized perturbation: a hybrid approach for privacy-preserving recommender system, in *Database Systems for Advanced Applications—22nd International Conference, DASFAA 2017, Suzhou, China, March 27–30, 2017, Proceedings, Part I*, volume 10177 of Lecture Notes in Computer Science, ed. by K.S. Candan, L. Chen, T.B. Pedersen, L. Chang, W. Hua (Springer, Berlin, 2017), pp. 576–591

[238] Y. Liu, X. Cao, Y. Yu, Are you influenced by others when rating? Improve rating prediction by conformity modeling, in *Proceedings of the 10th ACM Conference on Recommender Systems, Boston, MA, USA, September 15–19, 2016*, ed. by S. Sen, W. Geyer, J. Freyne, and P. Castells (ACM, 2016), pp. 269–272

[239] Y. Liu, T.N. Pham, G. Cong, Q. Yuan, An experimental evaluation of point-of-interest recommendation in location-based social networks. Proc. VLDB Endow. **10**(10), 1010–1021 (2017)

[240] Y. Liu, R. Zhang, J. Guo, M. de Rijke, W. Chen, Y. Fan, X. Cheng, Topic-oriented adversarial attacks against black-box neural ranking models, in *Proceedings of the 46th International ACM SIGIR Conference on Research and Development in Information Retrieval, SIGIR 2023, Taipei, Taiwan, July 23–27, 2023*, ed. by H. Chen, W.E. Duh, H. Huang, M. P. Kato, J. Mothe, B. Poblete (ACM, New York, 2023), pp. 1700–1709

[241] Z. Liu, Y. Fang, M. Wu, Mitigating popularity bias for users and items with fairness-centric adaptive recommendation. ACM Trans. Inf. Syst. **41**(3), 55:1–55:27 (2023)

[242] P. Lops, F. Narducci, C. Musto, M. de Gemmis, M. Polignano, G. Semeraro, Recommendations biases and beyond-accuracy objectives in collaborative filtering, in *Collaborative Recommendations—Algorithms, Practical Challenges and Applications*, ed. by S. Berkovsky, I. Cantador, D. Tikk (World-Scientific, Singapore, 2018), pp. 329–368

[243] H. Lu, W. Ma, Y. Wang, M. Zhang, X. Wang, Y. Liu, T. Seng Chua, S. Ma, User perception of recommendation explanation: are your explanations what users need? ACM Trans. Inform. Syst. **41**, 1–31 (2022)

[244] L. Lyu, N. Roy, H. Oosterhuis, A. Anand, Is interpretable machine learning effective at feature selection for neural learning-to-rank? in *European Conference on Information Retrieval* (Springer, Berlin, 2024), pp. 384–402

[245] A. Machanavajjhala, J. Gehrke, D. Kifer, M. Venkitasubramaniam, l-diversity: privacy beyond k-anonymity, in *Proceedings of the 22nd International Conference on Data Engineering, ICDE 2006, 3–8 April 2006, Atlanta, GA, USA*, ed. by L. Liu, A. Reuter, K. Whang, J. Zhang (IEEE Computer Society, 2006), p. 24

[246] A. Madry, A. Makelov, L. Schmidt, D. Tsipras, A. Vladu, Towards deep learning models resistant to adversarial attacks, in *6th International Conference on Learning Representations, ICLR 2018, Vancouver, BC, Canada, April 30–May 3, 2018, Conference Track Proceedings* (2018)

[247] L. Marconi, R. Matamoros Aragon, F. Epifania, et al., Discovering the unknown suggestion: a short review on explainability for recommender systems, in *CEUR Workshop Proceedings*, vol. 3463 (CEUR-WS, 2023), pp. 1–15

[248] B.M. Marlin, R.S. Zemel, S.T. Roweis, M. Slaney, Collaborative filtering and the missing at random assumption, in *UAI 2007, Proceedings of the Twenty-Third Conference on Uncertainty in Artificial Intelligence, Vancouver, BC, Canada, July 19–22, 2007*, ed. by R. Parr and L.C. van der Gaag (AUAI Press, 2007), pp. 267–275

[249] C. Marsh, D.P. Payne, The globalization of human rights and the socialization of human rights norms. BYU L. Rev. 665 (2007)

[250] S. Masoudian, C. Volaucnik, M. Schedl, S. Masoudian, Effective controllable bias mitigation for classification and retrieval using gate adapters (2024). CoRR, abs/2401.16457

[251] P. Massa, P. Avesani, Trust-aware recommender systems, in *Proceedings of the 2007 ACM Conference on Recommender Systems, RecSys 2007, Minneapolis, MN, USA, October 19–20, 2007*, ed. by J. A. Konstan, J. Riedl, B. Smyth (ACM, New York, 2007), pp. 17–24

[252] B. McMahan, E. Moore, D. Ramage, S. Hampson, B.A. y Arcas, Communication-efficient learning of deep networks from decentralized data, in *Proceedings of the 20th International Conference on Artificial Intelligence and Statistics, AISTATS 2017, 20–22 April 2017, Fort Lauderdale, FL, USA*, volume 54 of Proceedings of Machine Learning Research, ed. by A. Singh, X.J. Zhu (PMLR, 2017), pp. 1273–1282

[253] F. McSherry, I. Mironov, Differentially private recommender systems: building privacy into the netflix prize contenders, in *Proceedings of the 15th ACM SIGKDD International Conference on Knowledge Discovery and Data Mining, Paris, France, June 28–July 1, 2009*, ed. by J.F.E. IV, F. Fogelman-Soulié, P.A. Flach, M.J. Zaki (ACM, 2009), pp. 627–636

[254] N. Mehrabi, F. Morstatter, N. Saxena, K. Lerman, A. Galstyan, A survey on bias and fairness in machine learning. ACM Comput. Surv. **54**(6), 1–35 (2021)

[255] A.B. Melchiorre, D. Penz, C. Ganhör, O. Lesota, V. Fragoso, F. Fritzl, E. Parada-Cabaleiro, F. Schubert, M. Schedl, Emotion-aware music tower

blocks (emomtb): an intelligent audiovisual interface for music discovery and recommendation. Int. J. Multim. Inf. Retr. **12**(1), 13 (2023)

[256] A.B. Melchiorre, N. Rekabsaz, C. Ganhör, M. Schedl, ProtoMF: prototype-based matrix factorization for effective and explainable recommendations, in *Proceedings of the 16th ACM Conference on Recommender Systems* (2022), pp. 246–256

[257] A.B. Melchiorre, N. Rekabsaz, E. Parada-Cabaleiro, S. Brandl, O. Lesota, M. Schedl, Investigating gender fairness of recommendation algorithms in the music domain. Inf. Process. Manag. **58**(5), 102666 (2021)

[258] A.B. Melchiorre, N. Rekabsaz, E. Parada-Cabaleiro, S. Brandl, O. Lesota, M. Schedl, Investigating gender fairness of recommendation algorithms in the music domain. Inform. Process. Manag. **58**(5), 102666 (2021)

[259] F.A. Merra, V.W. Anelli, T.D. Noia, D. Malitesta, A.C.M. Mancino, Denoise to protect: a method to robustify visual recommenders from adversaries, in *Proceedings of the 46th International ACM SIGIR Conference on Research and Development in Information Retrieval, SIGIR 2023, Taipei, Taiwan, July 23–27, 2023*, ed. by H. Chen, W.E. Duh, H. Huang, M.P. Kato, J. Mothe, B. Poblete (ACM, 2023), pp. 1924–1928

[260] E.L. Merrer, R. Pons, G. Trédan, Algorithmic audits of algorithms, and the law (2022). arXiv preprint arXiv:2203.03711

[261] A.-K. Meßmer, M. Degeling, Auditing recommender systems–putting the DSA into practice with a risk-scenario-based approach (2023). arXiv preprint arXiv:2302.04556

[262] Meta, Introducing 22 system cards that explain how ai powers experiences on Facebook and Instagram (2023). https://ai.meta.com/blog/how-ai-powers-experiences-facebook-instagram-system-cards/

[263] M. Millecamp, R. Haveneers, K. Verbert, Cogito ergo quid? The effect of cognitive style in a transparent mobile music recommender system, in *Proceedings of the 28th ACM Conference on User Modeling, Adaptation and Personalization* (2020), pp. 323–327

[264] M. Minkkinen, J. Laine, M. Mäntymäki, Continuous auditing of artificial intelligence: a conceptualization and assessment of tools and frameworks. Digit. Soc. 1 (2022)

[265] M. Mitchell, S. Wu, A. Zaldivar, P. Barnes, L. Vasserman, B. Hutchinson, E. Spitzer, I.D. Raji, T. Gebru, Model cards for model reporting, in *Conference on Fairness, Accountability, and Transparency* (2019), pp. 220–229

[266] S. Mitchell, E. Potash, S. Barocas, A. D'Amour, K. Lum, Algorithmic fairness: choices, assumptions, and definitions. Ann. Rev. Stat. Appl. **8**, 141–163 (2021)

[267] B. Mitra, N. Craswell, An introduction to neural information retrieval. Found. Trends Inf. Retr. **13**(1), 1–126 (2018)

[268] A. Mojzisch, S. Schulz-Hardt, Knowing others' preferences degrades the quality of group decisions. J. Pers. Soc. Psychol. **98**(5), 794 (2010)

[269] C. Molnar, *Interpretable Machine Learning* (Lulu.com, 2020)

[270] K. Muhammad, A. Lawlor, R. Rafter, B. Smyth, Great explanations: opinionated explanations for recommendations, in *International Conference on Case-Based Reasoning* (Springer, Berlin, 2015), pp. 244–258

[271] S. Mukherjee, R. Walch, F. Meisingseth, E. Lex, C. Rechberger, Hiding your awful online choices made more efficient and secure: a new privacy-aware recommender system, in *IFIP International Conference on ICT Systems Security and Privacy Protection* (Springer, 2024), pp. 353–366

[272] P. Müllner, E. Lex, M. Schedl, D. Kowald, Differential privacy in collaborative filtering recommender systems: a review. Front. Big Data **6**, 1249997 (2023)

[273] P. Müllner, E. Lex, M. Schedl, D. Kowald, ReuseKNN: neighborhood reuse for differentially private KNN-based recommendations. ACM Trans. Intell. Syst. Technol. **14**(5), 1–29 (2023)

[274] P. Müllner, E. Lex, M. Schedl, D. Kowald, The impact of differential privacy on recommendation accuracy and popularity bias, in *European Conference on Information Retrieval* (Springer, 2024), pp. 466–482

[275] J. Murphy, C.F. Hofacker, R. Mizerski, Primacy and recency effects on clicking behavior. J. Comput. Mediat. Commun. **11**(2), 522–535 (2006)

[276] D.M. Murungi, D.J. Yates, S. Purao, J. Yu, R. Zhan, Factual or believable? Negotiating the boundaries of confirmation bias in online news stories, in *52nd Hawaii International Conference on System Sciences, HICSS 2019, Grand Wailea, Maui, Hawaii, USA, January 8–11, 2019*, ed. by T. Bui (ScholarSpace, 2019), pp. 1–10

[277] M. Naghiaei, H.A. Rahmani, Y. Deldjoo, CPFair: personalized consumer and producer fairness re-ranking for recommender systems, in *SIGIR '22: The 45th International ACM SIGIR Conference on Research and Development in Information Retrieval, Madrid, Spain, July 11–15, 2022*, ed. by E. Amigó, P. Castells, J. Gonzalo, B. Carterette, J. S. Culpepper, G. Kazai (ACM, 2022), pp. 770–779

[278] T. Ngo, J. Kunkel, J. Ziegler, Exploring mental models for transparent and controllable recommender systems: a qualitative study, in *Proceedings of the 28th ACM Conference on User Modeling, Adaptation and Personalization* (2020), pp. 183–191

[279] T. Nguyen, M. Rosenberg, X. Song, J. Gao, S. Tiwary, R. Majumder, L. Deng, MS MARCO: a human generated machine reading comprehension dataset, in *Proceedings of the Workshop on Cognitive Computation: Integrating neural and symbolic approaches 2016 co-located with the 30th Annual Conference on Neural Information Processing Systems (NIPS 2016), Barcelona, Spain, December 9, 2016*, volume 1773 of *CEUR Workshop Proceedings*, ed. by T.R. Besold, A. Bordes, A.S. d'Avila Garcez, G. Wayne (CEUR-WS.org, 2016)

[280] R.S. Nickerson, Confirmation bias: a ubiquitous phenomenon in many guises. Rev. Gener. Psychol. **2**(2), 175–220 (1998)

[281] M. Nilashi, D. Jannach, O. bin Ibrahim, M.D. Esfahani, H. Ahmadi, Recommendation quality, transparency, and website quality for trust-building in recommendation agents. Electron. Commer. Res. Appl. **19**, 70–84 (2016)

[282] X. Ning, G. Karypis, SLIM: sparse linear methods for top-n recommender systems, in *Proceedings of the 11th IEEE International Conference on Data Min-*

ing, ICDM 2011, Vancouver, BC, Canada, ed. by D.J. Cook, J. Pei, W. Wang, O. R. Zaïane, X. Wu (IEEE Computer Society, 2011), pp. 497–506
[283] T.D. Noia, N. Tintarev, P. Fatourou, M. Schedl, Recommender systems under european AI regulations. Commun. ACM **65**(4), 69–73 (2022)
[284] I. Nunes, D. Jannach, A systematic review and taxonomy of explanations in decision support and recommender systems. User Model. User-Adapt. Interact. **27**, 393–444 (2017)
[285] R. Nyathani, Ai-powered recruitment the future of hr digital transformation. J. Artif. Intell. Cloud Comput. **1**(4), 1–5 (2022)
[286] M. O'Brien, M.T. Keane, Modeling result-list searching in the world wide web: The role of relevance topologies and trust bias, in *Proceedings of the 28th Annual Conference of the Cognitive Science Society*, vol. 28, pp. 1881–1886 (Citeseer, 2006)
[287] OECD, OECD framework for the classification of ai systems (323) (2022)
[288] C.I.I. Office, The cyberspace administration of China and three other departments issued the "regulations on the management of deep integration of internet information services" (2022). https://www.cac.gov.cn/2022-12/11/c_1672221949318230.htm Accessed 17 Mar 2024
[289] T.B. Ogunseyi, C.B. Avoussoukpo, Y. Jiang, A systematic review of privacy techniques in recommendation systems. Int. J. Inf. Sec. **22**(6), 1651–1664 (2023)
[290] E.U. Osiobe, S. Malallah, N.E. Osiobe, Enhancing data visualization accessibility: a case for equity and inclusion. Eng. Technol. Q. Rev. **7**(2) (2024)
[291] D. Pager, H. Shepherd, The sociology of discrimination: racial discrimination in employment, housing, credit, and consumer markets. Annu. Rev. Sociol. **34**, 181–209 (2008)
[292] S. Pandian, D. Ganguly, S. MacAvaney, Evaluating the explainability of neural rankers, in *European Conference on Information Retrieval* (Springer, Berlin, 2024), pp. 369–383
[293] D.H. Park, Y. Chang, Adversarial sampling and training for semi-supervised information retrieval, in *The World Wide Web Conference, WWW 2019, San Francisco, CA, USA, May 13–17, 2019* (2019), pp. 1443–1453
[294] A. Parry, M. Fröbe, S. MacAvaney, M. Potthast, M. Hagen, Analyzing adversarial attacks on sequence-to-sequence relevance models, in *Advances in Information Retrieval—46th European Conference on Information Retrieval, ECIR 2024, Glasgow, UK, March 24–28, 2024, Proceedings, Part II*, volume 14609 of Lecture Notes in Computer Science, ed. by N. Goharian, N. Tonellotto, Y. He, A. Lipani, G. McDonald, C. Macdonald, I. Ounis (Springer, Berlin, 2024), pp. 286–302
[295] E.A. Pascoe, L. Smart Richman, Perceived discrimination and health: a meta-analytic review. Psychol. Bull. **135**(4), 531 (2009)
[296] G.K. Patro, A. Biswas, N. Ganguly, K.P. Gummadi, A. Chakraborty, FairRec: two-sided fairness for personalized recommendations in two-sided platforms, in *WWW '20: The Web Conference 2020, Taipei, Taiwan, April 20–24, 2020*,

ed. by Y. Huang, I. King, T. Liu, M. van Steen (ACM/IW3C2, 2020), pp. 1194–1204

[297] J.W. Payne, J.R. Bettman, E.J. Johnson, *The Adaptive Decision Maker* (Cambridge University Press, Cambridge, 1993)

[298] E. Perez, F. Strub, H. de Vries, V. Dumoulin, A.C. Courville, Film: visual reasoning with a general conditioning layer, in *Proceedings of the Thirty-Second AAAI Conference on Artificial Intelligence, (AAAI-18), the 30th innovative Applications of Artificial Intelligence (IAAI-18), and the 8th AAAI Symposium on Educational Advances in Artificial Intelligence (EAAI-18), New Orleans, Louisiana, USA, February 2–7, 2018*, ed. by S. A. McIlraith and K. Q. Weinberger (AAAI Press, 2018), pp. 3942–3951

[299] J. Piao, J. Liu, F. Zhang, J. Su, Y. Li, Human–ai adaptive dynamics drives the emergence of information cocoons. Nat. Mach. Intell. **5**(11), 1214–1224 (2023)

[300] K. Prinz, A. Flexer, G. Widmer, On end-to-end white-box adversarial attacks in music information retrieval. Trans. Int. Soc. Music. Inf. Retr. **4**(1), 93 (2021)

[301] Product liability directive (PLD) - directive 85/374/eec. https://eur-lex.europa.eu/legal-content/EN/TXT/?uri=celex%3A31985L0374. Accessed 23 June 2024

[302] Provisions on the Administration of Algorithm Recommendations for Internet Information Services. https://www.cac.gov.cn/2022-01/04/c_1642894606364259.htm. Accessed 15 Mar 2024

[303] P. Pu, L. Chen, R. Hu, Evaluating recommender systems from the user's perspective: survey of the state of the art. User Model. User-Adapt. Interact. **22**(4–5), 317–355 (2012)

[304] A. Qi, G. Shao, W. Zheng, Assessing China's cybersecurity law. Comput. Law Secur. Rev. **34**(6), 1342–1354 (2018)

[305] L. Quillian, D. Pager, O. Hexel, A.H. Midtbøen, Meta-analysis of field experiments shows no change in racial discrimination in hiring over time. Proc. Natl. Acad. Sci. **114**(41), 10870–10875 (2017)

[306] H.A. Rahmani, Y. Deldjoo, T.D. Noia, The role of context fusion on accuracy, beyond-accuracy, and fairness of point-of-interest recommendation systems. Expert Syst. Appl. **205**, 117700 (2022)

[307] I.D. Raji, A. Smart, R.N. White, M. Mitchell, T. Gebru, B. Hutchinson, J. Smith-Loud, D. Theron, P. Barnes, Closing the ai accountability gap, in *Proceedings of the 2020 Conference on Fairness, Accountability, and Transparency* (2020)

[308] I.D. Raji, A. Smart, R.N. White, M. Mitchell, T. Gebru, B. Hutchinson, J. Smith-Loud, D. Theron, P. Barnes, Closing the ai accountability gap: defining an end-to-end framework for internal algorithmic auditing, in *Proceedings of the 2020 Conference on Fairness, Accountability, and Transparency* (2020), pp. 33–44

[309] Regulation (EU) 2016/679 of the European Parliament and of the Council of 27 April 2016 on the protection of natural persons with regard to the processing of personal data and on the free movement of such data, and repealing Directive

95/46/EC (General Data Protection Regulation). https://eur-lex.europa.eu/legal-content/EN/TXT/PDF/?uri=CELEX:32016R0679. Accessed 15 Mar 2024

[310] Regulation (EU) 2022/1925 of the European Parliament and of the Council of 14 September 2022 on contestable and fair markets in the digital sector and amending Directives (EU) 2019/1937 and (EU) 2020/1828 (Digital Markets Act). https://eur-lex.europa.eu/legal-content/EN/TXT/PDF/?uri=CELEX:32022R1925. Accessed 15 Mar 2024

[311] Regulation (EU) 2022/2065 of the European Parliament and of the Council of 19 October 2022 on a Single Market For Digital Services and amending Directive 2000/31/EC (Digital Services Act). https://eur-lex.europa.eu/legal-content/EN/TXT/PDF/?uri=CELEX:32022R2065. Accessed 15 Mar 2024

[312] N. Rekabsaz, S. Kopeinik, M. Schedl. Societal biases in retrieved contents: measurement framework and adversarial mitigation of BERT rankers, in *SIGIR '21: The 44th International ACM SIGIR Conference on Research and Development in Information Retrieval, Virtual Event, Canada, July 11–15, 2021*, ed. by F. Diaz, C. Shah, T. Suel, P. Castells, R. Jones, T. Sakai (ACM, New York, 2021), pp. 306–316

[313] N. Rekabsaz, O. Lesota, M. Schedl, J. Brassey, C. Eickhoff, TripClick: the log files of a large health web search engine, in *Proceedings of the 44th International ACM SIGIR Conference on Research and Development in Information Retrieval*, SIGIR '21 (Association for Computing Machinery, New York, 2021), pp. 2507–2513

[314] N. Rekabsaz, M. Schedl, Do neural ranking models intensify gender bias? in *Proceedings of the 43rd International ACM SIGIR conference on research and development in Information Retrieval, SIGIR 2020, Virtual Event, China, July 25–30, 2020*, Ed. By J.X. Huang, Y. Chang, X. Cheng, J. Kamps, V. Murdock, J. Wen, Y. Liu (ACM, New York, 2020), pp. 2065–2068

[315] S. Rendle, C. Freudenthaler, Z. Gantner, L. Schmidt-Thieme, BPR: Bayesian personalized ranking from implicit feedback, in *UAI 2009, Proceedings of the Twenty-Fifth Conference on Uncertainty in Artificial Intelligence, Montreal, QC, Canada, June 18–21, 2009*, ed. by J.A. Bilmes, A.Y. Ng (AUAI Press, 2009), pp. 452–461

[316] S. Rendle, L. Schmidt-Thieme, Pairwise interaction tensor factorization for personalized tag recommendation, in *WSDM* (ACM, 2010), pp. 81–90

[317] P. Resnick, N. Iacovou, M. Suchak, P. Bergstrom, J. Riedl, GroupLens: an open architecture for collaborative filtering of netnews, in *Proceedings of the 1994 ACM conference on Computer supported cooperative work* (1994), pp. 175–186

[318] M.T. Ribeiro, S. Singh, C. Guestrin, "why should i trust you?" Explaining the predictions of any classifier, in *Proceedings of the 22nd ACM SIGKDD International Conference on Knowledge Discovery and Data Mining* (2016), pp. 1135–1144

[319] F. Ricci, L. Rokach, B. Shapira (eds.), *Recommender Systems Handbook* (Springer, Berlin, 2015)

[320] F. Ricci, L. Rokach, B. Shapira (eds.), *Recommender Systems Handbook* (Springer, New York, 2022)

[321] F. Ricci, L. Rokach, B. Shapira, P.B. Kantor (eds.), *Recommender Systems Handbook*, 3rd edn. (Springer, Berlin, 2022)

[322] R.L. Rivest, L. Adleman, M.L. Dertouzos, On data banks and privacy homomorphisms, in *Foundations of Secure Computation* (Academia Press, New York, 1978), pp. 169–179

[323] H. Roberts, J. Cowls, E. Hine, J. Morley, V. Wang, M. Taddeo, L. Floridi, Governing artificial intelligence in china and the european union: comparing aims and promoting ethical outcomes. Inform. Soc. **39**(2), 79–97 (2023)

[324] R. Robertson, D. Lazer, C. Wilson, Auditing the personalization and composition of politically-related search engine results pages (2018)

[325] F. Rossetto, J. Dalton, R. Murray-Smith, Generating multimodal augmentations with LLMs from song metadata for music information retrieval, in *Proceedings of the 1st Workshop on Large Generative Models Meet Multimodal Applications, LGM3A 2023, Ottawa ON, Canada, 2 November 2023*, ed. by Z. Wang, C. Long, S. Xu, B. Gan, W. Shi, Z. Cao, T. Chua (ACM, New York, 2023), pp. 51–59

[326] A. Rozsa, E.M. Rudd, T.E. Boult, Adversarial diversity and hard positive generation, in *2016 IEEE Conference on Computer Vision and Pattern Recognition Workshops, CVPR Workshops 2016, Las Vegas, NV, USA, June 26– July 1, 2016* (IEEE Computer Society, 2016), pp. 410–417

[327] C. Rudin, Stop explaining black box machine learning models for high stakes decisions and use interpretable models instead. Nat. Mach. Intell. **1**(5), 206–215 (2019)

[328] C. Sagan, *The Demon-Haunted World: Science as a Candle in the Dark* (Ballantine Books, 2011)

[329] Y. Saito, S. Yaginuma, Y. Nishino, H. Sakata, K. Nakata, Unbiased recommender learning from missing-not-at-random implicit feedback, in *WSDM '20: The Thirteenth ACM International Conference on Web Search and Data Mining, Houston, TX, USA, February 3–7, 2020*, ed. by J. Caverlee, X.B. Hu, M. Lalmas, W. Wang (ACM, New York, 2020), pp. 501–509

[330] J. Salas, Sanitizing and measuring privacy of large sparse datasets for recommender systems. J. Ambient Intell. Humaniz. Comput. **14**(11), 15073–15084 (2023)

[331] C. Sandvig, K. Hamilton, K. Karahalios, C. Langbort, Auditing algorithms: research methods for detecting discrimination on internet platforms, in *Data and Discrimination: Converting Critical Concerns into Productive Inquiry* (2014)

[332] B. Sarwar, G. Karypis, J. Konstan, J. Riedl, Item-based collaborative filtering recommendation algorithms, in *Proceedings of the 10th International Conference on World Wide Web*, WWW '01 (Association for Computing Machinery, New York, 2001), pp. 285–295

[333] M. Schedl, The LFM-1b dataset for music retrieval and recommendation, in *Proceedings of the 2016 ACM on International Conference on Multimedia*

Retrieval, ICMR 2016, New York, New York, USA, June 6–9, 2016, ed. by J.R. Kender, J.R. Smith, J. Luo, S. Boll, W.H. Hsu (ACM, New York, 2016), pp. 103–110

[334] M. Schedl, S. Brandl, O. Lesota, E. Parada-Cabaleiro, D. Penz, N. Rekabsaz, Lfm-2b: a dataset of enriched music listening events for recommender systems research and fairness analysis, in *CHIIR '22: ACM SIGIR Conference on Human Information Interaction and Retrieval, Regensburg, Germany, March 14–18, 2022*, ed. by D. Elsweiler (ACM, New York, 2022), pp. 337–341

[335] M. Schedl, E. Gómez, J. Urbano, Music information retrieval: Recent developments and applications. Found. Trends Inf. Retr. **8**(2–3), 127–261 (2014)

[336] M. Schedl, D. Hauger, J. Urbano, Harvesting microblogs for contextual music similarity estimation: a co-occurrence-based framework. Multim. Syst. **20**(6), 693–705 (2014)

[337] M. Schedl, P. Knees, B. McFee, D. Bogdanov, Music recommendation systems: Techniques, use cases, and challenges, in *Recommender Systems Handbook*, ed. by F. Ricci, L. Rokach, B. Shapira (Springer, New York, 2022), pp. 927–971

[338] M. Schedl, N. Rekabsaz, E. Lex, T. Grosz, E. Greif, Multiperspective and multidisciplinary treatment of fairness in recommender systems research, in *UMAP '22: 30th ACM Conference on User Modeling, Adaptation and Personalization, Barcelona, Spain, July 4–7, 2022, Adjunct Proceedings* (ACM, New York, 2022), pp. 90–94

[339] M. Schedl, M. Tkalcic, Genre-based analysis of social media data on music listening behavior: are fans of classical music really averse to social media? in *Proceedings of the First International Workshop on Internet-Scale Multimedia Management, WISMM '14, Orlando, Florida, USA, November 7, 2014*, ed. by R. Zimmermann, Y. Yu (ACM, New York, 2014), pp. 9–13

[340] M. Schedl, H. Zamani, C. Chen, Y. Deldjoo, M. Elahi, Current challenges and visions in music recommender systems research. Int. J. Multim. Inf. Retr. **7**(2), 95–116 (2018)

[341] L. Schelenz, A. Segal, O. Adelio, K. Gal, Transparency-check: An instrument for the study and design of transparency in ai-based personalization systems. ACM J. Responsible Comput. **1**(1), 1–18 (2024)

[342] T. Schnabel, S. Amershi, P. N. Bennett, P. Bailey, T. Joachims, The impact of more transparent interfaces on behavior in personalized recommendation, in *Proceedings of the 43rd International ACM SIGIR Conference on Research and Development in Information Retrieval* (2020), pp. 991–1000

[343] C. Schwind, J. Buder, Reducing confirmation bias and evaluation bias: when are preference-inconsistent recommendations effective—and when not? Comput. Hum. Behav. **28**(6), 2280–2290 (2012)

[344] A.Y. Seita, Globalization and the convergence of values, in *International Law of Human Rights* (Routledge, London, 2017), pp. 449–471

[345] Y. Seki, T. Maehara, A method to anonymize business metrics to publishing implicit feedback datasets, in *RecSys 2020: Fourteenth ACM Conference on Recommender Systems, Virtual Event, Brazil, September 22–26, 2020*, ed. by

R.L.T. Santos, L.B. Marinho, E.M. Daly, L. Chen, K. Falk, N. Koenigstein, E.S. de Moura (ACM, New York, 2020), pp. 4–12
[346] S. Seo, J. Huang, H. Yang, Y. Liu, Interpretable convolutional neural networks with dual local and global attention for review rating prediction, in *Proceedings of the Eleventh ACM Conference on Recommender Systems* (2017), pp. 297–305
[347] L.S. Shapley, et al., *A Value for n-Person Games* (1953)
[348] A. Sharma, D. Cosley, Do social explanations work? Studying and modeling the effects of social explanations in recommender systems, in *Proceedings of the 22nd International Conference on World Wide Web* (2013), pp. 1133–1144
[349] R. Sharma, S. Ray, Explanations in recommender systems: an overview. Int. J. Bus. Inform. Syst. **23**(2), 248–262 (2016)
[350] M. Sheehan, China's new ai governance initiatives shouldn't be ignored (2022). https://carnegieendowment.org/2022/01/04/china-s-new-ai-governance-initiatives-shouldn-t-be-ignored-pub-86127. Accessed 13 Feb 2024
[351] M. Sheehan, Tracing the roots of China's AI regulations (2022). https://carnegieendowment.org/research/2024/02/tracing-the-roots-of-chinas-ai-regulations?lang=en. Accessed 13 Mar 2024
[352] M. Sheehan, China's ai regulations and how they get made. Carnegie Endowment Int. Piece **2**, 2003 (2023)
[353] W. Shen, Y. Liu, China's normative systems for responsible ai: from soft law to hard law (2022), pp. 150–166
[354] Y. Shen, H. Jin, Privacy-preserving personalized recommendation: an instance-based approach via differential privacy, in *2014 IEEE International Conference on Data Mining, ICDM 2014, Shenzhen, China, December 14–17, 2014*, ed. by R. Kumar, H. Toivonen, J. Pei, J.Z. Huang, X. Wu (IEEE Computer Society, 2014), pp. 540–549
[355] D. Shin, Toward fair, accountable, and transparent algorithms: case studies on algorithm initiatives in Korea and China. Javnost-The Public **26**(3), 274–290 (2019)
[356] D.D. Shin, *Algorithms, Humans, and Interactions: How Do Algorithms Interact with People? Designing Meaningful ai Experiences* (Taylor & Francis, London, 2023)
[357] H. Shin, S. Kim, J. Shin, X. Xiao, Privacy enhanced matrix factorization for recommendation with local differential privacy. IEEE Trans. Knowl. Data Eng. **30**(9), 1770–1782 (2018)
[358] E. Shmueli, T. Tassa, Secure multi-party protocols for item-based collaborative filtering, in *Proceedings of the Eleventh ACM Conference on Recommender Systems, RecSys 2017, Como, Italy, August 27–31, 2017*, ed. by P. Cremonesi, F. Ricci, S. Berkovsky, A. Tuzhilin (ACM, New York, 2017), pp. 89–97
[359] E. Shmueli, T. Tassa, Mediated secure multi-party protocols for collaborative filtering. ACM Trans. Intell. Syst. Technol. **11**(2), 15:1–15:25 (2020)
[360] B. Shneiderman, *Human-Centered AI* (Oxford University Press, Oxford, 2022)

[361] C. Siepmann, M.A. Chatti, Trust and transparency in recommender systems, in *ACM CHI Workshop Human-Centered Perspectives in Explainable AI (HCXAI)* (2023)

[362] J. Singh, A. Anand, Exs: explainable search using local model agnostic interpretability, in *Proceedings of the Twelfth ACM International Conference on Web Search and Data Mining* (2019), pp. 770–773

[363] R. Sinha, K. Swearingen, The role of transparency in recommender systems, in *CHI '02 Extended Abstracts on Human Factors in Computing Systems*, CHI EA '02 (Association for Computing Machinery, New York, 2002), pp. 830–831

[364] Z. Siting, H. Wenxing, Z. Ning, Y. Fan, Job recommender systems: a survey, in *Proceedings of the 7th International Conference on Computer Science & Education (ICCSE)* (2012), pp. 920–924

[365] R. Smirke, Five Takeaways From the 2023 IFPI Global Music Report. Billboard Bulletin, 2023. https://www.billboard.com/wp-content/uploads/2023/03/march-22-2023-billboard-bulletin.pdf

[366] S.L. Smith, M. Choueiti, K. Pieper, H. Clark, A. Case, S. Villanueva, Inclusion in the recording studio, in *USC Annenberg* (2018), p. 32

[367] N. Sonboli, J.J. Smith, F. Cabral Berenfus, R. Burke, C. Fiesler, Fairness and transparency in recommendation: the users' perspective, in *Proceedings of the 29th ACM Conference on User Modeling, Adaptation and Personalization* (2021), pp. 274–279

[368] D. Spagnuelo, G. Lenzini, Transparent medical data systems. J. Med. Syst. **41**, 1–12 (2016)

[369] H. Steck, Evaluation of recommendations: rating-prediction and ranking, in *Seventh ACM Conference on Recommender Systems, RecSys '13, Hong Kong, China, October 12–16, 2013*, ed. by Q. Yang, I. King, Q. Li, P. Pu, G. Karypis (ACM, New York, 2013), pp. 213–220

[370] E. Storms, O. Alvarado, L.M. Krebs, 'transparency is meant for control' and vice versa: learning from co-designing and evaluating algorithmic news recommenders, in *Proceedings of the ACM on Human-Computer Interaction* (2022)

[371] H. Suresh, J.V. Guttag, A framework for understanding unintended consequences of machine learning (2019). CoRR, abs/1901.10002

[372] M. Suzuki, Y. Yamamoto, Analysis of relationship between confirmation bias and web search behavior, in *Proceedings of the 22nd International Conference on Information Integration and Web-Based Applications & Services*, iiWAS '20 (Association for Computing Machinery, New York, 2021), pp. 184–191

[373] L. Sweeney, k-anonymity: a model for protecting privacy. Int. J. Uncertain. Fuzziness Knowl. Based Syst. **10**(5), 557–570 (2002)

[374] C. Szegedy, W. Zaremba, I. Sutskever, J. Bruna, D. Erhan, I.J. Goodfellow, R. Fergus, Intriguing properties of neural networks, in *ICLR* (2014)

[375] O. Tal, Y. Liu, J. Huang, X. Yu, B. Aljbawi, Neural attention frameworks for explainable recommendation. IEEE Trans. Knowl. Data Eng. **33**(5), 2137–2150 (2019)

[376] B. Tan, B. Liu, V.W. Zheng, Q. Yang, A federated recommender system for online services, in *RecSys 2020: Fourteenth ACM Conference on Recommender Systems, Virtual Event, Brazil, September 22–26, 2020*, ed. by R.L.T. Santos, L.B. Marinho, E.M. Daly, L. Chen, K. Falk, N. Koenigstein, E.S. de Moura (ACM, 2020), pp. 579–581

[377] J. Tang, X. Du, X. He, F. Yuan, Q. Tian, T. Chua, Adversarial training towards robust multimedia recommender system. IEEE Trans. Knowl. Data Eng. **32**(5), 855–867 (2019)

[378] J. Tang, X. Du, X. He, F. Yuan, Q. Tian, T. Chua, Adversarial training towards robust multimedia recommender system. IEEE Trans. Knowl. Data Eng. **32**(5), 855–867 (2020)

[379] N. Thalpage, Unlocking the black box: Explainable artificial intelligence (XAI) for trust and transparency in ai systems. J. Digit. Art Hum. **4**(1), 31–36 (2023)

[380] The algorithmic accountability act (AAA). https://www.wyden.senate.gov/imo/media/doc/algorithmic_accountability_act_text.pdf. Accessed 29 Feb 2024

[381] The California privacy rights act of 2020. https://thecpra.org/. Accessed 13 Feb 2024

[382] N. Tintarev, Explanations of recommendations, in *Proceedings of the 2007 ACM conference on Recommender systems* (2007), pp. 203–206

[383] N. Tintarev, J. Masthoff, A survey of explanations in recommender systems, in *2007 IEEE 23rd International Conference on Data Engineering Workshop* (IEEE, Piscataway, 2007), pp. 801–810

[384] N. Tintarev, J. Masthoff, Explaining recommendations: design and evaluation, in *Recommender Systems Handbook* (Springer, Berlin, 2015), pp. 353–382

[385] F. Tomasi, J. Cauteruccio, S. Kanoria, K. Ciosek, M. Rinaldi, Z. Dai, Automatic music playlist generation via simulation-based reinforcement learning, in *Proceedings of the 29th ACM SIGKDD Conference on Knowledge Discovery and Data Mining, KDD 2023, Long Beach, CA, USA, August 6–10, 2023*, ed. by A.K. Singh, Y. Sun, L. Akoglu, D. Gunopulos, X. Yan, R. Kumar, F. Ozcan, J. Ye (ACM, Berlin, 2023), pp. 4948–4957

[386] T. Tran, R. Sweeney, K. Lee, Adversarial Mahalanobis distance-based attentive song recommender for automatic playlist continuation, in *Proceedings of the 42nd International ACM SIGIR Conference on Research and Development in Information Retrieval, SIGIR 2019, Paris, France, July 21–25, 2019* (2019), pp. 245–254

[387] Translation: Internet information service algorithmic recommendation management provisions (draft for comment) – Aug. 2021. https://digichina.stanford.edu/work/translation-internet-information-service-algorithmic-recommendation-managemen-t-provisions-opinon-seeking-draft/. Accessed 29 Feb 2024

[388] Translation: Personal information protection law of the people's republic of China – effective Nov. 1, 2021. https://digichina.stanford.edu/work/ transla-

tion-personal-information-protection-law-of-the-peoples-republic- of-china–effective-nov-1-2021/. Accessed 13 Feb 2024

[389] T.R. Tyler, C.J. Wakslak, Profiling and police legitimacy: procedural justice, attributions of motive, and acceptance of police authority. Criminology **42**(2), 253–282 (2004)

[390] P.M. Vaidya, Speeding-up linear programming using fast matrix multiplication (extended abstract), in *30th Annual Symposium on Foundations of Computer Science, Research Triangle Park, North Carolina, USA, 30 October–1 November 1989* (IEEE Computer Society, 1989), pp. 332–337

[391] A.C. Valdez, M. Ziefle, The users' perspective on the privacy-utility trade-offs in health recommender systems. Int. J. Hum. Comput. Stud. **121**, 108–121 (2019)

[392] L. Valentine, S. D'Alfonso, R. Lederman, Recommender systems for mental health apps: advantages and ethical challenges. AI Soc. **38**(4), 1627–1638 (2023)

[393] B. Vecchione, K. Levy, S. Barocas, Algorithmic auditing and social justice: lessons from the history of audit studies, in *Equity and Access in Algorithms, Mechanisms, and Optimization* (2021)

[394] M. Verma, D. Ganguly, LIRME: locally interpretable ranking model explanation, in *Proceedings of the 42nd International ACM SIGIR Conference on Research and Development in Information Retrieval* (2019), pp. 1281–1284

[395] C. Vernotti, Digital policy experts weigh in on China's new algorithm regulation (2022). https://technode.com/2022/04/05/digital-policy-experts-weigh-in-on-chinas-new-algorithm-regulation. Accessed 13 Feb 2024

[396] U. von Luxburg, B. Schölkopf, Statistical learning theory: models, concepts, and results, in *Inductive Logic*, volume 10 of Handbook of the History of Logic, ed. by D.M. Gabbay, S. Hartmann, J. Woods (Elsevier, Amsterdam, 2011), pp. 651–706

[397] E.M. Voorhees, The evolution of Cranfield, in *Information Retrieval Evaluation in a Changing World—Lessons Learned from 20 Years of CLEF*, volume 41 of The Information Retrieval Series, ed. by N. Ferro, C. Peters (Springer, Berlin, 2019), pp. 45–69

[398] S. Wachter, B. Mittelstadt, C. Russell, Counterfactual explanations without opening the black box: automated decisions and the GDPR. Harv. JL Tech. **31**, 841 (2017)

[399] O.A. Wahab, G. Rjoub, J. Bentahar, R. Cohen, Federated against the cold: a trust-based federated learning approach to counter the cold start problem in recommendation systems. Inf. Sci. **601**, 189–206 (2022)

[400] A. Wang, An industrial strength audio search algorithm, in *Proceedings of the 4th International Conference on Music Information Retrieval (ISMIR 2003)* (2003)

[401] C. Wang, K. Wang, A. Bian, R. Islam, K.N. Keya, J.R. Foulds, S. Pan, Do humans prefer debiased AI algorithms? A case study in career recommendation, in *IUI 2022: 27th International Conference on Intelligent User Interfaces, Helsinki, Finland, March 22–25, 2022*, ed. by G. Jacucci, S. Kaski, C. Conati, S. Stumpf, T. Ruotsalo, K. Gajos (ACM, New York, 2022), pp. 134–147

[402] D. Wang, Y. Chen, A novel many-objective recommendation algorithm for multistakeholders. IEEE Access **8**, 196482–196499 (2020)

[403] D. Wang, Y. Chen, A novel cascade hybrid many-objective recommendation algorithm incorporating multistakeholder concerns. Inf. Sci. **577**, 105–127 (2021)

[404] N. Wang, H. Wang, Y. Jia, Y. Yin, Explainable recommendation via multi-task learning in opinionated text data, in *The 41st International ACM SIGIR Conference on Research & Development in Information Retrieval* (2018), pp. 165–174

[405] Q. Wang, H. Yin, T. Chen, J. Yu, A. Zhou, X. Zhang, Fast-adapting and privacy-preserving federated recommender system. VLDB J. **31**(5), 877–896 (2022)

[406] S. Wang, X. Zhang, Y. Wang, F. Ricci, Trustworthy recommender systems. ACM Trans. Intell. Syst. Technol. **15**(4), 1–20 (2024)

[407] T. Wang, D. Wang, Why amazon's ratings might mislead you: the story of herding effects. Big data **2**(4), 196–204 (2014)

[408] W. Wang, Y. Huang, Y. Wang, L. Wang, Generalized autoencoder: A neural network framework for dimensionality reduction, in *Proceedings of the IEEE Conference on Computer Vision and Pattern Recognition Workshops* (2014), pp. 490–497

[409] X. Wang, Q. Li, D. Yu, Q. Li, G. Xu, Reinforced path reasoning for counterfactual explainable recommendation. IEEE Trans. Knowl. Data Eng. (2024)

[410] H. Watson, C. Nations, Addressing the growing need for algorithmic transparency. Commun. Assoc. Inf. Syst. **45**, 26 (2019)

[411] E.-M. Weiß, Österreichische Arbeitsagentur veroeffentlicht fragwuerdigen KI-Chatbot (2024). https://www.heise.de/news/Oesterreichische- Arbeitsagentur-veroeffentlicht-fragwuerdigen-KI-Chatbot-9588098.html

[412] C. Wilkie, L. Azzopardi, Retrievability and retrieval bias: a comparison of inequality measures, in *Advances in Information Retrieval—37th European Conference on IR Research, ECIR 2015, Vienna, Austria, March 29–April 2, 2015. Proceedings*, volume 9022 of Lecture Notes in Computer Science, ed. by A. Hanbury, G. Kazai, A. Rauber, N. Fuhr (2015), pp. 209–214

[413] D.R. Williams, S.A. Mohammed, Discrimination and racial disparities in health: evidence and needed research. J. Behav. Med. **32**, 20–47 (2009)

[414] Workshop on ExplainAble Recommendation and Search (EARS 2018) at SIGIR 2018. *Posthoc Interpretability of Learning to Rank Models using Secondary Training Data* (2018)

[415] C. Wu, D. Lian, Y. Ge, Z. Zhu, E. Chen, Triple adversarial learning for influence based poisoning attack in recommender systems, in *KDD '21: The 27th ACM SIGKDD Conference on Knowledge Discovery and Data Mining, Virtual Event, Singapore, August 14–18, 2021*, ed. by F. Zhu, B.C. Ooi, C. Miao (ACM, New York, 2021), pp. 1830–1840

[416] C. Wu, D. Lian, Y. Ge, Z. Zhu, E. Chen, S. Yuan, Fight fire with fire: Towards robust recommender systems via adversarial poisoning training, in *SIGIR '21: The 44th International ACM SIGIR Conference on Research and Development*

in Information Retrieval, Virtual Event, Canada, July 11–15, 2021, ed. by F. Diaz, C. Shah, T. Suel, P. Castells, R. Jones, T. Sakai (ACM, New York, 2021), pp. 1074–1083

[417] C. Wu, F. Wu, X. Wang, Y. Huang, X. Xie, Fairness-aware news recommendation with decomposed adversarial learning, in *Thirty-Fifth AAAI Conference on Artificial Intelligence, AAAI 2021, Thirty-Third Conference on Innovative Applications of Artificial Intelligence, IAAI 2021, The Eleventh Symposium on Educational Advances in Artificial Intelligence, EAAI 2021, Virtual Event, February 2–9, 2021* (AAAI Press, 2021), pp. 4462–4469

[418] C. Wu, R. Zhang, J. Guo, M. de Rijke, Y. Fan, X. Cheng, PRADA: practical black-box adversarial attacks against neural ranking models. ACM Trans. Inf. Syst. **41**(4), 89:1–89:27 (2023)

[419] F. Wu, C. Lu, M. Zhu, H. Chen, J. Zhu, K. Yu, L. Li, M. Li, Q. Chen, X. Li, et al.. Towards a new generation of artificial intelligence in China. Nat. Mach. Intell. **2**(6), 312–316 (2020)

[420] H. Wu, C. Ma, B. Mitra, F. Diaz, X. Liu, A multi-objective optimization framework for multi-stakeholder fairness-aware recommendation. ACM Trans. Inf. Syst. **41**(2), 47:1–47:29 (2023)

[421] Y. Wu, J. Cao, G. Xu, Y. Tan, TFROM: a two-sided fairness-aware recommendation model for both customers and providers, in *SIGIR '21: The 44th International ACM SIGIR Conference on Research and Development in Information Retrieval, Virtual Event, Canada, July 11–15, 2021*, ed. by F. Diaz, C. Shah, T. Suel, P. Castells, R. Jones, T. Sakai (ACM, New York, 2021), pp. 1013–1022

[422] Y. Wu, L. Zhang, U. A. Bhatti, M. Huang, Interpretable machine learning for personalized medical recommendations: a lime-based approach. Diagnostics **13**(16), 2681 (2023)

[423] C. Xu, W. Wang, Y. Li, L. Pang, J. Xu, T. Chua, Do LLMs implicitly exhibit user discrimination in recommendation? An empirical study (2023). CoRR, abs/2311.07054

[424] Y. Xu, L. Chen, F. Xie, W. Hu, J. Zhu, C. Chen, Z. Zheng, Directional adversarial training for recommender systems, in *ECAI 2020* (2020)

[425] F. Yang, Y. Yao, A new regulatory framework for algorithm-powered recommendation services in China. Nat. Mach. Intell. **4**(10), 802–803 (2022)

[426] L. Yang, B. Tan, V.W. Zheng, K. Chen, Q. Yang, Federated recommendation systems, in *Federated Learning—Privacy and Incentive*, volume 12500 of Lecture Notes in Computer Science, ed. by Q. Yang, L. Fan, H. Yu (Springer, Berlin, 2020), pp. 225–239

[427] P. Yu, R. Rahimi, J. Allan, Towards explainable search results: a listwise explanation generator, in *Proceedings of the 45th International ACM SIGIR Conference on Research and Development in Information Retrieval* (2022), pp. 669–680

[428] F. Yuan, L. Yao, B. Benatallah, Adversarial collaborative auto-encoder for top-n recommendation, in *International Joint Conference on Neural Networks, IJCNN 2019 Budapest, Hungary, July 14–19, 2019* (2019), pp. 1–8

[429] F. Yuan, L. Yao, B. Benatallah, Adversarial collaborative neural network for robust recommendation, in *Proceedings of the 42nd International ACM SIGIR Conference on Research and Development in Information Retrieval, SIGIR 2019, Paris, France, July 21–25, 2019* (2019), pp. 1065–1068

[430] H. Zamani, M. Schedl, P. Lamere, C. Chen, An analysis of approaches taken in the ACM RecSys challenge 2018 for automatic music playlist continuation. ACM Trans. Intell. Syst. Technol. **10**(5), 57:1–57:21 (2019)

[431] H. Zarzour, Y. Jararweh, M.M. Hammad, M. Al-Smadi, A long short-term memory deep learning framework for explainable recommendation, in *2020 11th International Conference on Information and Communication Systems (ICICS)* (IEEE, Piscataway, 2020), pp. 233–237

[432] M. Zehlike, F. Bonchi, C. Castillo, S. Hajian, M. Megahed, R. Baeza-Yates, Fa*ir: a fair top-k ranking algorithm, in *Proceedings of the 2017 ACM on Conference on Information and Knowledge Management, CIKM 2017, Singapore, November 06–10, 2017*, ed. by E. Lim, M. Winslett, M. Sanderson, A. W. Fu, J. Sun, J.S. Culpepper, E. Lo, J.C. Ho, D. Donato, R. Agrawal, Y. Zheng, C. Castillo, A. Sun, V.S. Tseng, C. Li (ACM, New York, 2017), pp. 1569–1578

[433] J. Zeng, Artificial intelligence and China's authoritarian governance. Int. Affairs **96**(6), 1441–1459 (2020)

[434] F. Zhang, V.E. Lee, R. Jin, S. Garg, K.R. Choo, M. Maasberg, L. Dong, C. Cheng, Privacy-aware smart city: a case study in collaborative filtering recommender systems. J. Parallel Distrib. Comput. **127**, 145–159 (2019)

[435] J. Zhang, K. Bao, Y. Zhang, W. Wang, F. Feng, X. He, Is ChatGPT fair for recommendation? Evaluating fairness in large language model recommendation, in *Proceedings of the 17th ACM Conference on Recommender Systems, RecSys 2023, Singapore, Singapore, September 18–22, 2023*, ed. by J. Zhang, L. Chen, S. Berkovsky, M. Zhang, T.D. Noia, J. Basilico, L. Pizzato, Y. Song (ACM, 2023), pp. 993–999

[436] S. Zhang, Measuring algorithmic bias in job recommender systems: an audit study approach (2021)

[437] S. Zhang, L. Yao, A. Sun, Y. Tay, Deep learning based recommender system. ACM Comput. Surv. **52**(1), 1–38 (2019)

[438] Y. Zhang, X. Chen, et al., Explainable recommendation: a survey and new perspectives. Found. Trends® Inform. Retrieval **14**(1), 1–101 (2020)

[439] Y. Zhang, G. Lai, M. Zhang, Y. Zhang, Y. Liu, S. Ma, Explicit factor models for explainable recommendation based on phrase-level sentiment analysis, in *Proceedings of the 37th International ACM SIGIR Conference on Research & Development in Information Retrieval* (2014), pp. 83–92

[440] H. Zhao, S. Fu, X. Chen, Promoting users' intention to share online health articles on social media: the role of confirmation bias. Inf. Process. Manag. **57**(6), 102354 (2020)

[441] A. Zharova, Achieving algorithmic transparency and managing risks of data security when making decisions without human interference: legal approaches. J. Digit. Technol. Law **1**(4), 973–993 (2023)

[442] J. Zheng, J. Mai, Y. Wen, Explainable session-based recommendation with meta-path guided instances and self-attention mechanism, in *Proceedings of the 45th International ACM SIGIR Conference on Research and Development in Information Retrieval* (2022), pp. 2555–2559

[443] Y. Zheng, C. Gao, X. Li, X. He, Y. Li, D. Jin, Disentangling user interest and conformity for recommendation with causal embedding, in *WWW '21: The Web Conference 2021, Virtual Event/Ljubljana, Slovenia, April 19–23, 2021*, ed. by J. Leskovec, M. Grobelnik, M. Najork, J. Tang, L. Zia, (ACM/IW3C2, 2021), pp. 980–2991

[444] Y. Zheng, J.R. Toribio, The role of transparency in multi-stakeholder educational recommendations. User Model. User-Adapt. Interact. **31**(3), 513–540 (2021)

[445] A. Zien, N. Krämer, S. Sonnenburg, G. Rätsch, The feature importance ranking measure, in *Machine Learning and Knowledge Discovery in Databases: European Conference, ECML PKDD 2009, Bled, Slovenia, September 7–11, 2009, Proceedings, Part II 20* (Springer, Berlin, 2009), pp. 694–709

Index

M. Schedl et al., *Technical and Regulatory Perspectives on Information Retrieval and Recommender Systems*, The Information Retrieval Series 50,
https://doi.org/10.1007/978-3-031-69978-8

SPRINGER NATURE

GPSR Compliance

The European Union's (EU) General Product Safety Regulation (GPSR) is a set of rules that requires consumer products to be safe and our obligations to ensure this.

If you have any concerns about our products, you can contact us on ProductSafety@springernature.com

In case Publisher is established outside the EU, the EU authorized representative is:

Springer Nature Customer Service Center GmbH
Europaplatz 3
69115 Heidelberg, Germany

The manufacturer's authorised representative in the EU is Springer Nature Customer Service Centre GmbH, Europaplatz 3, 69115 Heidelberg, Germany. If you have any concerns regarding our products, please contact ProductSafety@springernature.com

Printed and bound by CPI Group (UK) Ltd, Croydon, CR0 4YY
01/10/2026
02225913-0009